LOST CHORDS

LOST CHORDS

THE DIVERTING STORY OF AMERICAN POPULAR SONGS

DOUGLAS GILBERT

COOPER SQUARE PUBLISHERS, INC., NEW YORK, 1970

Originally Published 1942
Copyright © 1942 by Douglas Gilbert
Reprinted by Permission of Mrs. Douglas Gilbert
Published 1970 by Cooper Square Publishers, Inc.
59 Fourth Avenue, New York, N. Y. 10003
International Standard Book No. 0-8154-0370-4
Library of Congress Catalog Card No. 74-139203

Printed in the United States of America

For Marguerite

49242

THE SONG HISTORY of America, when some day it gets written, will accomplish two things. It will give the feel and atmosphere, the layout and lingo, of regions, of breeds of men, of customs and slogans, in a manner and air not given in regular history, to be read and not sung.

CARL SANDBURG
The American Songbag

FOREWORD

THIS IS A BOOK *about* songs, specifically an examination and analysis of the American "pop" tune as a social expression in the lives of our people since the Civil War. My reference to Harrigan and Hart is sparing because their highly specialized numbers, of specific New York locales, have been analyzed elsewhere abundantly. I have not dealt with Stephen Collins Foster, with the Negro spirituals, with folk songs. Their bibliography is immense. And they are not pop tunes. I have used none of the melodies. Such examinations are profitless. Music, however banal, is the most abstract of expressions, its interpretation often an impertinence. True, our popular music does reflect our social changes. Jazz, and the development of swing, are intense illustrations. But the words are the thought and the feeling of the times of a song, and I have purposely stressed this throughout my book. To fashion it, I have, in short, taken Carl Sandburg's advice in his introduction to *The American Song-bag.* I have tried to write a book about songs—to be read. And I have been able to attempt it largely through the kindness of Jack Murphy, whose prodigious memory of songs and events is mainly responsible for the first half; of Elliott Shapiro, always available for information, who placed his prized collection of De Marsan's *Singer's Journal* and the Delaney song books at my disposal; of Harry T. Peters, authority on the lithography of America, who gave me carte blanche with his collection of song covers; of Edward B. Marks, Jay Witmark, John J. O'Connor, and Leslie H. Bradshaw. All these are more steeped in the lore of our songs than I. Each shared his knowledge with me with unfailing courtesy.

DOUGLAS GILBERT

CONTENTS

xi

The Sound and the Fury—Juke Box, Jazz, Swing, and Boogie-Woogie

THE HEARTH—AND THE TAVERN

OVERTURE

THE AMERICAN POPULAR SONG, the strictly "pop" tune—"After the Ball," "Let Me Call You Sweetheart," "Alexander's Ragtime Band," "Dardanella," "My Blue Heaven," and the million-odd more—is now become nostalgic in essence, a peg upon which to hang memories. The popular song: a bit of doggerel—moral, sentimental, or topically comic—and set to a maudlin, lively, or reminiscent melody, is written no more in the genre as we knew it, partly because of a changed social and economic pattern, mostly because America is no longer a melodic nation. America now is a rhythmic nation. We dance. We do not sing any more; we are sung at. Contemporary songs are written for bands or performers; "production numbers" is the trade term. During the months of the impasse between the American Society of Composers, Authors and Publishers and the broadcasting chains who refused to play ASCAP-controlled popular music because they deemed the demanded fees were excessive, this, as a music-publisher executive admitted, typified the complaints of the listening public: "Why can't I hear Benny Goodman play 'Twelfth Street Rag'?" True, the old tunes still are played today, over the radio chains and on the 500,000 juke boxes for ear entertainment—and dancing—in as many bars and grills and dance halls throughout the nation. But are they always recognizable? Swing strangles melody; and the hep-cats and jive-hounds like to be in at the death.

The musical expression of the popular song is bastard. Many of their melodies were deliberately lifted from or inspired by more dignified originals—grand opera arias; the saccharinities of

3

Chopin; Tchaikovsky, an especial crutch; the themes of Mendelssohn or Schumann—retouched, drawn, and quartered by adept if unimaginative pop-tune masters who often filched from one another.

> Composer (auditioning his newest): It's a good tune.
> Publisher: It always was.

This was a standard jest for fifty years in Tin Pan Alley.

As a contribution to the country's culture, the pop tune rates with the comic strip, to whose values it is akin. Both are topical, occasionally satirical, often sentimental or mock-heroic, always essentially superficial. In our songs, every facet of normal interest that made up our daily lives—our manners, slang, dress, deportment, business, entertainment—is mirrored in the periods of their popularity. A reasonably accurate history of American morals derives from them.

They have no relation to our folk tunes, except the occasional illegitimacy of a prairie lament or a hillbilly ballad introduced into their ditties. They do have the virtue of social authenticity. However unwittingly, the writers of our pop tunes reflected their environment. They delivered, deliberately, to the mass taste of their day because they were a part of it. They were incapable of being vicarious, and a certain honesty of effort thus inheres to them for inscribing, in tune and assonance, generally accurate data of past times.

The speak-easies, night clubs, and clip joints in the "noble experiment" days of the 1920s, the helling around of those times, were contrary, in their subterfuge, in the deceit and wicked puissance of the bootlegger and highjacker, to the halcyon courtship of "Sunbonnet Sue." The Coolidge-Hoover era of bathtub gin and "Hello, sucker" necessarily spawned such stuff as "I Faw Down and Go Boom" and "Yes, We Have No Bananas." It was a sultry sophistication, jittery and befuddled. How foreign to the bathetic lamppost genialities that flourished in the early 1900s and are the flavor of 1903's "Sweet Adeline!"

When beer came back in 1933, it was the prediction of many

that the old tunes would come back with it, "sailing home on a sea of foam," crossing the bars with legal impunity to the accompaniment of barbered harmony. "Down Where the Würzburger Flows," "Sweet Rosie O'Grady," and "When You Were Sweet Sixteen" again were to be the chants of fellowship, the themes for rendezvous. Alas! the thought was as idle as noble. Nostalgic wishful thinking stays not the pointers of Kronos, which marched on with relentless beat to the mounting cacophonies of social and political upheaval that nine years later sent the world into its tailspin, quite properly to the *marche funèbre* of swing.

What more fitting hymns to contemporary barbarism than Gene Krupa's tom-tom, "Drumboogie"; or "Beat Me, Daddy, Eight to the Bar"? Current at this writing are "Abercrombie Had a Zombie," the "Hut Sut Song," "Shoot the Meat Balls to Me, Dominick," and "Alexander Is a Swoose"—all of equal mental strain.

Jeannette Illion, in 1940, wrote, to the music of Elliot Lawrence and Don Arres:

> I can't sleep and I can't eat;
> Something's burning at my feet.
> Call the wagon, tie me tight,
> Or those mad maracas will drag me out tonight. Oh![1]

The "Oh!" is Miss Illion's, and her song is "Conga Fever, La Boom Ba." Double talk? It is the current Esperanto.

To every age its gaucheries:

HAM FAT MAN

> Pig's meat is nice and sweet—Ham Fat!
> Pig's meat is good to eat—Ham Fat!
> Smell it fryin' in the pan—Ham Fat!
> Good enough for any man—Ham Fat!

Chorus: Ham fat, ham fat, zuka zicka zang.
> Ham fat, ham fat, tingly and a-tang.
> Get into the kitchen just as quickly as you can
> For the gravy's mighty hot in the Ham Fat Pan.

[1]Copyright, 1940, Broadcast Music, Inc. Used by permission.

This was a diverting *lied* of the 1860s; sung everywhere—in the free and easies of eastern cities, in western mining camps, and down the Mississippi; in kitchen, parlor, and 'round the boardinghouse square pianner. Its crudities are obvious, but it at least makes gustatory sense. And it is precise to a period when tables groaned from larders that were constantly replenished.

In the post-Civil War industrial centers, a workingman's board cost him three dollars weekly. His room furnishings were meager—a rag carpet, usually threadbare, a wooden bedstead with tricky slats, a feather mattress, a bowl and pitcher on a washstand whose closet concealed a chamber, or "thunder mug." There were a table, bureau, and one chair. Breakfast was served at 6 A.M. and varied little: pancakes, sausage, fried ham, fried eggs, fried pork, enormous leathery doughnuts—all heaped upon the table and help yourself. The landlady herself poured the coffee into huge china mugs from a two-gallon smoke-blackened pot.

Dinner (midday) was served in these establishments only on Sundays. On weekdays the workingmen carried enormous pails of beef or pork and bread, the pails packed and set in a row in the hallway near the door. Supper was a heavy meal. Boiled fresh or corned beef was served, or boiled pork, onions, potatoes, cabbage, parsnips, boiled apple dumplings, boiled puddings, gingerbread, and coffee or tea. Sliced bread was sissy; broken loaves were strewn about the table in large hunks. This peasant opulence was often molded into character songs in the '60s—boisterous, sometimes vulgar, yet nonetheless reflecting the stomachic influence. Everybody knew "Simon Johnson's Ball" and dinned its chorus with gusto.

SIMON JOHNSON'S BALL

Oh, down at Simon Johnson's house we had a gay old time,
With a gal in the corner chewing soap and a mouth like a hash
    house sign.
Miss Julia Johnson she was there with ears as big as a whale—

She'd just broke loose with a boil on her tooth from out of the
county jail.

Chorus: Pass around the gin and make the fiddle ring,
       Stay out all night till broad daylight
       If we all go to Sing Sing Sing.
       We're bound to have our fun,
       And make the money run,
       It's no use, we're bound to be loose
       At Simon Johnson's ball.

For supper we had cocoanut soup, mosquitoes fried in sand,
An elephant stuffed with bootjacks, the finest in the land.
Miss Julia Johnson she took sick, her blood began to boil,
She took syrup of squills and sixteen pills and finished on kerosene
   oil.

Chorus (Repeat)

When lunch was done the dance begun to the music of the band.
Then one-legged Carey tried to waltz with a hambone in each hand.
Mayor Blank got up to make a speech but the people all turned pale.
They knocked out his eye with a huckleberry pie and packed him
   off to jail.

These are but two of a welter of songs that suggested, and
sometimes burlesqued, the trencherman prowess of our forebears. Yet it is astonishing that "Ham Fat" was so popular, for
it was "plugged" (we shall come to know that word better)
mainly by the banjo players of the period, and the banjo player
then—as, indeed, most performers—was in ill repute. His instrument was despised and himself generally regarded as a
low fellow. Actually, to strum a banjo beneath the window of
a house where neighbors had gathered for an informal function of mixed ale (half ale, half porter), onion sandwiches, and
songs about the "pianofortay" (there was even a song about
that) was a social affront. Old ballads, say "Kitty Clyde," or
"Not So Young As I Used to Be" (a parlor song esteemed by
amateurs for its business with an old hat, a cane, and a rheumatic
limp), were popular at these shindigs:

      Now I'm an old man as you can see,
      Some seventy-odd years of age am I,

My teeth are all gone, I can scarcely see,
For now I am very near blind of an eye. . . .

Chorus: Oh, fol-de-dol-doodle-de-doot-de-doo,
How I love to sing to you.
And many a song would I sing with glee
If I was as young as I used to be.

When I was young and in my prime
I was chasing the girls the most of my time.
I often took them out for a ride
And I always had one of them by my side.
I hugged and kissed them just for fun,
And I haven't forgotten the way it is done.
And if any young girl here would like to try me,
She'll find me as young as I used to be.

Well, as such were delivered to the accompaniment of an accordion, an instrument *de rigueur,* some near-by hellion with deliberate intent would sound a banjo at a pause in the frolic—and that's how the fight would start.

The hostess, infuriated by the insult, would excuse herself to her guests, repair to the domicile of the offending neighbor, and neatly toss a brick through his window. The neighbor, in turn, would respond with a can of garbage, to even greater devastation. It added zest to the parties, but it often required the arbitration of police.

Conversely, legitimate serenades were institutions in the '60s and '70s highly esteemed by the recipient young ladies as a complimentary gesture. Often a quartet would assemble under the window of some popular girl at midnight (odd hour, but so) and sing plaintive ballads. Sometimes a string quartet would oblige, but more often a single admirer, breaking the stillness with voice and guitar. An old gentleman whose recollections of the times are still vivid recently recalled for the writer an experience of his own. He was a banjo player. But he obviated the stigma by sliding two pennies under the banjo's bridge, which gave the instrument the tone quality of a guitar. Thus strumming, he took up beneath the window of his affections, offering "Nellie Gray" or some such dolorous ditty. In a little while the window of a neighbor was raised, and a matronly voice called down: "Young man, your music is very nice, but the young lady has gone to the seashore with her folks, and we should like to go back to sleep."

GLORIOUS PORK—AND DIXIE

JOHNNY FORBES, an eccentric and popular banjoist and singer around the beer halls and wine rooms of the '60s and '70s was largely responsible for the success of "Ham Fat." Until he tired of touring, Forbes sang it all over with such mounting response that a hundred variants were devised by as many of his trouping colleagues, all extolling the virtues of pork as a victual. Songs well into the '70s reeked of lard. So pronounced was the sway of its theme and subject, variety singers who continued to glorify the pig became known as "ham fatters," an egregious term that persisted for years and may well be the origin of the contemporary "ham" characterizing the inferior actor.

Forbes played a five-string banjo and played it old style, with a thimble, and he made of "Ham Fat Man" a compelling rhythm with the improvisation of an ingenious obligato. In technique it was really a 12/8 accompaniment against a 4/4 melody. He always disliked the road, and his reason was well grounded—a disastrous tour with a honky-tonk troupe that featured a cancan act. During an evening performance in a midwestern whistle stop, the police looked in on the show, arrested the entire company, and clapped them in jail. Forbes was assigned to the cellar, and early in the morning he made his escape through the coal hole. Blackened beyond recognition, he jumped town on a freight. But he never recovered his trunk, and thereafter, to his final curtain, he used a market basket for luggage, slinging his banjo from a shoulder as a soldier sometimes carries a musket.

The popular song as we were to know it in after years grew out of the post-Civil War period. Jubilation makes for song, and the termination of the bloodletting loosed a furore of abandon that was to suppurate in the tragedy of the Reconstruction. The news of Lee's surrender reached the eastern seaboard at dawn. The war was over! People of the towns and cities, many in night clothes, swarmed into the streets. Strangers embraced, sobbing hysterically. Urchins kindled bonfires, joined by unreckoning adults, caring nothing. Bedsteads, quilting frames, and stepladders were lugged from homes. Window shutters were torn from houses and tossed upon the roof-high flames along with commodes, whalebone umbrellas, straw bonnets, and pickle kegs. Officials strutted through the streets, ordering a general illumination. Complying, townspeople everywhere set candles in small sconces attached to window sashes, a lighted candle for each pane. The glowing houses and flaming fires turned streets into golden rivers, a fierce setting for the mobs' song snatches, which soon rose to chants—hoarse, strident, hysterical—of "Rally 'Round the Flag."

This immediate and volatile hysteria, an affront to Grant's plea that there should be no rejoicing, crystallized in hymns of hate—an unusual quality, for the popular song, save for a few vicious political tunes, while often a satirical or critical rib, is almost never hateful—after the murder of Lincoln. The first reaction, of course, was one of profound sorrow, and soon after the tragedy, Beadle's *Fifth Avenue Songster* published "Little Tad," which not only echoed the common man's feeling but gave an unusual, if permissible, twist to the word "orphan."

LITTLE TAD

God bless the little orphan boy,
A father's darling pride.
May heaven guard his youthful form
And be his hope and guide.
May that pure love and honest worth
Which filled his parent's heart,
Be his inheritance in life,
The good and generous part.

Bereft of a fond father's love
And his paternal care,

Without his sacred teachings
Or his warm, devoted prayer.
Oh, earth must seem so dreary now
To that dear orphan child—
How he will miss the loving one
That so often on him smiled!

But yet there's left a mother's love
To watch his youthful years.
For them a nation's sympathy;
For them a nation's tears.
Columbia never can forget
The kindred of her friend.
And for the little orphan boy
E'er will her love extend.

With the exception of Lee, the South and its leaders were pilloried, excoriated, satirized, and ridiculed in songs sung everywhere throughout the North. One of them, built on a canard, was extraordinarily popular—"Jeff in Petticoats." It was written by George Cooper and Henry Tucker, both prolific tune writers, and was published in 1865 by William A. Pond, a leading contemporary music house, the purveyors of Harrigan and Hart.

"Jeff in Petticoats" was critical, boastful, a bone for New York's victory crowds. It alluded to Davis's supposed attempt to escape from his captors, the 4th Michigan Cavalry, Colonel Pritchard commanding. The presence of the Federal troopers was observed by Jim Jones, Davis's Negro coachman who, with Mrs. Davis, whom he had accompanied by another route from Richmond, met Davis's party near Irwinsville, Georgia. Jones roused Davis, who went to his wife's tent to warn her of the cavalry, which he assumed encircled his camp. There troopers apprehended him. Davis reached for a cloak and caught hold of his wife's raglan, which he donned as he was taken into custody. Soldiers then opened Mrs. Davis's trunk and removed a hoop skirt, another raglan, and a shawl. (It cost a soldier his hand, which was blown off by the accidental firing of his carbine during the examination.) Out of this incident, the South has always insisted, grew the canard that was exploited, in raucous burlesque by P. T. Barnum and in vicious cartoons, especially those of Frank Bellew, a New York artist and publisher. Bellew lampooned Davis in six caricatures showing various phases of the Confederate President's Civil War tenure, all uncomplimentary and with a final panel labeled "The End of Jeff." This showed the vanquished leader dangling from a scaffold, the wire frame of a hoopskirt belted to his middle, upon which were perched crows against a background of the Capitol in Washington.

Here are two verses of "Jeff in Petticoats":

> Jeff Davis was a hero bold, you've heard of him I know,
> He tried to make himself a king where southern breezes blow;
> But Uncle Sam he laid the youth across his mighty knee,
> And spanked him well, and that's the end of brave old Jeffy D

Chorus: Oh! Jeffy D. You "flow'r of chivalree,"
> Oh! royal Jeffy D!
> Your empire's but a tinclad skirt,
> Oh, charming Jeffy D.

> This Davis, he was always full of bluster and of brag,
> He swore on all our northern walls he'd plant his rebel rag;
> But when to battle he did go, he said "I'm not so green;
> To dodge the bullets I will wear my tinclad crinoline."

In its tease of Southern sympathizers, its tweak of a fallen, albeit honorable, foe, the lines are unfair. They are only an earnest of unmannerly times.

But the glut of victory soon gave way to the respite of peace, and a resultant expression more wholesome became manifest around the nation's pianos, on its barrel organs, its tavern accordions and banjos, and in the people's throats. Minstrelsy was at its peak; the ballad days were come. Professionals, amateurs, parlor entertainers, any in the mood of tune, all sang "Little Bunch of Roses." It was whistled and hummed in workshops, factories, on the streets, probably because of its simple words and music, possibly because its sentiment was attuned to the recoil from blood.

> I am waiting here to meet my darling,
> My heart is in a flutter of delight.
> For we kissed last night when we parted,
> And this is where she bade me come tonight.
> She promised surely she would meet me,
> In yonder shady lane.
> With smiles and kisses she will greet me,
> When we meet once again.
> She has such a pretty little dimple;
> Her smile is brighter than the day.
> Her manner is bewitching and so simple;
> And swiftly the hours they pass away.

The professionals, as well as gifted "cards," gave it a twist at the close—coy, and with a step or two in dance:

> There's one thing now I must not tell, (*Break*)
> And that is where this maid doth dwell. (*Break*)
> In her hair she wears a white camelia;
> Dark blue is the color of her eyes.
> I call her my little bunch of roses,
> My darling, charming, captivating prize. (*Dance*)

(A "break" is four bars of music at the end of a line—or step, if dancing—and done in the same time as the song. The music and dance continue, but the singer does not sing.)

As though in general atonement, "Dixie" was taken up by the North; indeed, was virtually kidnaped and legitimatized as a true hymn of the Blue. Northern zealots to this day have been its champions. Daniel Decatur Emmett, a violin player who earlier had been a drummer in Southern circuses, wrote it as a "walk around" for a minstrel show. The walk around was the invariable finale to the first part of the early-day minstrels. It was presented like this: At a chord from the orchestra, the company rose to their feet. As the orchestra began a lively tune in 2/4 time, one of the company would step down stage from the semicircle, walk around for sixteen bars of the music and do one step of a reel, finish with a break, then resume his place

in the semicircle as another stepped out and repeated the performance, varying, though, with a different step. This would
continue until six or more dancers had appeared. Then all the
dancers came down stage and danced together while the rest
of the company patted time and shuffled. Curtain.

"Dixie's" popularity was spontaneous, and it is still a de-
pendable rouser. The words don't mean anything, but there is
a skin-prickling element in the melody. No song is better known,
not even the "Star Spangled Banner." In St. Louis, in 1908, the
women of the Confederate Choir of America replaced its words
because they were not suited "to the grandeur of the song or
the cause for which it stands." Veteran soldiers and sympathizers on both sides protested, but the belles were firm. And
here is their version:

> Oh, Dixie is the land of glory,
> The land of cherished song and story,
> Look away, look away, look away, Dixie Land.
> 'Tis the land that patriots love to dwell in,
> The land our fathers fought and fell in,
> Look away, look away, look away, Dixie Land.

Chorus: I'm glad I live in Dixie. Hurrah! Hurrah!
    (*Rest unchanged*)

The insistence of the Confederate Choir drew nationwide publicity, and the editorial writers leaped to their pens. "Don't
mutilate 'Dixie'! It means much. It is a part of our history,"
screamed the Rochester (N. Y.) *Chronicle*. To which the
New York *Herald* added: "It is a very cold-blooded Northerner
who does not tingle at the sound of the stirring Southern melody.
Already it is as much the nation's possession as 'America.' Let
it alone." This proved the *coup-de-grâce*, and the lines were
scrapped.

The flippancy the belles associated with the lyric was out of
keeping with Dan's character. He was a deeply religious man,
spent hours poring over a well-thumbed Bible, and at his death
left a set of prayers presumably written by himself. One was
a grace some construe as ironic and of possible reference to his

wn poverty. It thanked God "for this frugal meal Thou hast
)ermitted me to enjoy."

Dan wrote "Dixie" on a cold, bleak day in New York while
hinking of his warm Southern tours as a circus drummer. The
)hrase, "I wish I was in Dixie" occurred to him as an actual
)hysical reminder. He responded to the cue, developed the song,
nd it was first played, September 19, 1859, at a performance
)f Bryant's Minstrels, then appearing at 472 Broadway. His
)riginal opening, sung at rehearsal, was never repeated, because
Mrs. Bryant, as the belles did later, balked at its supposed
flippant Biblical reference. The original lines:

> Dis worl' was made in jiss six days,
> An' finish'd up in various ways;
> Look away! Look away! Look away!
> Dixie Land!
> Dey den made Dixie trim and nice,
> But Adam call'd it "Paradise."
> Look away! Look away! Look away!
> Dixie Land!

There are skeptics today who protest that Dan did not write
the song, although throughout these years his name as author
appears on the title page. Their point seems to derive from some
verses written for the song by General Albert Pike. They first
appeared in the Natchez *Courier*, April 30, 1861, and here
they are:

> Southrons, hear your country call you!
> Up, lest worse than death befall you!
> To arms! To arms! To arms, in Dixie!
> Lo! all the beacon fires are lighted,
> Let all hearts be now united!
> To arms! To arms! To arms, in Dixie.

> *Chorus:* Advance the flag of Dixie! Hurrah! Hurrah!
> For Dixie's land we take our stand,
> And live and die for Dixie!
> To arms! To arms! And conquer peace for Dixie!
> To arms! To arms! And conquer peace for Dixie!

The general doth exclaim too much. And his "falling close," "in Dixie," has not only no relation to the beauty of the Horatian poetic form—it ruins the beat of the tune.

Nearly all know the lines as they were originally sung, but some memories may need prodding. They are:

> Way down South in the fields of cotton,
> Cinnamon seed and sandy bottom,
> Look away, look away, look away, Dixie land.
> In Dixie land where I was born in,
> Early on one frosty mornin',
> Look away, look away, look away, Dixie land.

Chorus: I wish I was in Dixie. Hooray! Hooray!
In Dixie land I'll take my stand
And live and die in Dixie.
Away, away, away down South in Dixie.
Away, away, away down South in Dixie.

For many years Dan Emmett lived in retirement on a little farm near Mount Vernon, Ohio. He was eighty when Al G. Fields, a popular minstrel manager and performer, induced Dan to travel with his show in 1895. Dan rode in the street parade in an open barouche with banners on its side proclaiming

DAN EMMETT—COMPOSER OF DIXIE

He was introduced to the audience at the finale of the first part and then the band played and the company sang Dixie with the inevitable instantaneous response, while Dan bowed feebly. He was a good draw, but troublesome to care for on the road, and Fields only took him out that one season.

Dan died in 1904 in his Mount Vernon shack at the age of eighty-nine. And for the forty-five years of his song—in his lifetime—he received a total of $300 for it, which was the original selling price of the copyright.

Most of the Negro songs of the '60s were lively rhythms fitted to nonsense verse. Except for Stephen C. Foster's laments, it was almost twenty years before the doleful, ol'-massa-faithful-slave tunes were introduced, a natural delay. Retrospection was rare throughout the incredible decade of the Reconstruction, and the Negro of the Carpetbaggers—pillaging, swaggering, brutish—was by no means popular. Yet no songs the writer has examined portray him in this evil, and miscast, role. It is curious that so pronounced a phase of such bitter days found no response from so topical an expression as the popular song.

FANCY LITTLE COON

JIM CROW, whose meaning today is so racially significant, was the name of an erratically rhythmed Negro tune which was exceedingly popular throughout the '60s, although it had been introduced in 1828 by Thomas D. Rice. Its jabber and dance influenced the entertainment of America for forty years. Supposedly, it is the first Negro song sung in public in this country. Cincinnati, Louisville, and Pittsburgh contend for its origin, but it is the consensus of old variety performers to whom the legend was handed down that Rice, a dramatic actor, fell upon the song, quite by accident, while he was appearing in Baltimore. In the stableyard of the hotel where Rice was stopping (so runs the theatrical version), an eccentric Negro hostler accompanied his chores with a grotesque hop, skip, and twist to a lively song with senseless words. His gyrations amused Rice, who, after studying the Negro's antics, added some verses to the two-line chorus. The hostler was a local character, and on a night during his engagement, Rice gave an impersonation of him in his show. To Rice's astonishment, the song and dance not only set Baltimore on its ears, it swept the country, exactly as "Yes, We Have No Bananas" did in our time. (But Jim Crow lasted much longer than the banana song.)

Wherever Rice appeared in a Negro part, his "Jim Crow" specialty ran away with the show. This inspired the hurried writing and production of countless melodramas with Negro leads. Hundreds of verses—local, political, and personal—were written during the life of the song, and when Rice took it to England, it was as popular there. Here are three of the original verses:

JIM CROW

Come listen all you gals and boys I'm just from Tuckahoe,
I'm going to sing a little song, my name's Jim Crow.
Went down to the river but I didn't mean to stay,
When I seen so many gals I couldn't get away.

Chorus: I wheel about I twist about I do just so,
Every time I turn about I jump Jim Crow.

After I been there awhile I jump a river boat,
I fell into the water and I found myself afloat.
And when I got to New Orleans I felt so full of fight,
They put me in the calaboose and kept me there all night.

The other day I hit a man and he was mighty fat,
I hit so hard I knocked him in an old cocked hat.
I sit upon a hornets' nest, I dance upon my head
I tie a viper round my neck and then I go to bed.

Perusing these lines, one may well ask, why all the furore? It is that man finds his release in just such nonsense—the *raison d'être* of popular songs, which are essentially the adult's *Mother Goose*. Almost a hundred years after the original Jim Crow, Sigmund Romberg adapted Rice's idea for an effective number in *Maytime* called "Jump Jim Crow," an eccentric dance, but to different music.

This type of Negro tune continued well on into the '70s and '80s, a popular reaction that talented variety performers made much of. Delehanty and Hengler, a great, versatile song-and-dance team of the '70s and '80s and a headline act, specialized in the Negro tune, were virtual crusaders in preserving its popularity, a turnabout aspect, for it maintained their own. In 1868, Ned Straight wrote and published a song called "Pickaninny Nig." It was admirable for the art of Delehanty and Hengler, and they promptly took it over.

PICKANINNY NIG

I'm a Pickaninny Nig,
I am somewhat on a jig,
I'm a fancy little coon
And I doesn't care a fig.
I can beat old Uncle Snow,
De best way he can go.
I will clean de whole caboodle,
Den ye peoples watch my toe.
Den open up your eyes,
And watch me do a jig,
I know I'll please you all
In de Pickaninny Nig.
I will try to please you all
With this my rattling jig.
I'll tear myself to pieces
In the Pickaninny Nig.

The popularity of the song was largely due to the inimitable presentation of Delehanty and Hengler, and it branded that type of dancing throughout their period in vaudeville as the "pickaninny." There were, incidentally, many kinds of black-face song-and-dance specialties in the '70s and '80s—the acrobatic, the rival, the flirtation, the old slave, the contraband, the buck and wench, the knockabout, the neat, the singles, doubles, and fours. Delehanty and Hengler introduced many of these varieties in their prodigious repertoire, and they could also play tambourines, bones, and banjos expertly. Their pickaninny number was a strip from "dandy darkies" to the irresponsible, rollicking black-boy type, and their make-up for this was short and rather baggy pants, hickory shirts wide open at the neck, and old straw hats. The music was the familiar swinging 4/4 time, and the dancing was of the slide, skip, and slap technique, covering a lot of stage. As a by-product and to cash in on their success, the New York Popular Publishing Co., then at 32 Beekman St., issued *Delehanty and Hengler Songsters*, small paper-covered books giving the words to various songs written, sung, and popularized by the team, with some songs of other composers and performers, and sold them for twenty-five cents. It was the practice of the day for many headliners.

These songsters, those issued under the names of important vaudeville performers, and those published as legitimate popular "hymnals," by Beadle, De Marsan, Wehman, Delaney, and Tousey, were an effective agency for the dissemination of songs. But the songs first had to be popularized, and in this effort the tavern, the free and easy, and vaudeville were the greatest factors. Vaudeville was intimate entertainment with a homespun quality that reached the hearts of the people, and its influence cannot be overestimated in the sixty-odd years of its expression (incredible brevity for so lusty an art!) before it was slain by invention and science that may well someday do for us all.

Negro songs of the type of "Jim Crow" and "Pickaninny Nig" fill these songsters throughout the '60s, and it is interesting—and delightful—as one hums through their pages, to come upon "The Yellow Rose of Texas." This is an unusual Negro song. Although published by William A. Pond in 1858, it was popular throughout the post-Civil War period and well on into the '80s. Not only is it not written in dialect; its lyric is above the doggerel and nonsense jingle of those times. Its lines scan, its sentiment is genuine and plaintive, and albeit "Rosa Lee" and "Tennessee" would never be admitted by the purists, the assonance, favorite cliché of the songwriter, is absent.

THE YELLOW ROSE OF TEXAS

> There's a yellow rose in Texas that I am going to see,
> No other darky knows her, no darky only me;
> She cried so when I left her, it like to broke my heart,
> And if I ever find her, we never more will part.

Chorus: She's the sweetest rose of color this darky ever knew,
> Her eyes are bright as diamonds, they sparkle like the dew.
> You may talk about your Dearest May, and sing of Rosa Lee,
> But the yellow rose of Texas beats the belles of Tennessee.

Where the Rio Grande is flowing, and the starry skies are
    bright,
She walks along the river in the quiet summer night;
She thinks if I remember when we parted long ago,
I promised to come back again, and not to leave her so.

Oh! now I'm going to find her, for my heart is full of woe,
And we'll sing the song together, that we sung so long ago,
We'll play the banjo gaily, and we'll sing the songs of
    yore,
And the yellow rose of Texas shall be mine forever more.

It is said this is the favorite song of President Franklin D.
Roosevelt, but Stephen Early, his secretary, says it is one of several favorites—"Anchors Aweigh," "Happy Days Are Here
Again," and "Home on the Range"—of all of which the President is fond. Who knows who wrote "The Yellow Rose of
Texas"? This writer has never been able to find out. The title
page of the original issue in the collection of Elliott Shapiro—
of Shapiro, Bernstein, music publishers—gives only the initials
—"J.K."—as the composer. Years of research by Shapiro, en-
tailing much correspondence, have never disclosed the identity
of J.K. From its treatment and publication in New York, it
would seem to be of Northern origin.

In the music of the lay people are their lives. Popular music
is not even arty. It is banal, silly, often vulgar; its tunes alloy.
But it is simple, an extension of runes and ballads sung in work
and play and sorrow, since men have toiled and laughed and
wept. The child, the courtship, the marriage—the child, the
mother, the father, the home, the grave—that is the span of man
in his melodies as in his life and death.

J. A. Butterfield got a good deal of this feeling into "When
You and I Were Young Maggie," one of the best of the nostalgic songs, thriving today in its eighty-fifth year, in a world of
terror, its homely sentiment still shining, a mocking reminder
of gentler times, kindlier thoughts.

WHEN YOU AND I WERE YOUNG MAGGIE

I wandered, today, to the hill, Maggie,
To watch the scenes below;
The creek and the creaking old mill, Maggie,
As we used to, long ago.
The green grove has gone from the hill, Maggie,
Where first the daisies sprung:
The creaking old mill is still, Maggie,
Since you and I were young!

Chorus: And now we are aged and gray, Maggie,
And the trials of life nearly done:
Let us sing of the days that are gone, Maggie,
When you and I were young!

A city so silent and lone, Maggie,
Where the young and the gay and the best
In polished white mansions of stone, Maggie,
Have each found a place of rest,
Is built where the birds used to play, Maggie,
And join in the songs that were sung—
For we sang as gay as they, Maggie,
When you and I were young!

They say I am feeble with age, Maggie,
My steps are less sprightly than then:
My face is a well-written page, Maggie,
But time alone was the pen!
They say we are aged and gray, Maggie,
As sprays by the white breakers flung:
But to me you're as fair as you were, Maggie,
When you and I were young!

Butterfield was not only a prolific composer, he had a sound musical background unusual for the pop-tune composer. He was born in Great Berkhampstead, England, in 1837, took violin lessons when he was four years old, and when he was eight was a proficient player. He had a fine, true soprano before adolescence and was one of five boys named for the Westminster Abbey choir, but his parents, for some curious reason, refused to let him sing. But he kept on with his music, and at the age of ten, as a pupil of John Hullah, conducted a performance of *The Messiah*. He came to America when he was eighteen, and save for a brief home visit, remained here the rest of his life, teaching music in Indianapolis, later becoming the director of the Chicago Oratorio Society. When he relinquished his post he came back East and settled in Norwich, Connecticut. He was the composer of four operas, one of which, *Belshazzar*, was popular, and of some seventy songs. Maggie was tremendously popular, selling 250,000 copies up to 1873, immense for those times.

LOVE AMONG THE ROSES

THE GOOD DOUCE FAMILIES of the '60s lived largely in rented houses. Rents were low of necessity. An apprentice at any of the trades—carpenter, mechanic, painter, cobbler, slater, coppersmith, cooper, mason—received about $12 weekly, the standard wage for journeymen. When and if he became foreman, his wage was $15, and he was considered prosperous. The term of courtship varied from three to seven years, and elopements were rare. A young married couple could rent a six-room house in a reputable neighborhood for $8.00 monthly. There was no gas, heat, bath, or toilet in these houses; taps and toilets were out-of-doors. In emergency or sickness, a "pot chair" was used. They were generally homemade, a round hole sawed in the seat of a wooden chair, and a chamber fitted under the hole. The sides and back of the chair were masked with cloth, and the seat covered with a thick cushion. This not only made another piece of furniture, it attempted to disguise its utility. No one was fooled. Oil lamps and candles were used for illumination, and these were lighted from spills made of twisted paper which were ignited at the kitchen stove because of the scarcity of matches.

Heating stoves were used in all the rooms. These were dismantled in the spring, wrapped in newspapers, and stowed in the cellar. When they were set up again in the fall, the stovepipes never fit, no matter how carefully sorted and marked when put away. Coal was inexpensive, but a great deal of wood was burned, hauled in from the country by farmers, who dumped it in cordwood lengths upon the sidewalk in front of the dwelling of the purchaser. There it would lie until some old fellow came along with a saw and buck and cut it into stove lengths.

A cord of wood is eight feet long, four feet high, and four feet wide, and each four-foot length had to be cut into three pieces to fit the stoves. For his work, the sawyer received twenty-five cents per cord—a lot of backache for a shinplaster, as the paper money of the period was called.

Many people walked long distances to their work, but if it was several miles, they boarded horsecars. When the cars got stuck in the snow or ran off the track, as they often did, the male passengers would alight and unite in a mighty push to re-track the car. This was deemed a lark, not a hardship: jokes, laughter, and badinage accompanied their efforts to restore transportation to normal conditions and thus permit resumption of their journey to their ten-hour-a-day jobs.

The women worked harder.

> Man works from sun to sun,
> Woman's work is never done.

Thus an old saw.

It is incredible to us today that an old woman of the '60s and '70s—though not, of course, among the gentry—could, and did, unaided, cook, sew, wash, bake, and darn for a family of seven or eight persons and in her spare time put up preserves and make soap, medicines, and shirts for her menfolk and bachelor friends. They were fearsome things, those shirts. They were very full, reached below the knee in length, their bosoms pleated and their cuffs turned. One of them contained enough cloth to make a fair-sized awning. But what was really appalling were the homemade medicines and remedies. Each fall a number of old women from the country peddled roots, seeds, herbs, and berries from house to house, which were purchased and brewed or stewed into concoctions for Johnny's cold, Uncle Amos' rheumatism, Aunt Sophrony's asthma, Father's vapors, or Mother's sciatica.

Prickly ash berries combined with gin was deemed a panacea for all irregularities. Balsam apple and brandy were used for cuts and bruises. Blackberries, quassia, burdock, sage, stillingia, and rhubarb—all were blended with brandy for general aches and pains. A murderous tea of mullein root and yarrow seasoned with honey was deemed sovereign for the nerves. And a veritable witch's brew called spice bitters was considered infallible as a remedy for colds. It contained all the breath-taking and throat-searing compounds aforesaid, served boiling hot in large mugs.

After supper, the old ladies relaxed by cutting carpet rags, knitting pulse warmers, or making spills while crooning, perhaps,

BARBARA ALLEN

In Scarlet town where I was born,
There was a fair maid dwellin',
Made every youth cry "where away?"
Her name was Barbara Allen.
All in the merry month of May
When green buds were a-swellin',
Young Jamie Gay on death bed lay,
For love of Barbara Allen.

And death is printed on his face,
And o'er his heart is stealin',
Then haste away to comfort him
Oh, lovely Barbara Allen.
So slowly, slowly she came up
And slowly she came nigh him,
And all she said when there she came,
"Young man, I think you're dying."

When he was dead and laid in grave,
Her heart was struck with sorrow,
Oh, mother, mother, make my bed
For I shall die tomorrow.

Farewell, she said, ye virgins all,
And shun the fault I fell in;
Henceforth take warning by the fall
Of cruel Barbara Allen.

(Many versions exist of this old ballad. The writer has given it as sung in the '60s, when it was still a favorite, especially of older folk with a lass to admonish. In its Scottish reversion and swift recompense in death it is superior to the version used by Carl Sandburg, in his *American Songbag*, which closes with the dead lovers united as rose vines clinging atop the church tower.)

Then maybe an old friend would drop in for a bit of gossip or to pass along news of the outside world, and if the season was winter and the night bitter, they would all have a "stone fence," a potent but agreeable mixture of hard cider, brown sugar, and apple brandy, served hot. Brandy was the great tipple; it was not until the '70s that the use of whisky became general. And it cost but $2.00 per gallon, still less if purchased from smugglers, and much of it was.

The more pretentious homes were lighted with gas and enjoyed bathtubs made of wooden boxes about three feet wide and seven feet long and lined with copper. A typical parlor of the better class homes was adorned with heavy crystal chandeliers and side brackets. Carpet covered the entire floor. Under the chandelier stood a rickety carved walnut center table with a heavy white marble top, and a photograph album and a few daguerreotypes in cases were invariably on it. Likely, in a corner stood a whatnot. This contained seashells, a carved fan Uncle Manlius had brought back from China, some specimens of moss agate, quartz crystals, iron pyrites, a penwiper made by Aunt Cynthia when she was only six years old, probably two battered Gettysburg bullets, an Indian arrowhead Uncle Chester sent from out West, and a couple of keys to fit heaven knows what locks.

On a small stand between windows one could be certain of finding a music box—out of order—and a case of stuffed birds or crystallized leaves. A handsome clock, also out of order, occupied the mantel, over which hung a large, stern-faced oil portrait of Grandma Greene. On a corner cabinet rested stereoscopic views of Niagara Falls, the Leaning Tower of Pisa and the steamship *Great Eastern.*

Wallpapers with atrocious color combinations—maroon and gilt, reds and splotchy yellows—frequently covered the walls, and a large, square piano was the *pièce de résistance* of all genteel parlors. It was a respected fixture, no catchall. No shawls, scarves, vases, autographed photographs ever were placed on the piano; only music on the rack: Robinson's "Schottische," say, or songs of "Lorena," or "Flow Gently, Sweet Afton," or the "Mabel Waltz." The "Mabel Waltz" was so excessively popular that it was referred to in other songs, notably one sung by Tony Pastor, which he called the "Mabel Waltz" but whose lyric was adapted to an air called the "Naval Waltz."

Tony introduced his "Mabel" night upon night at his Pastor's Opera House, 201 Bowery, which had been an unsavory beer hall for the bibulous called Volk's Garden and where, so is the legend, the indecent gag originated that characterized the free-and-easy variety shows of the period. During the course of the bill, the manager announced to his beer-sodden audience: "And now, gents, Miss Lillian McTwobucks will sing 'Love Among the Roses.' " Whereupon a drunk arose and in stentorian tones replied, "She is a whore." Unabashed, the manager dismissed the interruption. "Nevertheless," he said, "Miss Lillian Mc-Twobucks will still sing 'Love Among the Roses' ":

> *Chorus:* Now I hate to tell, but then I must—
> Within her heart I placed my trust
> She was sitting in the garden,
> Where the little butterfly reposes:
> And how we met, I'll ne'er forget—
> 'Twas love among the roses!

Tony's "Mabel Waltz," if not so universal in its sentiment, or so colorful in its background, was more topical. Here it is:

THE MABEL WALTZ

(Tony Pastor's)
I once did know a pretty girl,
She dressed so very neat;
She used to run a sewing machine,
Down in Chatham Street.
Her eyes were bright, complexion light,
Her cheeks were like the rose;
She'd a dimple chin, and pouting lips,
And a beautiful turned up nose.
I never can forget the night
I met her at a ball:
'Twas a fancy hop, a dollar a head,
Up at Irving hall.

Chorus: She looked so neat, I never thought
She ever would prove false;
Her step was light as the bounding fawn,
Dancing the Mabel Waltz.

Alas for the aberrations of affections!—no novelty in Tony's time, just as they were a commonplace in Ptolemy's. Mabel, the wretch, was faithless, and Tony, after bewailing spent sums on lavished finery, the wrench of heart and mental anguish suffered, comes, not too speedily, to the denouement:

And when a year had passed away,
At a window I did see,
My fair, but false one sitting,
With a baby on her knee.
I quickly marched into the house,
And, there, what met my view!
'Twas a tall policeman, six feet high,
He was her husband, too!
He collared me, and then commenced
A series of assaults—
I never chassezed it so fast before,
While dancing the Mabel Waltz.

Odd twist; the incongruities of pop-tune lyrics are never to be analyzed. They abridge poetic license, are held by writers in fief. What is wrong with Mabel's Tony waltzing from his burly assailant? It fills out the line, doesn't it? And cued his following dance.

The tonal quality of the household squares in Tony's day was invariably inferior to those in the sporting houses which, by the way, we shall occupy later—in a quite disinterested and sociological analysis, to be sure; you will find the bawdyhouse an important factor in the annals of our pop tunes if you will tool along with us—but they were, these parlor pianos, in the cliché of the drama reviewer, adequate. And so prevalent (people amused *themselves* in other days) that those American Gilbert and Sullivans of the '70s, Harrigan and Hart, could scarcely fail us with a satirical reference. They did not fail, and one of their earliest songs drew immediate response from a public who understood and appreciated a genial jest of

MISS BRADY'S PIANO FORTAY

If you're fond of real classical music,
Come over to our tenement.
Drop in of a Saturday evening,
And listen to Caroline Bent.
She's lately come over from Europe,
From a musical conservortray,
She plays polkas and waltzes and didos,
On Miss Brady's piano fortay.

Chorus: Up and down, all around
Then she'll hammer away like a nailer.
One, two, three, can't you see,
Her German professor would say.
Pinafore, by the score
Olivette and the late Billie Taylor;
Allegro, de capo, on Miss Brady's piano fortay.

Folks who could not afford a pianofortay, and some who could, favored the melodeon or a harp. But this was generally a gesture; like the ornate mantel clock and the music box, they were usually in need of repair.

In winter—and in summer too, when the chandeliers, side brackets, mirrors, and paintings were covered with fly netting and the furniture disguised under linen coverings—young folks assembled in these parlors. Surprise parties, serenades, wooden weddings, tin weddings, birthdays, troths, picnics, were plotted and celebrated in them. It was a great unbosoming, ripe for melody, and everybody sang. It was fun, also, to examine the gifts for the celebrants—clothespins, ax helves, cradles, and kegs for the couple wedded five years; pie pans, toy fiddles of tin, muffin rings for the ten-year couples—all piled deep on the haircloth sofas and chairs.

This was the life of the ballad age; the fine old ballads (many of them were), which were such favorites eighty years ago; ballads that show the unmistakable antiquity—yes, and authenticity—of their Scottish and English forebears. The ballad, of course, was never completely expunged from the pop-tune genre. Yet, though it exists, it is devitalized, maudlin; popular still in the 1920s, it is now moribund.

THE OLD FOLKS ABROAD

Many of the ballads were popularized by the "Old Folks' Concerts," chief of which was "Father Kemp's Ye Olde Folkes' Concerts." Its success was sensational, and the copycat show world hastened to exploit that type of entertainment, flooding the nation with fifty-odd old folks' concerts troupes. Kemp owned a boot-and-shoe shop in Boston, and to advertise his store he put on amateur song festivals in the fall and winter. They were popular, and Kemp soon established them on a professional basis, although maintaining his store. He had a company of about fifteen performers arrayed in colonial costumes. They sang ballads, played instruments, delivered recitations, and for variety interpolated comic interludes portraying mock courtships or two-part humorous songs. A customary finale for the old folks' concerts was the "Tin Maker Man," in which the entire company joined. In the chorus, small mallets were used to pound on tin pans, and the audience gleefully joined in. Having no mallets, they clapped hands to the rhythm. Modern night clubs supply mallets to their customers, and there the resemblance ends. The general admission for these and other "concerts" was twenty-five cents. Father Kemp became a by-word in show business of the times, enjoyed the distinction of having himself and his troupe burlesqued and lampooned by other companies. The Morris Brothers' Minstrels ribbed his specialty mercilessly, Lon Morris, as "Father Kemp," introducing his burlesque with the lines: "We do not give these concerts to make money, but we do keep a boot-and-shoe store on Hanover St." Kemp, a shrewd showman, loved it for the ad it proved. He did such capacity business, his fame spread abroad. He knew it, and in the '60s took his company to England, returning with pockets jingling.

Many of the tunes of the old folks' concerts were delivered as duets, and their presentation, with a sort of Quakerish, Biblical touch, was as quaint as the colonial costumes. Simple, and rendered with apparent sincerity, they were extraordinarily popular throughout the '60s. And odd as it may seem when you read the following lines, the singers often responded to three or four encores of the same song. Such a song:

Joshua: Dost thou love me Sister Ruth? Say, say, say.
Ruth: As I fain would speak the truth, Yea, yea, yea.
Joshua: Long my heart hath yearned for thee, pretty sister Ruth.
Ruth: That has been the case with me, dear engaging youth.

Joshua: Wilt thou promise to be mine? Maiden fair?
Ruth: Take my hand, my heart is thine. There, there, there.
Joshua: Let us thus the bargain seal. Oh, dear me, hi ho.
Ruth: Laws how very odd I feel. Oh, dear me, hi ho.

Joshua: Love like ours can never cloy. Hum, hum, hum.
Ruth: While no jealous fears annoy. Hum, hum, hum.
Joshua: Oh how blest we both should be. Hey down ho down hey.
Ruth: I could almost dance with glee. Hey down ho down hey.

The "old folks" made much of these naïve lines. Sighs, embarrassment, archness, inhibitions were adroitly blended with eye work, facial expression, and stage business unique in the balladry of the day.

Undoubtedly the first of the "family" troupes was the Peak, a related band of psalm singers who began as troubadours in 1829, pioneers in a form of entertainment that was to become so enormously popular in the '60s and whose appeal lasted well into the '70s. But the idea, subsequently exploited with such pronounced success by the Peaks, was that of John B. Gough, probably the most influential white-ribbon rabble rouser in this most susceptible of rabble-roused nations. At the time, William Peak was organist of a church in Medford, Massachusetts, and his wife sang in the choir. Gough, a good showman, as are all successful exhorters, had heard the Peaks play and sing. It occurred to him that he might even increase his hold on his temperance audiences if he varied his lectures with an interlude of song. He put it up to the Peaks, and they said yes, provided Gough didn't book them so far away they couldn't get back to Medford for Sunday services. Gough agreed, and they started out. The venture was immediately successful, and Peak, no dolt, quit Gough and went out on his own—or, rather, the Peak family's own, for he gathered for his initial troupe his sons, William, Jr., and Eddie, and his daughters, Julia, Fannie, and Lizetta. All of them sang well and were talented performers on harp, organ, and guitar.

Peak, Jr., inherited his father's showmanship. Wandering afield one day (for the Peak recitals were godly), he slipped into a free and easy in Milwaukee, where an obscure comic, Sol Smith Russell, was doing a razzle-dazzle act of songs and character impersonations. Almost at the same time a family of juvenile musicians named Berger crossed paths with the Peaks. They were Fred, Louisa, Anna, and Henry Berger, brothers and sisters who had been playing with the Carter Zouave Troupe—twenty children who drilled, formed a brass band, and put on vaudeville specialties. The Bergers played well, were attractive on stage, and Peak, Jr., joined them and Sol Smith Russell to his family troupe of singers, musicians, and bell ringers.

The Bergers, which now included Sol Smith Russell, who married Louisa, remained with the Peaks until 1869, when they went out under their own management. They were public favorites until the '80s, largely owing to the artistry of Sol Smith Russell, one of the greatest of America's singing comedians and one whom we shall meet again.

As in all affairs, you wane, too, in show business, and when the Peaks petered out, the Hutchinson Family took over. This outstanding and significant troupe was popular some thirty years, and their heydays were the '60s. The Hutchinsons originated in Milford, N. H., and comprised the tribes of Asa, John, and Judson Hutchinson. Later a sister, Abby, and Asa's wife, Lizzie, were added. After they were well established ("well established" is an understatement; they were immense, so highly regarded that towns were named for them in Kansas and Minnesota), Asa and Lizzie's children, Abby, Freddie, and "Little Dennett," as he was billed, started a troupe of their own and, exploiting the nationally known family name, soon reaped the capacity business previously enjoyed by their father and mother, uncles and aunts.

Asa was a hell of a fellow. As with the Peaks, the Hutchinsons' presentation of song and recitation was semi-religious. But Asa could get more come-to-Jesus into his work than any of his colleagues, a quality that impressed Harriet Beecher Stowe with repercussions and considerable importance. As were 150,-000 others, Hutchinson was deeply shaken by *Uncle Tom's Cabin* (and what a raft of songs that book inspired! "I Am Going There," "Death of St. Clare," "Uncle Tom's Glimpse of Glory," etc., etc.; even Whittier wrote one—"Little Eva"—but then the great Quaker humanist could write a political campaign song, and did), and asked her to permit its dramatization. He need not have asked her. After running serially, *Tom* was published, March 20, 1852, and an author's dramatic rights were not included in his copyright until 1870. Harriet replied to Hutchinson in a characteristic, and little-known, letter:

I have considered your application and asked advice of my different friends, and the general sentiment of those whom I have consulted so far agrees with my own, that it would not be advisable to make that use of my work which you propose. It is thought, with the present state of theatrical performances in this country, that any attempt on the part of Christians to identify themselves with them will be productive of danger to the individual character, and to the general cause. If the barrier which now keeps young people of Christian families from theatrical entertainments is once broken down by the introduction of respectable and moral plays, they will then be open to all the temptations of those which are not such, and there will be, as the world now is, five bad plays to one good. However specious may be the idea of reforming dramatic amusements, I fear it is wholly impracticable, and as a friend to you should hope that you would not run the risk of so dangerous an experiment. The world is not good enough yet for it to succeed. I preserve a very pleasant recollection of your family, and of the gratification I have derived from the exercise of your talents, and it gives me pleasure to number you among my friends.

Prissy Harriet! Uncle Tom was dramatized, whether by Harriet's express permission to Hutchinson or pure piracy is not known. M. B. Leavitt, in his autobiography, *Fifty Years in Theatrical Management*, says that she did give Hutchinson permission. But Leavitt—and what chronicler does not?—nodded. At any rate, it was produced at the Museum Theater in Boston in August 1852, and the late Forrest Wilson, Harriet's latest biographer, says that from that year to 1931 it was never off the boards of the American stage. If Harriet yielded to the theatrical seduction of Hutchinson, she maintained stolidly her puritanical aversion for the theater for six years until, in 1858, Francis Underwood carried her off to Boston's National Theater, not only to see for the first time a performance of the play made from her famous book—it was the first time she had ever soiled her skirts in that den of iniquity, the theater itself.

Many a ballad listened to and sung by people of the '6os

and '70s, who shared not Harriet's sawtoothed religion, had little story substance, albeit their themes stressed moral delinquencies and the harrowing punishment that was the inevitable lot of offenders. A number of them, especially those sung in the taverns and free and easies, were lyric relics of traditional origin; "antiques," showmen of the '60s called them. And one was beautiful:

THE GYPSY DAVY

There was a lord, a highborn lord,
He married a highborn lady.
She up and left her bed and board
And eloped with the Gypsy Davy.

Chorus: Ri too ral loo ral loo ral lay,
Beware of the Gypsy Dávy.

His lordship came back from the hunt,
Inquiring for his lady.
The serving maid to him she said,
She's gone with the Gypsy Davy.

How could she leave her highborn lord?
How could she leave her baby?
How could she leave her bed and board
And elope with the Gypsy Davy?

Last night she slept in a feather bed,
Along with her lord and her baby,
Tonight she sleeps on the cold, cold ground
In the arms of the Gypsy Davy.

In lyric quality, poignancy, and suspense of sentiment, this ballad is unsurpassed by any of contemporary popularity, its assonances justified. The taste was not all for the bathetic and banal.

The wages of sin were strictly adhered to in another:

THE HOUSE CARPENTER AND THE SHIP CARPENTER

There was a jolly ship carpenter
Who sailed upon the sea.
Fell in love with the wife of a house carpenter,
And a fine young woman was she.

If you will leave your house carpenter
And sail along with me,
I'll take you where the grass grows green
In lands you never did see.

If I should leave my house carpenter,
And sail along with thee,
What would become of my keepsakes dear,
Also my little ba-bee?

Said he I've a hundred ships or more
All sailing for dry land.
Three thousand and ten of your countrymen—
Love, they shall be at your command.

They had not sailed two weeks or more,
Two weeks, or scarcely three,
When the ship struck a rock and sprung a leak,
And they went to the bottom of the sea.

Oh, cursed be the ship carpenters,
Oh, cursed be their lives,
For invading the homes of the house carpenters
And coaxing away their wives.

Recognition of the facts of life and man's errant way with woman is further developed in "The Sailor and the Tailor," an interesting ballad for its Americanizations. No doubt it is an "antique" as the two that have been quoted. But "canoodled," and "what the hell," and "hog in a stall" are hardly British locutions of whatever century. They are the vulgate of America's '60s' and '70s' menfolk, and the version given, that of Jack Murphy, himself a trouper for more than half a century, would seem to be the emendation of some colloquial-minded performer in the free and easies, or as rendered to his banjo by some tavern busker, a hail fellow of airs and rough graces we have yet to meet. And one can only forgive the juxtaposition of "sweat" and "chest."

THE SAILOR AND THE TAILOR

Oh, there was a jolly boatswain, in London he did dwell,
He had a charming wife and the tailor loved her well.

They had a merry time when the sailor was at sea,
They kissed and canoodled just as happy as could be.

Chorus: Naw tee toodin naddin naddy naw tee toodin naddy ay,
Naw tee toodin naddin naddy naw tee toodin naddy ay.

When the sailor came ashore he brought home his chest,
And he kept it at home till he sailed for the west.
So he waited with his mates till the turning of the tide,
Then he knocked on the door and the tailor had to hide.

Don't worry now my love, I will not disturb your rest,
But my ship's about to sail and I've come for my chest.
The weather being cold they were muffled to the chin;
They opened the door and they walked right in.

The sailors being stout and the sailors being strong,
They picked up the chest and they carried it along.
But they laid their burden down while they wiped away
the sweat,
Says one to the other, "what the hell's in the chest?"

So they opened up the chest and there before them all,
Lay the tailor just as snug as a hog in a stall.
Says he now that I've got you I'll take you out to sea,
And I'll soon teach you how to make tailor boys for me.

It should be apparent that the foregoing were no part of the balladry of the psalm-singing Hutchinsons, the clans of Peak, or the "Olde Folkes" of the canny Kemp. They did, though, these semi-salvationists, foster a liking for the ballad, kept alive its musical story, even in their sedate and dignified renditions, which the free-and-easy performer, and his freer and easier cousin, the busker, rough-hewed for the rowdy stag audiences they played to in the taverns and wine rooms of the nation. The Carroll Family, for that matter, an Irish troupe, less prim and extraordinarily popular in the '60s and '70s, had a repertoire that closely shaded that of the buskers. A lively favorite of the Carrolls was:

THE LANDLADY OF FRANCE

A landlady of France loved an officer, 'tis said,
And this officer he dearly loved her brandy-o.

Now said she, "I dearly love this officer although his nose is re{
And his legs are what the regiment calls bandy-o."

But when this bandy officer was ordered to the coast,
Then she tore her lovely locks that looked so sandy-o.
"Now goodby, my love," said she, "when you write pray pay th{
  post,
But before we part we'll take a drop of brandy-o."

"Take a bottle of it with you," to the officer she said,
"In your tent, you know, my love 'twill be the dandy-o."
"You're right, my dear," said he, "for a tent is very damp,
And 'tis better in my tent to take some brandy-o."

So she filled him up a bumper just before he left the town,
With another for herself so neat and handy-o.
And to keep their droopin' spirits up they poured the spirits dow{
For love is like the colic, cured with brandy-o.

To be sure, this is scarcely of a piece with some of the song{
we shall come upon that entertained the bibulous—and amorou{
—gentry of the taverns. But its implications and character woul{
have appalled the Peaks and the Hutchinsons, and its them{
was likewise shunned by the "Olde Folkes."

A feature of the Carroll Family's performance was the playing of the Irish pipes, and since both the Irish and Scotch bag-
pipes were often played in the taverns, the free and easies, a{
well as in more reputable halls of entertainment, and are related to the musical expression of the '60s and '70s, they rate
a page or so of description. They differ vastly.

The Scotch pipes is an instrument consisting of an airtight
leather bag about the size and shape of an ordinary ham. The
bag is carried under the left arm and filled with air by blowing
through a tube or mouthpiece attached to the top of the bag.
Four pipes, varying in length from about eighteen inches to
two feet six inches, are also attached to the top of the bag. They
look something like clarinets. They are the drones. They are
tuned in fifths and are of a set tone, keeping up a constant,
sustained chord or drone as long as there is any air in the bag to
vibrate the reeds. The chanter, upon which the melody is played,

s attached to the bag near the top and held in a vertical position by the player. The chanter resembles the oboe, but it has a range of only nine notes of the diatonic scale; that is, no half tones are possible. Half tones are slurred over, or faked, by playing triplets, for there are no keys on the chanter, just eight holes. The higher notes of the register are achieved by squeezing the bag harder, which forces additional air through the chanter's reed. It is a double reed, like that on a bassoon.

The Irish pipes are not operated by lung power. A small leather bag is strapped under the left arm. This is inflated by a powerful bellows which is fastened under the right arm. The player assumes a sitting position, and the drones extend from a finger board placed on the right knee. The drones do not sound continuously; they are controlled by the keys on the finger board. The chanter is placed in an upright position on the left knee. It is fitted with keys and pads, like a flute, and a valve, or stop, on the end of the chanter can be closed by pressing down on the knee. This is used to increase the range. The drones can be operated when the right hand is not in use or, as some expert players do, by using the wrist of the right hand to depress the keys. Because of their arrangement, the Irish pipes are not so practical for marching as the Scotch pipes are. But for reels, jigs, and strathspeys they never fail "to get the feet going." Pat Touhey, who was one of the best Irish pipers ever to appear in America, once teamed with Joe Burke for a vaudeville tour. The managers were a bit skeptical of the appeal of such exotic jig and music, but they were finally penciled in for an emergency date at the American Theater, then at Eighth Avenue and Forty-second Street in New York and now the site of the Franklin Savings Bank. The dubious management just hoped, for the type of audience was largely Jewish. But when Pat went into "Before the Daylight in the Morning" on his pipes, the audience almost kicked down the building marking time.

A PENNY FOR YOUR SONG

ALL THE FOREGOING SONGS, and many we shall come to learn, were known to the young folks of the '60s. Their social position was curious, an astonishing contrast to our own flotsam. The explanation is simple: they had virtually no place to go but home. Variety halls were taboo, and the free and easies were "hell holes for harlots." (An exaggeration of the reformers. Girls who attended the free and easies were of the "good time," promiscuous type. But they were not strictly pro.) The legitimate theaters, what few there were, were expensive for their meager pocket money. And there were no movies, no radio (to each age a benison), no amusement parks. Sports consisted of skating, sledding, riding, and swimming, and most of these required an excursion of a whole day. So they met at one another's homes for euchre, dominoes, or charades; arranged surprise parties or serenades—and sang songs and songs and more songs while lemonade, or perhaps a glass of Aunt Euphemia's currant wine, was served.

Printed music was not common, but the words of songs in penny ballad form—broadsides—hawked by old men and women on the street corners were always available. They fastened the broadsides to a rack, and when a potential customer paused, and perhaps chose a ballad for its words, the hawker would hum, whistle, or sing the melody until the purchaser memorized it. Paying his penny, he went off singing. Singing on the streets was a casual practice. The young folks were quick to catch choruses and would sing them riding on the horsecars or while walking home.

These hawkers persisted well into the '80s in New York, but on a roving basis and in a manner close to racketeering. The "industry," known as the "song sheet men," was controlled by one Michael Cregansteine, "King of the Song Sheet Men," a picaresque and dissolute character with headquarters at 25

Bowery, a flophouse where he cradled his two hundred-odd henchmen and there recruited, drilled, and assigned them to districts. They were exclusively hawkers, not alley or street singers, and generally worked in pairs after obtaining their songs from Cregansteine, who in turn got them from the publishers. Cregansteine paid the publishers (when he paid) forty cents per hundred for his sheets, and his hawkers sold them for from one to five cents, or more if they could get it. They worked Broadway, the side streets, even the water front—colorful figures in an expressive town.

Cregansteine was a rare fellow. He lived at 25 Bowery, where beds were a dime a night. Despite the bastard teutonism of his name, Cregansteine was an Irishman, Dublin born. He was a great, if misspent, organizer who had drifted into his unusual role because of drink. A long career of failures and disappointments dogged him. He was educated for the priesthood, but his exercising elbow thwarted his ordination and he became a policeman. When the Franco-Prussian war began, he quit the force, went to France, and joined up, winning a commission for bravery in action. Then drunkenness provoked an escapade for which he was court-martialed, and, to salvage what he could from the disgrace, he resigned.

Returning to America, he taught languages for a while in a private school, lasting until his alcoholic addiction became apparent. How he got into the song-sheet racket is not clear anywhere, but he was an ace man himself and, even after he organized his gang, often peddled music, working the saloons at night, singing the melodies he sold, varying his whisky tenor with recitations from the poets—Moore's "Lalla Rookh," Poe's "Raven," and passages from Shakespeare.

He had an amazing accent—a mixture of French, German, and English with a touch o' brogue—that somehow gave emphasis to his renditions and always amused or astonished his sodden listeners. Occasionally he would dismay his barroom patrons with passages from Sallust, Caesar, or Virgil's *Bucolics*. One day he was picked up drooling by a policeman who hustled him over to Blackwell's (now Welfare) Island. The policeman thought him demented, and so did the doctor on first examination. The physician turned to an assistant and muttered, in Latin: "His face and voice are those of a lunatic; as such he is condemned." Whereupon Cregansteine came out of his stupor, translated the passage (as given), and began a poetic discourse. The physician, astounded, freed him. The quote was right about his face. Distorted by drink, only an acute observer could see the vanishing marks of culture that twenty-five years of dissipation had not entirely erased. He would go down to his Bowery dump, befuddled with drink, and awaken even the gutter drunks with a stentorian rendition of the "Marseillaise," his favorite song. What became of him, no one knows. One can be certain only that he is dead.

Everybody knew a lot of songs in those days. A good song lived for years instead of being mechanically murdered in a few weeks. At the home gatherings about the square piano, or accompanied by flute, guitar, or accordion, the young folks—elders too—would always oblige with a popular ballad, or perhaps Uncle Ned would prefer his own delivery of "Daniel O'Connell." Songs with gibberish choruses (some we already know) were popular, especially:

POLLY WON'T YOU TRY ME O

Way down South where I was born,
Sing song kitchie can't you ki me O,
I chopped the wood and I shucked the corn,
Sing song Polly won't you ki me O?
Ki mo nero dar a woo,
Ma hee ma hi ma rump sutta puddle wuddle linkum nit cut,
Sing song kitchie won't you ki me O?

Impromptu duos, trios, or quartets were always willing, and often harmonized quite well. And no bass at any gathering ever had to be coaxed to sing

CAPTAIN KIDD

Oh my name is Captain Kidd and I sailed,
My name is Captain Kidd and I sailed,
My name is Captain Kidd,
Many wicked deeds I did,
And a heap of gold I hid as I sailed as I sailed,
And a heap of gold I hid as I sailed.

Many gallant ships I sank,
Many kegs of rum I drank,
And I made 'em walk the plank as I sailed.

I sank 'em great and small
And I never cared at all
For their shot or cannon ball as I sailed.

And of course there was always a whistler in the party. If Jack, the bass, could entertain, well, so would Bill, who could whistle, and did, "Listen to the Mocking Bird." Sep Winner, a Philadelphia music dealer and publisher, wrote and "arranged," as it says on the title cover, the song under the name of Alice Hawthorne, possibly the name of his mother. But an additional name—Richard Milburn—appears on the original issues. He may be the Negro for whom Winner arranged the "Mocking Bird." The Negro sold candy on the street and whistled remarkably well to his own guitar accompaniment. He was a character well known to Winner, and their collaboration is probable.

Home was where the fun was, and the music. Variety halls, the wine rooms, the free and easies, the taverns, socially barred to the young people and ladies as disreputable rendezvous, which they usually were, were popular with menfolk of all classes, and an infiltration into the home of tavern songs, often "blue" and sometimes downright bawdy, became gradual though never, of course, pronounced. The elders patronized the theaters, but attendance was not habitual. Still, almost every adult knew *London Assurance* and the *Lady of Lyons*, and only dolts or paupers missed the performances of Edwin Forrest.

And although the variety halls flourished, and were to become of vast importance in the social structure after Tony Pastor swept them clean with his shows in the '80s, entertainment for mixed audiences was available in the '60s and '70s. The circus, the minstrels, the "museum" show, which was a combination of side-show freaks and variety-hall performers whose patter and songs were censored, the specialty and caravan shows of Washburn, the Lingards, Pastor himself, Sol Smith Russell, William J. Scanlan, and many others—all these were presentations women and children could attend unblushingly.

Comedy male quartets were popular in these shows, and it is curious that they were not organized as a definite entertaining unit until the middle '80s. Those of the '60s were never a permanent partnership or distinct act, but an impromptu assembly of four performers in the show who would introduce an utterly senseless routine of burlesqued tragedy, operatic numbers, nursery rhymes, magic, anything ridiculous they could think of. They were the precursors of the later day "nut" comics. A quartet of this kind was used as a "comic interlude" and billed as, say, "The Four Prophets," and a song they invariably sang, achieving the comic effect by a dead pan delivery of intense seriousness, was

WING WANG WADDLE

When I was a little boy I lived all by myself,
And all the bread and cheese I got I put upon the shelf.
The rats and the mice they led me such a life
I had to go to London to buy myself a wife.

Chorus: Wing, wang, waddle, to my ding, dong doodle,
O my fim, fum foodle, it's a long ways home.

The lanes were so long and the streets were so narrow,
I had to bring her home in an old wheelbarrow.
The wheelbarrow broke and my wife got a fall,
Down came wheelbarrow, little wife and all.

Swapped wheelbarrow and got myself a sheep,
The doggoned thing went fast asleep.
Swapped my sheep and got me a hen,
The crazy critter wouldn't stay in her pen.

Swapped my hen and got me a rat,
Put it on the housetop away from the cat.
Swapped the rat and got me a mole,
Doggoned thing ran straight to its hole.

This was a "mixed audience" song, its jingle a favorite of the
children.

MAIDENS NOT SO COY

ON SEPTEMBER 12, 1866, a theatrical event occurred whose influence upon our songs and entertainment was considerable and
is still effective. This was the opening at Niblo's Garden, then at
Broadway and Prince St., of the *Black Crook*. It was a daring
exhibition of tighted thighs and ladies *voluptés* that inaugurated
sophisticated musicals in the United States, a heritage made
brazen and profitable by today's Buddy De Sylva, Dwight
Deere Wiman, Max Gordon, and George Abbott. The ladies of
the *Black Crook*—and this is a sad corrective better speedily forgotten—were (alas!) not a bevy of brewery blondes of billowy
bosom and fattish rump. They were, actually, except for the
period's fashion, even as the girls of today—slender, modeled to
nature's wont. Give no heed to the pictures. Their bosoms and
buttocks were phonies—padded by Dazian, the theatrical cos-
tuming house still in existence at 142 West Forty-fourth Street,
New York, with what were known as "symmetricals," lumps of
batting strategically placed, distorting the girls' natural curves
to the masculine truck-horse taste of the times.

Fantastic itself was the *Black Crook*, a shot in the dark by an
apathetic manager who paled for years with the recollection of
how nearly he missed a half interest of the $650,000 profit in
its four years of successful operation. (The run, however, was
not continuous. The *Black Crook* played 475 performances
after its initial presentation and was revived again in the '70s.)
It was produced by Henry C. Jarrett, who was of the theater,
and Harry Palmer, a Wall Street broker who occasionally
angeled shows. With what?—Jarrett was soon to inquire, for

when the money was needed for production (it cost $30,000 a lot for a show in those days), Palmer didn't have a nickel and his share was supplied by Leonard Grover, actor, playwright, and manager, who was really responsible for the presentation of a show which yielded him not a pennyworth of its profits. He had no piece of the play, presumably taking other security for his loan to Palmer.

One Charles M. Barras, an actor, had written a play. He submitted it to his friend, William Wheatley, then manager of Niblo's Garden. Wheatley paid no attention to it, but out of his regard for Barras he agreed to bring the actor and Grover, whom Wheatley knew, together for a reading. The three met the following day, and in the balcony of Niblo's Garden, Barras read them his script of the *Black Crook*. Wheatley slept soundly throughout the reading, but Grover at once saw its merit. He roused Wheatley, praised the script highly, and solely upon Grover's recommendation, Wheatley blindly agreed to stage it at Niblo's Garden with the backing of Jarrett and Palmer, who, recall, was fortified by the loan from Grover.

The opening was a sensation. It was the first "girlie" type show New York had ever witnessed, and when word got around of its naughty exposé of breasts and buttocks (untrue), of its suggestive songs, of the girls' prancing legs flung cancan high with deliberate, if graceful, assault upon decorum, an enraged pulpit and press denounced it for its harlotrous obscenities and called for the noose and the rack. The result, of course (even as today), sent a never-ending stream of eager patrons to Wheatley's boxoffice.

There was another immediate reaction: the *Black Crook* girls were all blondes—among the most important props of the company were several gallons of peroxide—and a rage for "flaxen" hair ensued, inspired by the show, which was a musical extravaganza with the threat of the Evil Genius (the Black Crook) woven through it. Alas for the perversity of fate! So enormous was the success of the *Black Crook* that Spalding, Bidwell and McDonough, New York theatrical managers, bought the South

American rights to the production, and scarcely had the company disembarked when the damsels' golden hair proved as the strands of Lilith to the unfortunate entrepreneurs. The Latins, whose zeal for blondes is fanatic, carried off all but one of the girls, ending the tour. The lone lady, faithful to a New York fiancé, was Augusta Chambers, a comely and clever soubrette.

The tirade of the Grundys of the '6os against the *Black Crook*, whose girls truly exposed no more skin than that upon their face, neck, and arms, is to us both funny and preposterous —until the social and religious setting of the period—a period whose thought and belief was virtually dominated by Henry Ward Beecher, forensic pseudo-moralist—is realized. Yet even stronger than the tablets of the hairshirts are the passions of man. Forever will he yield to the female body—even as Beecher to Lib Tilton's. (He was soundly slapped in song for this, as we shall see.) Beecher suffered acutely from the Puritan's complaint, which was, in Mark Twain's diagnosis, his denial for centuries that fornication is fun. Thus were the blasts of the reformers ineffective in the '6os, as they were unavailing in our own time to make permanent the thirteen-year crime of prohibition.

The *Black Crook* and succeeding burlettas—*Lydia Thompson's British Blondes* was an immediate successor—not only withstood the trumpetings of the self-anointed, they profited excessively by them. And they became a factor in the life of those days with a potency heretofore too little regarded. The effect of the *Black Crook* on our songs was immense. Almost overnight the influence of this extravaganza blanketed the American ballad, stimulated a pronounced change in pop-tune style to the comic, the satirical, the flirtatious. "You naughty, naughty men," caroled Millie Cavendish, the Carline of the *Black Crook* musical on that opening September night in Niblo's Garden, and who then proceeded to justify the accusation with rhymed premise in what may well be the first sophisticated song to be introduced in America. It bore the title of the quoted refrain, and its lyric and music, written by T. Kennick and G. Bicknell, is of a true

strain retained to this day by Cole Porter and Rodgers and Hart
Here is the song she sang (the last two lines of each verse were
repeated in the singing):

YOU NAUGHTY, NAUGHTY MEN

I will never more deceive you, or of happiness bereave you,
But I'll die a maid to grieve you, oh, you naughty, naughty men!
You may talk of love and sighing, say for us you're nearly dying
All the while you know you're trying to deceive, you naughty men.

When you want a kiss or favor you put on your best behavior,
And your looks of kindness savor, oh, you naughty, naughty men!
Of love you set us dreaming, and when with hope we're teeming
We find you are but scheming, you naughty, naughty men!

If a fortune we inherit, you see in us every merit,
And declare we're girls of spirit, oh, you naughty, naughty men!
But too often matrimony is a mere matter of money;
We get bitters, 'stead of honey from you naughty, naughty men!

And when married how you treat us, and of each fond wish defeat
us,
And some will even beat us, oh! you naughty, naughty men!
You take us from our mothers, from our sisters and our brothers;
When you get us—flirt with others; oh, you cruel, wicked men!

But with all your faults we clearly love you wicked fellows dearly,
Yes, we dote upon you dearly, oh, you naughty, naughty men!
We've no wish to distress you, we'd sooner far caress you,
And when kind we'll say, 'Oh, bless you,' you naughty, dear, de-
lightful men!

The imperfections of the lines are atomic in relation to the
drool of contemporaneous "lyrics." What is graver is its astonishing realism. Here is no coy maid of blushing mien and
downcast eyes contemplating a love everlasting from a marriage
made in heaven with the swain of her choice and whose vows
have been sanctified by the angels. How stabbing, then, is this
Black Crook lyric at this, the popular virginal conception of the
'6os' popular song writers!

Within two years of that September evening in 1866 in

Niblo's Garden, W. H. Gove, a song writer and publisher of Boston, wrote and published:

THE CHARMING YOUNG WIDOW I MET IN THE TRAIN

I live in Vermont and one morning last summer,
A letter informed me my Uncle was dead,
And also requested I'd come down to Boston
As he left me a large sum of money it said;
Of course I determ'd on making the journey
And to book myself by the "first class" I was fain,
Though had I gone "second" I had never encountered
The Charming Young Widow I met in the Train.

Yet scarce was I seated within the compartment,
Before a fresh passenger enter'd the door,
'Twas a female—a young one—and dressed in deep mourning,
An infant in long clothes she gracefully bore.
A white cap surrounded a face oh so lovely!
I never shall look on one like it again,
I fell deep in love overhead in a moment,
With the Charming Young Widow I Met in the Train.

The Widow and I side by side sat together,
The carriage containing ourselves and no more,
When silence was broken by my fair companion
Who inquired the time by the watch that I wore.
I of course satisfied her, and then conversation
Was freely indulged in by both, 'till my brain
Fairly reeled with excitement, I grew so enchanted
With the Charming Young Widow I Met in the Train.

We became so familiar I ventured to ask her
How old was the child that she held at her breast.
"Oh, Sir," she responded, and into tears bursting,
Her infant still closer convulsively pressed.
"When I think of my child I am well nigh distracted,
Its Father—my Husband—oh my heart breaks with pain."
She choking with sobs leaned her breast on my waistcoat—
Did the Charming Young Widow I Met in the Train.

By this time the train had arrived at the station
Within a few miles of the great one in town,
When my charmer exclaimed as she looked through the window—
"Good gracious alive! why there goes Mr. Brown,

He's my late Husband's Brother—dear Sir would you kindly
My best beloved child for a moment sustain?"
Of course I complied—then off on the platform
Tripped the Charming Young Widow I Met in the Train.

Three minutes elapsed when the whistle it sounded,
The Train began moving—no Widow appeared,
I bawled out "Stop! Stop!" but they paid no attention,
With a snort and a jerk, started off as I feared.
In this horrid dilemma I sought for the hour—
But my watch! Ha! where was it? Where, where was my chain?
My purse too, my ticket, gold pencil-case—all gone,
Oh that Artful Young Widow I Met in the Train.

While I was my loss thus so deeply bewailing,
The train again stopped and I "ticket please" heard,
So I told the Conductor while dandling the infant,
The loss I'd sustained—but he doubted my word.
He called more officials—a lot gathered round me—
Uncovered the child—oh how shall I explain!
For behold 'twas no baby—'twas only a dummy!
Oh that Crafty Young Widow I Met in the Train.

Satisfied I'd been robbed they allowed my departure
Though of course I'd to settle my fare the next day.
And I now wish to counsel young men from the country
Lest they should get served in a similar way.
Beware of Young Widows you meet on the Railway
Who lean on your shoulder—whose tears fall like rain;
Look out for your pockets in case they resemble
The Charming Young Widow I Met in the Train.

This was 1868. And for several years thereafter, Gove's
young widow, whose charms were but the veneer of deceit, was
a popular new-type ballad, daring in its flaunt of hitherto un-
assailable feminine virtues. It is quite possible Gove never saw
the *Black Crook;* and even if he did, he might never have written the song. But it is inconceivable that it would have been
popular had he, by some strange anachronistic urge, turned it
out in the early '60s. A number of songs of this type followed
Gove's not-so-charming young widow. And Gove himself, if
one be not unfair to a buried man, may have borrowed his idea
from an earlier English song, "The Dark Girl Dressed in Blue,"

which was written and sung with immeasurable success by
Harry Clifton, a popular British music-hall performer in the
6os. Indeed, there is an Americanized version of the song
which delighted the free-and-easy patrons of those days. Like
Jove's widow, Clifton's girl in blue was a gay deceiver who
induced an impromptu escort she had met on the train to pass a
counterfeit $10 bill, the change from which she pocketed and
fled. So from the frail woman type, ripe, perhaps eager, for seduction, the bards of the period, prodded by a public equally
eager in its response, passed on to the brazen hussy.

Observe this illustration of abandon:

GIRL OF THE PERIOD
(Late '6os)

I am a girl of this period, and I am not afraid to venture
That I am just the gayest girl of this the nineteenth century.
Some gents think they are very fast, but this is all con-
ceited;
Give us gay girls but a square chance and we are bound to
beat 'em.

Chorus: I am just sixteen and from Mama,
With little poodle and cigar,
I strut the street with a flourishing cane,
And the Girl of the Period is my name.

Now all you chaps that's twenty or more,
And don't want to be on the bachelor's score,
For heaven's sake don't longer tarry
But come to me—for I'm bound to marry.
I'm handsome, and I know it, too;
With a waterfall of a golden hue;
With a Grecian Bend and a heavy frill—
I'll tell you I'm a sweet little pill.

This little tramp is as atrocious as the "lyric" that characterizes
her. It is quite apparent she is well on the way to a couch other
than the marriage bed. Where were the songs of yesteryear?

Let us sing of the days that are gone, Maggie,
When you and I were young!

"Girl of the Period" is a baffling song, the allusions in it
chorus surprising. Few expressions are more factual than ou:
popular songs; even their exaggerations, for comic or satirica
effect, can be analyzed, traced. There is no explanation fo:
the cigar. Save for a few old pipe smokers, women did no
smoke in the '60s, '70s, or '80s, and never in public. Prostitute:
would occasionally take snuff, which they rolled in a smal
piece of cheesecloth or tissue paper and placed behind the lowe:
lip, and for a lark might try a puff or two on a cigar. It was no
a practice. Nor did women carry canes.

And here (oh, fie for shame!) is the pansy!

THE BUTTERFLY DUDE

He's his mama's own sweet little pet.
He can smoke a real strong cigaret,
A sweet scented dandy,
A sugar and candy;
He'd melt if he ever got wet.
He's a birdie that's fond of his ease.
He tries very hard for to please.
He's a delicate duck,
And he plays in great luck
For he'd fall all apart if he'd sneeze.

Chorus: Oh the dude, the butterfly dude,
Sweet little dolly, he talks like a Polly.
The dude, the dude, the butterfly dude—
Oh, say, did you ever get on to the dude?

The "waterfall of golden hue" is, in the "Girl of the Period,"
of course, a reference to the hair-dos of the day, and not so unlike our own, for the "waterfall" draped down en masse, so to
say, over the fair one's shoulders, where it was caught and held
with a net. It resembled the snood of the 1940s. The Greciar
Bend was a silly, strutting, camel-like walk, the fashionabl
feminine stride of the day. The press hooted at it, and th
thoroughly aroused song writers, and their exponents, the performers, jibed at it mercilessly.

It was a natural target for William H. Lingard, a female

mpersonator who, with his brother, Dick, were a popular
eam throughout the decade of the '70s. When its silly contor-
ion was being practiced extensively by women all over the East
(especially in Saratoga and Long Branch, N. J., then summer
social capitals), Lingard seized upon it for one of his best
satirical characterizations:

THE GRECIAN BEND

(Lingard's version)
Good evening to one and all;
I hope I don't intrude,
Dressed in this quiet fashion:
Pray do not think me rude.
I always study Le Follet,
The fashion to amend;
So I introduce you, ladies, to
This graceful Grecian Bend.

Chorus: The Grecian Bend, as I now show,
You must admit is all the go;
The head well forward, and the body you extend,
To be perfect in the Grecian Bend.

'Twas raining hard the other day:
So, I got into a stage.
Some little boys began to shout
Which put me in a rage.
The driver, too, said: "Really, miss,
You've room enough for ten!"
And actually charged me double,
On account of my Grecian Bend.

Then Lingard introduced this patter:

I wouldn't mind it so much, only there was Ann Jenkins, who
lives next door to me, in the same stage; she began to laugh at me.
She's been practising the Grecian Bend for three weeks, but she
can't do it. She's jealous of me, because I took her young man
away. One gent had the audacity to tell me that the Grecian Bend
was nothing more or less than a spasmodic movement of the third
rib in connection with the left shoulder, in fact I need not tell you
that. . . . (*Then into the chorus*).

The Lingards often appeared at Jim Fisk's Grand Opera House (Jim himself was exploited in song—how could they overlook him?) when it was customary to produce a farce, or afterpiece—*Box and Cox, Handy Andy*, the *Limerick Boy*, or *Troublesome Lodgers*—at the close of the main performance, which might have been tragedy, heavy melodrama, or opera. The Lingards produced skits, travesties, or farces for these aftershows.

When two dramas or other productions were presented on one bill, the Lingards appeared between the first and second sections of the program. These shows ran late, customers always got the worth of their money—in length, at least. Aimee often appeared with the Lingards on the Grand Opera House's bills. She was French, a natural comedienne, and professional oldsters recalled her work as unmatched by contemporary artists. Every one loved her "Pretty As a Picture" number. It was not much of a song, but its tune was catchy, and largely through her artistry she made it quite popular.

PRETTY AS A PICTURE

Oh my heart is gone and I'm forlorn,
Such a darling smile has won me.
Such a pretty girl with teeth of pearl—
I met her down by the brook.
She's the prettiest (la, la, la, la, la)
And the wittiest (la, la, la, la, la)
And I never miss the sunshine when she's by me.
She's the merriest (la, la, la, la, la)
And the cheeriest (la, la, la, la, la)
She's as pretty as the picture on the wall.

This approximation to gibberish Aimee sang as best she could (she was not much of a singer) and danced as best she could (she was not much of a dancer). But she was Aimee. Her eye work, body movement, expression, and gestures seemed spontaneous, and no one could get near her in portraying a risqué situation in the most innocent manner. Her popularity lasted well into the '80s. She died in Paris in 1887 and willed $50,000 to an actor in her company, one Sig. del Campo (nee Albertini). Before the '6os, the popular song was usually ballad style, in essence a homely characterization of the sentimental verities— young love, mother and child, home and hearth—and a great renascence of this expression occurred in the '8os, sniffling out in the early '9os. (Millions whimpered at the excruciating pathos of "The Little Lost Child," which Edward B. Marks and his partner, Joseph W. Stern, published in 1894.) But the severely critical flavor of the late '6os and '7os songs was never wholly recaptured. It was immense after "The Grecian Bend."

The foible of women's fashions: bustles and stays, hair-dos, chignons; posture and mincing manners, drunkenness (among women, too!), gambling, fornication (the Beecher-Tilton scandal furnishing *that* motif)—the gamut of social and political expression was pilloried, flayed, mocked, and derided in hundreds of songs that for zest, vigor, lustiness, and ribaldry have never been equaled in our melodic history.

The reaction to Lingard's "Grecian Bend" was immediate, and the whole silly business exploded in one derisive guffaw. The issue of the New York *Herald* on September 2, 1868, thus facetiously referred to the posture in a social note from Saratoga:

> The Grecian Bend with its ridiculous attire "behind and before" has been voted vulgar even at Saratoga. Miss Flora McFlimsey regrets this as she thinks the most "statuesque pose" a body of grace can assume as that which her favorite poodle exhibits when requested to elevate himself on his hind legs and trot staggering across the piazza and back. We are firmly persuaded that if fashion should decree that her votaries should imitate the walk of a porcine order of four-footed beasts there is not a woman in the land but in a fortnight would pride herself on the elegance of her "grunt."

THE INCREDIBLE BEADLE

PUBLISHER BEADLE, whose innumerable magazines, dime novels, and songsters brought him wealth, was quick to exploit this incidental publicity. He issued a "Grecian Bend" songster and in-cluded a variant which he called the

GRECIAN BEND, NO. 2

The world is taken all aback,
The doctors looking solemn,
To see the fearful curvature
In woman's spinal column.
Clear the track now, gentlemen,
Move a little faster,
The *train* is going 'round a *curve*
Look out for a disaster.

Chorus: Clear the track, gentlemen,
Move a little faster;
When you see the Grecian curve
Look out for a disaster.

Beadle's publications were almost as fantastic as his career. In his score of pamphlets, songsters, magazines, dime novels, and "guides" is an exhaustive summary of America's folkways—its mores for four decades, the '50s, '60s, '70s, and '80s, exposed. In a brochure on the Beadle Collection of dime novels, handbooks acquired in 1922 through the munificence of Dr. Frank P. O'Brien, the New York Public Library describes the songsters thus:

The song literature it [the collection] contains discloses, in strik-ing manner, the prevailing thoughts and manners of society [in the late '70s]. Many of the songs themselves, both in title and text, reveal the prevalence of an artificial sentimentality, a tolerance of crime and vulgarity, a worship of alcohol, and a laxity of morals decidedly in contrast with ideas now prevailing.

The rather naïve conclusion, written in 1922, when our girls were displaying practically their thighs in the "rehearsal" dresses of the flapper period and getting drunk on bathtub gin, does not weaken the soundness of the library's general observa-tion.

During some forty-odd years he issued successively *Beadle's Dime Ballplayer, Beadle's Dime Biographical Library, Beadle's*

Dime Book of Fun (Mark Twain's "Jumping Frog" made its first appearance in print in this), *Beadle's Dime Book of Verses, Beadle's Guide to Dressmaking and Millinery, Beadle's Dime Handbook of Riding and Driving, Beadle's Dime Ladies Letter Writer,* etc., etc. His digest of the airs and graces, functions practical and decorous of our lay public, was complete. That so little is known of the man is a tragic lacuna in our historical memoirs. This astonishing man with his brother, Irwin P. Beadle, was the inventor of the dime novel, and through this medium he influenced the English-reading public more than Shakespeare. The Beadle dime novels were shipped to the Union lines in carload lots during the Civil War, and their circulation in England was almost as great.

Public knowledge of Erastus Flavel Beadle is confined to an illuminating article in the October 1929 *Bookman* (now defunct), by Henry Morton Robinson; a reference under the heading, "Dime Novel King," in *New York History,* Vol. 22, Cooperstown, 1941, by Della Lutes; and *Dime Novels,* a book Edmund Pearson published also in 1929. Beadle began his career with the publication of songs (words only) in Buffalo in 1851 —songs he reprinted from the broadsides hawked by the penny-a-sheet street-corner sellers. That is the date of his first *Dime Song Book.* It marked the publication of some 2,000 subsequent songs and ballads. In 1860 he issued his first dime novel, *Malaeska, the Indian Wife of the White Hunter,* a reprint from a periodical serial, and an American literary event damnably ignored. It was written by Ann S. Stephens. She received $250 for the reprint rights, and it sold more than 65,000 copies. Here was the forerunner of bite-the-dust fiction that exploited the derring-do of Dan'l Boone, Kit Carson, Davy Crockett, and Sam Houston. "It is probably no exaggeration," wrote Robinson, "to say that much of our pioneer nationalism, hitherto inarticulate, found its first utterance in the dime chronicles published by Erastus Beadle."

Malaeska and its vigorous followers spiked the lit'ry cambric tea of the times with a veritable Mickey Finn—a gesture lusty, ill-mannered, possibly, yet a necessary goosing of such period fal-lal as *The Young Ladies Tea Tray: a Monthly Bonbonniere of Spiritual Delicacies: the Seminarian's Confidante*—a contemporary magazine.

Beadle soon quit Buffalo for New York, where he established an immense business. He must have made a vast amount of money. At the peak of his thriving business, an ungrateful hireling, one George Munro, who had been Beadle's book-keeper, took in a partner and in open competition originated the Old Cap Collier series. Munro retired in 1893 with $10,-000,000, a logical yardstick to measure Beadle's wealth. Beadle ended his business in 1889; died, probably in 1897. Even then the frontier dime novel was become decadent; its coonskin-capped hero with fringed leggings and unerring rifle sissyfied into city-slicker types of con men, sharpers, and gyps. The West had been won—at any rate, from the Indians.

Beadle's editor was Orville J. Victor, a scholarly man, a fairish writer of acute perception, and it is likely that the success of the magazines during the late '60s was due to Victor's efforts. As the editor of *Beadle's Monthly*, he was on top of every expression, was actually excited by the mode and manners of the day. One of his most vigorous lampoons he leveled at the "waterfall," a silly hair-do of the period that had been the butt of songs and to which we have already referred.

In an article dated 1866 and labeled, "Old Style and New Style," Victor (presumably; it is unsigned) wrote:

Now seriously, my dear female, is there not a vast want of good taste in your present moment of dressing the head? Is not the "waterfall" a slovenly dodge to get rid of putting up the hair? Are the jaunty cap and feather woman's right to do as she may please? The law of good taste, of propriety, of modesty, of folly, fit only for flirts—are not these gigantic hairpins, headed with glass jewels, and woven with gold made out of iridium, too much of a good thing?

The song writers said as much in their medium, often more deftly, and sometimes with pretty conceit. The "jaunty cap

and feather" of the jaundiced Victor is an allusion to the jockey
hat so favored by the post Civil War ladies. A pleasant jingle
survives that was as popular in the late '6os as the style itself:

JOCKEY HAT AND FEATHER

As I was walking out one day
And thinking about the weather,
I saw a pair of laughing eyes
Beneath a hat and feather.
I looked at her, she looked at me,
It made my heart pit-pat.
And turning 'round she said like this,
"How do you like my hat?"

Chorus: I said, "It's gay, and pretty, too—
They look so well together,
Your coal black curls and jockey hat
Trimmed with rooster's feather."

She kissed her hand, said "au revoir,"
And then I was a goner,
Before I'd time to say goodbye
She'd skipped around the corner.
And all that night I could not sleep,
So up in bed I sat.
And right in front of me I thought
I saw that jockey hat.

Like the Grecian Bend, the waterfall hairdress soon succumbed to public ridicule. But bangs, which were much affected in the late '6os (and still are worn by some young ladies),
persisted, although subjected to continual digs by comics and
song writers.

About the time Beadle was printing his lament for the waterfall, De Marsan, in his *Singer's Journal*, issued

THE LADIES BANG THEIR HAIR

While promenading in the park,
One pleasant day in June,
My attention was attracted—
Now was it opportune.

> To see the ladies riding,
> In single and in pair,
> Now would you believe it really—they,
> The ladies bang their hair.

> *Chorus:* Yes bang it, yes bang it,
> Yes bang it, I declare.
> The ladies riding horseback,
> They—yes really bang their hair.

Indeed, fashions were a dominating topic in the songs of the late '60s. The feminine frivolity of wearing tassels on shoes was apparently an English importation, as was the song that made melodic memoranda of it. It was sung all over America—to the blush of many a lass who hid her tasseled shoes beneath voluminous skirts to forestall too personal reference. A verse and chorus of

TASSELS ON HER BOOTS

> It was at a fancy ball, I met this charmer fair,
> Mid howling swells and dashing belles
> The loveliest dancer there.
> I watched her while the band did play
> The latest waltz by Coots.
> I fell in love, no not with her,
> But the tassels on her boots.

> *Chorus:* Tassels on her boots,
> A style I'm sure that suits
> The English girls with wavy hair
> And tassels on her boots.

Another English song, popularized by Lingard, who changed the tense to fit his female impersonation, was

CHAMPAGNE CHARLIE

> Some time ago I had a beau and Charlie was his name,
> A fine young fellow fond of show who dearly loved champagne.
> When from my feet I spurned this swell as I will now explain,
> Although he loved me very well, he better loved champagne.

Chorus: Champagne Charlie was his name,
        Champagne Charlie was his name.
        Always making such a frightful noise,
        Kicking up a row at night, my boys.
        Champagne Charlie was his name,
        Champagne Charlie was his name.
        Kicking up a row at night, my boys,
        Always ready for a spree.

        He said he was an artist but I never saw his works.
        I think that he best understood the art of drawing corks.
        His studio was in the bar, his mahl stick was a cane;
        He had no palette for his paints but a palate for champagne.

For a time in the late '60s, levity was the note—girls, wine, the boulevards, the races, the gent in topper and Inverness, the smart rendezvous for gay times, the risqué wink, and the debonair fling—all are reflected, sometimes deftly, in the lyrics of those years. It had no effect on the vigor and ribaldry which was the general expression; rather balanced it—a neat foil. And a good deal of this sprightly character was furnished by the English importations. Curiously, many of these, written for and about men, and called "sports" songs, were adapted by seriocomics, who were women singers of both ballads and comic songs and who delivered them in masculine style. "Captain Jinks of the Horse Marines" was one, and a great favorite. It was sung by the girls almost always in military costume—rakish fur shako, sword-belt and sword and large gauntlet gloves.

Chorus: I'm Captain Jinks of the Horse Marines,
        I feed my horse good corn and beans.
        Of course it's quite beyond the means
        Of a captain in the army.

"Not for Joe," an English song of the "toff" type and vastly popular in America, was sung by nearly every seriocomic of the period in silk topper, light overcoat jauntily carried on arm, and a cane.

NOT FOR JOE

A friend of mine down in Pall Mall
The other night said, "Joe,
I'll introduce you to a girl
You really ought to know.
So you should set your cap, old pal
Oh that's what you should do.
A widow, and has lots of tin—
And only forty-two."

Spoken: Forty-two! What! Old enough to be my grandmother!
Oh, no, old chap.

Chorus: Not for Joe, not for Joe,
Not for Joseph if he knows it,
No, no, no, not for Joe,
Not for Joseph, oh, dear no!

Another of this type of song, apropos of the bibulous times,
was "I've Only Been Down to the Club," which was sung in
a battered plug hat, with broken cane, and the light overcoat
not so jauntily draped over an arm.

Chorus: The club had a meeting tonight, love,
Of business we had such a sight, love.
Don't think for a moment I'm tight, love,
I've only been down to the club.

The exotic qualities of the English music-hall songs, which
invariably characterized types and introduced slang with which
America was unfamiliar—the "toff," or dandy; the "bloke";
the "geezer" (which later became a part of our slang as an
opprobrious term for old men); the "doner," or girl friend;
"screw" for wages—were surprisingly popular here. One of the
"toff" songs, sung with silk hat, cane, and monocle, and an
immense favorite, was

LAH DE DAH

Let me introduce a fellah lah de dah,
A fellah quite a swellah lah de dah.
Though quite limited his screw,
Yet each week he wiggles through
For he knows the way to do,
Lah de dah, lah de dah.

Chorus: He wears a penny flower in his coat, lah de dah,
And a penny paper collar 'round his throat, lah de dah.
In his hand a penny stick,
In his teeth a penny pick,
And a penny in his pocket, lah de dah, lah de dah,
And a penny in his pocket, lah de dah.

THEY CALLED IT RECONSTRUCTION

I' FAITH, this is excellent fooling, but prettied up, a bit mincing for the callosity of the approaching '70s, when top hats were targets and the cane and monocle butts for jibes. We are come upon gutter days. Even Beadle, in his monthly magazine, could reply but faintly to a theme in another journal that published, in 1867, an article called "Drunkenness among American Women."

"How base!" trumpeted Beadle (or, more likely, Victor), which sums his entire reply. He could deny; he could not refute. The subtitle of the "offending" article (unnamed by Beadle throughout) apparently was, "Let the Truth Be Made to Appear." A purer and wiser principle, counseled *Beadle's Monthly*, is "Let No Scandal Be Made to Appear." Weak, this is, to the point of admission. But he was sound on the political skullduggery of the times, caught up fast with it. "We now understand 'politician' to mean not a statesman, but one who spends his time in partisan discussion; and, much to be regretted, it is fast having odium attached to it, in the estimation of a large body of the people." This he published in his *Monthly* for January 1866.

Drunkenness and politics—an aged blend—were an unneglected team of the song writers, and no moralizing either. In fact, drunkenness was often travestied in song. Just two years after Beadle's excoriation of the politician, he was reprinting in his songster (1868), a song published in Chicago by Root and Cady,

OUT OF THE TAVERN

> Out of the tavern I've just stepped to night,
> Street, you are caught in a very bad plight.
> Right hand and left hand are both out of place;
> Street, you are drunk, it's a very clear case.
>
> Moon, 'tis a very queer figure you cut,
> One eye is staring while the other is shut;
> Tipsy, I see, and you're greatly to blame,
> Old as you are, 'tis a terrible shame.
>
> And now the street lamps—what a scandalous sight!
> None of them soberly standing upright;
> Rocking and swaggering—why on my word,
> Each of the lamps is as drunk as a lord!
>
> All is confusion—now isn't it odd?
> I am the only one sober abroad;
> It would be rash with this crew to remain
> Better go back to the tavern again.

There is no repentance here; only frivolity, and an indicative crassness.

Everybody knew "Little Brown Jug"—knows it today, those who can recognize its recent swing version. In the late '6os it was a part of the life. Its simple tune made a perfect polka, a dance much favored then, and while that was an undoubted factor in its popularity, the words, too, were accepted. They had a certain apposite quality.

> My wife and I live all alone
> In a little log hut we call our own
> She loves gin and I love rum,
> I tell you what we've lots of fun!

Chorus: Ha ha ha, you and me,
 Little brown jug don't I love thee? (*Repeat*)

It's you that make me wear old clothes,
 It's you that caused all my woes.
 From you I got this bright red nose
 Tip her up and down she goes.

He is sorry, you think? Perhaps, for that moment, but he is
far from the pledge:

If I had a cow that gave such milk,
 I'd dress her in the finest of silk.
 Feed her on the choicest hay
 And milk her forty times a day.

Such a foible can scarcely herald a Neroic age. And yet it was
a spring song of what was to come, a harbinger of the change
in pop-tune style to the sinister, the cynical, the ribald, the
streetwalker, the recognition of life. The soil of the period was
right for this sowing. The decade of the Reconstruction was
the most vicious in our history—festering, corrupt, raucous,
brutal, with murder a pastime and ruin the cause of mirth.
Politicians and poseurs, pimps and prostitutes, sanctimonious
exhorters, name smearers, thieves prance across its stage, the
unholiest canto in the epic of America. And of these they sang.

The songs of the Presidential campaign of 1868 that returned
Grant and Colfax victors over Seymour and Blair are unequaled
in our political annals for their vulgarity and slander. Rapidly
the Reconstruction period was entering the fierce expression
of its political and social debauch. And the songs announced
this "black and bloody drama," as Claude Bowers calls the
twelve years that followed the murder of Lincoln in his remarkable history of the Reconstruction, *The Tragic Era*, with
a fidelity shameful in retrospect. Not even the tavern songs of
the '70s (dim-witted hired-man ditties of sex behind the barn),
not even the songs of the buskers (often as quaint in their
crudities as the lone, itinerant troubadours who sang them)
approach the scurrilities of the political songsters.

Here's to the man that pulled the trigger,
That killed the old cuss that freed the nigger.

This chorus is from a long melodic exhortation for Seymour and Blair from a political pen happily unidentified.

The intense bitterness that characterized that campaign makes a love feast of the 1940 dissension of Roosevelt and Willkie partisans, and it ranged from songs produced by bucolic bards in a doggerel gamut to a lyric of John Greenleaf Whittier. While the gentle, Quaker poet, whose interests often wandered from his wild flowers and the pastoral of his Puritan setting to penal reform and politics, was sounding thus against the times

Great Heaven! is this our mission?
End in this the prayers and tears?
The toils, the wars, the watchings,
Of our younger, better years?
Still as the Old World rolls in light,
Shall ours in shadow turn,
A beamless chaos, cursed of God,
Through outer darkness borne?
Where the far nations looked for night,
A blackness in the air,
Where for words of hope they listened,
The long wail of despair!

One William Hubbard left but this base record in the New York *Herald,* September 2, 1868, to salvage his obscurity:

WHO ARE THE USURPERS?

These are days of rough men and rough deeds and I'll use
Rough words in a song that I sing, if I choose.
Fair words are too precious on scoundrels to waste—
Rare vintage, which flows not for scullions to taste.
'Tis with felons I deal—
Thieves who break through and steal!
Such as Forney, who stole forty thousand at least!
And that millionaire burglar—Ben Butler, the Beast!

'Tis with wretches whose garments with murder are red!
All splattered and splotched with the blood they have shed!

Such as Bingham—whose eyeballs are scared with the sight
Of a ghost if he ventured out alone in the night!
The ghost of a woman all saintly and white!

    Poor Mary Surratt!
    Purer soul never sped
    To yon heav'n through the stars
    Beaming lustrous o'erhead
    Than thine, who wast strangled,
    And lain with the dead!
    Rest! Rest!
    With the martyred and blest!
    Murdered mother!
    Thy guiltlessness is now confessed.

Such as Stevens—corroded with lifelong remorse!
Whose sin-cankered heart has been long turned to gall—
For he sees, "in his mind's eye," the club-beaten corpse
Of a girl who for him gave up heaven and all.
Lured out to the brookside—the night dark and dread—
"Slain by some one unknown"—so the coroner said—
But the terrible spectre comes back from the dead!

Such as Sumner, the donkey, with leonine looks,
Clad in jacket of stripes which was given him by Brooks!
Such as Sumner, the Thing! neuter gender! who made
A mockery of marriage, and a woman betrayed!
Then tortured his victim, as a chief of the Crows
Does a victim he takes in a raid on his foes!

And the tumblebug filthmonger, blaspheming Wade!
Boss in chief, for long years, of the wench-hugger's trade!
Obscene as the Hun in his midsummer ride,
Who used beefsteak for saddle and supper beside!
A lowdown low fellow—low born and low bred!
With a fishwoman's tongue and a scalawag's head.

And these, oh my countrymen! these are the knaves
Who conspire to be masters when you shall be slaves.

Hubbard, whoever he was, is pretty harsh with his rogues'
gallery. But it was the temper of the times. Filth oozed from
heart and mind. There is no supporting record for Hubbard's
scurrilous accusations. Nor, incidentally, is there record of any
suit brought by those so viciously tarred against James Gordon

Bennett, owner and publisher of the New York *Herald*, who printed the slander under the facetious caption, "Campaign Minstrelsy." They were a sorry lot. Let us identify them in their order of mention.

Forney is Colonel John W. Forney, secretary of the United States Senate and owner and editor of the Washington *Chronicle* and the Philadelphia *Press*. Ben Butler is General Benjamin F. Butler, political conniver and rabble rouser who preached Negro superiority over the whites and to whom the political control of South Carolina by the blacks was a joyous advance in the nation's history. Bingham is Representative J. A. Bingham of Ohio, one of the eight congressmen accused in the steal of Crédit Mobilier. Mary Surratt, in whose H Street boardinghouse John Wilkes Booth and his companions hatched the assassination of Lincoln, was the only woman ever hanged by the United States Government. Stevens is Thaddeus Stevens, House leader of the Radical ("Rads," as they were called) Republicans; a vigorous hater of Lincoln, a sarcastic, cruel, and intelligent politician—a paradox who was honest in his knavery. Like Butler, he esteemed the Negro, accorded him virtues beyond equality, believed that the South should pay with its last drop of blood and with fiendish hatred endorsed and fought for a program that would have confiscated the plantations and given to each Negro forty acres of the white owners' land. The "club-beaten corpse" seems to be a deliberate fabrication, although it may well have been contemporary gossip in a Washington gassed with slanderous rumor. Every newspaper of any consequence in America printed stories of Thad Stevens' supposed mistress, a mulatto named Lydia Smith, and his housekeeper to his death, in the year of Hubbard's poisonous threnody, 1868.

Sumner is Charles Sumner, the Massachusetts Senator, and the reference to gender and "mockery of marriage" may be a fantastic allusion to Sumner's marriage to the lovely Mrs. Hooper. He was then fifty-five years of age, his bride many years younger, and in the winter of '67, when Washington drawing rooms cackled of his wife's association with a hand-some attaché of the Prussian Legation, the ladies giggled behind their fans that it was to solace with the virility of youth the small joy that was hers in an old man's bed. The reference to Brooks is more obscure. He is probably James Brooks, minority leader of the House, editor of the New York *Press* and more heavily involved in the scandal of the Crédit Mobilier than Bingham. Brooks, according to Bowers, in *The Tragic Era*, was a Tammany man—suave, courteous, not an orator, but plausible and persuasive—whose one distinction seems to be that he favored woman suffrage at a time when its mustered support comprised Elizabeth Cady Stanton, Susan B. Anthony, Lucretia Mott, and Isabella Beecher Hooker. Wade is Senator Benjamin F. Wade, another Lincoln hater, a ruthless ringleader of the Radicals, whose only apparent decent act throughout his pugnacious career was his failure to attend Lincoln's funeral. The "wench-huggers' trade," however, defies analysis in relation to him, albeit the "fishwoman's tongue" and "scalawag's head" are sound characterizations.

The fever of the campaign provoked even parodies of the "Star Spangled Banner":

> Oh say can you see since the war's deadly blight,
> Our time-honored flag without sadly regretting,
> The fate of a people who sold their birthright
> And behold now the sun of their liberty setting.
> And the tax we now pay (near two millions per day)
> Gives proof that fanatics and tyrants bear sway.
> While the Star Spangled Banner in mockery waves
> Over bondholding tyrants and tax-ridden slaves.

A more responsible Republican, one John Hopely, indited election lines that have meaning in our own time. He called his song the "Copperhead," and here are two of its five verses:

> Of all the factious men we've seen,
> Existing now or long since dead,
> No one was ever known so mean
> As him we call a copperhead.

A draft-evading copperhead;
A rebel-cheering copperhead;
A growling, slandering,
Scowling, pandering
Vicious state-rights copperhead.

When "Save the Union" was the cry,
And thousands for the Union bled,
The nation's right he did deny
To save itself—this copperhead.
A Son of Liberty copperhead,
A Golden Circle copperhead,
A scheming, lying,
Screaming, flying,
Mean, Canadian copperhead.

The "Mean, Canadian copperhead" is a specific reference to Clement L. Vallandigham, Democratic candidate for Governor in Ohio, and Number 1 Copperhead of the Civil War, who screamed his "near treason" from temporary exile in Canada. How certain is the political cycle! "The last vestiges of constitutional freedom are rapidly disappearing, and we are fast verging into centralization and despotism." Does it read like a quote from Herbert Hoover? It is the statement of Alexander H. Stephens, Vice-President of the Confederacy under Jeff Davis, taken from an interview in 1868. Songs have featured our national campaigns for a century, from "Tippecanoe and Tyler Too" (the tune of which Henry Ward Beecher thefted for his hymnal, *Plymouth Collection of Hymns and Tunes*, which flopped, to Henry Ward's disgust) to "Tammany" and the "Sidewalks of New York," which was Al Smith's campaign chant in 1928.

WILL YOU LOVE, CAN YOU LOVE?

THERE WERE FEW INHIBITIONS in the '70s; none whatever in the decade's tavern songs. They are dungboot, drunken revelry; antic madrigals with a surfeit of four-letter monosyllables which unfortunately prevents the reprinting of many. For however universal may be the use of the Anglo-Saxon onomatopoeia, they still seem indelicate in print. It is unfortunate, because the very crudities of the tavern songs' verse forms, their antiphonal gibberish, suggest interesting origins deep in folk balladry, marked with the influence of English and Scottish runes. Widely popular among the bibulous—gentry and peasant —was "You Know Very Well What I Mean Though." And it is an excellent example of the foregoing observation on balladry.

> There was an old woman lived under the hill,
> Green leaf, green low.
> She kept apples and cakes to sell—
> You know very well what I mean though.
> She had a daughter, Mary Ann,
> Green leaf, green low.
> She'd never known the pleasure of man—
> You know very well what I mean though.
> This young lady was taken with pain,
> Green leaf, green low.
> A young man in town he was taken the same—
> You know very well what I mean though.
> Sick and sick were put together,
> Green leaf, green low.
> Thinking that they might cure each other—
> You know very well what I mean though.

The refrain: "green leaf, green low," is certainly runic. And "sick and sick were put together" is arrestingly bucolic; it has a Chaucerian flavor. The last two verses are unprintable; the police power of Postmaster General Frank C. Walker is a potent force. But their omission should not confound any reasonably imaginative reader. If the tavern songs violated the conventions of polite society which, in passing, was not too polite in the unsavory '70s, they did face the moralities with a forthrightness uncommonly sound in its relation to life as it is. "Don't Wed An Old Man" is some unknown barroom laureate's sensible advice to a young girl. But if you do, so runs this tavern song, circumvention is not only easy but pleasant, as possibly Mrs. Sumner learned from her tall, dark, and handsome attaché. (Its two choruses are unprintable.)

> Now come all pretty maidens fair,
> Maids fair with golden hair,
> List to my story, poor fool that I am,
> When I was just sweet sixteen
> Fresh from the country green,
> I joined in marriage a wealthy old man.
>
> When the old man and I went to bed—
> Will you love, can you love?
> When the old man and I went to bed—
> Love if you can.
> When the old man and I went to bed
> There he lay like one dead—
> Maidens beware, don't wed an old man.
>
> When the old man he went to sleep—
> Will you love, can you love?
> When the old man he went to sleep—
> Love if you can.
> When the old man he went to sleep
> Out of the window I did creep
> Into the arms of a sporting young man.

If one can forget—or forgive—the realism, the song is a worthy lyric, its two moods excellently realized: the wistful beginning has a poignancy whose expiation in youth's desire is understandable to all but the hairshirts. And the archaic ache in "Will you love, can you love? Love if you can," is poetry.

A few of these songs were sung occasionally in the free and easies, large halls where entertainment of a "blue" type was offered the tosspots. But they originated in the taverns, and to them they specifically belong. No one knows who wrote the tavern songs; they are as anonymous as dirty jokes. Indeed, a number of the authors of the post-Civil War songs given in this book are unknown. They were introduced by some performer and taken up by others, with lines added or changed over the circuits, until the song sometimes became virtually a parody of its original. Yet few of the tavern songs were changed, probably because of their intimacy in subject and setting—a unique authenticity in so volatile an expression as the pop tune.

The old taverns flourished on the outskirts of every city of size, and they were largely patronized by farmers and city folk who drove out in summer or came a-sleighing in winter. Nor were the gentry slumming. Simple camaraderie was the motive, which resulted in an uninspired, delightful, and effective democratic fusion of classes, and all abetted by that most gregarious of agencies—the bottle. The farmers generally had disposed of their hay, grain, cord wood, live stock, or other commodities and were stopping overnight to rest their teams before the long drive home. All of the taverns had a large room on the first floor for a sitting room and a bar. In the center of the room stood an immense stove about six feet high, so adjusted that its top could be removed and a log of wood dropped in. A raised edge, or boxing, about five inches high and six feet square, was built around the stove, an enclosure that was filled with sand or sawdust to accommodate tobacco chewers. The floor was sprinkled with sand, and plenty of strong wooden chairs were available. The bar ran across one end of the room, and usually three bartenders presided. As their dispensations became more frequent, songs, candidly descriptive, as we have seen, inevitably followed. Say

SNAP POO

There was an old soldier came over the line,
Snap poo, snap poo.
There was an old soldier came over the line,
Snap poo.
There was an old soldier came over the line
With sweet cakes tied up in his shirttail behind.
Snap poo snap eater philanthy go peter snap poo.

Oh mother, dear mother, I'm not too young,
Snap poo, snap poo.
Oh mother, dear mother, I'm not too young,
Snap poo.

Oh mother, dear mother, I ache and I pine,
To go with the soldier from over the line,
Snap poo snap eater philanthy go peter snap poo.

Oh daughter, dear daughter, you are too young,
Snap poo, snap poo.
Oh daughter, dear daughter, you are too young,
Snap poo.
Indeed, dear daughter, you are too young,
To sit where you are, and stop twitching your bum.
Snap poo snap eater philanthy go peter snap poo.

When daughters are young then daughters will pout,
Snap poo, snap poo.
When daughters are young then daughters will pout,
Snap poo.
When daughters are young then daughters will pout,
The old woman dozed and her daughter slipped out.
Snap poo snap eater philanthy go peter snap poo.

Early next morning when daughter awoke,
Snap poo, snap poo.
Early next morning when daughter awoke,
Snap poo.
She found the old soldier had crept out of bed
And left the sweet cakes in his shirttail instead.
Snap poo snap eater philanthy go peter snap poo.

The vague denouement of "Snap Poo" is a subtlety generally
ignored, perhaps disdained is the word, by the tavern songsters.
But the moral, and the artifice by which it is overcome—the
common plot of the tavern songs—is plain enough. For this
reason, "Little Ball of Yarn" is a bit of tavern curiosa, albeit
with the usual erotica (in its three final stanzas) which again
must be omitted and imagined.

Oh 'twas in the month of May,
And the little lambs did play,
And the birds began to sing their merry song.
I met a charming maid
And thus to her I said,
May I wind up your little ball of yarn?

Oh no, kind sir, said she,
You are a stranger unto me,
And I fear that you might have some other charm.
You had better go to those
Who have money and fine clothes
And wind up their little balls of yarn.

Well, the maiden yielded—alas!—to a cad for he left her with a moralization to "sin" no more. Striking twist for a tavern tune whose ditties, if vulgar, were honest. Now examine these lines:

You had better go to those
Who have money and fine clothes
And wind up their little balls of yarn.

This can only be deliberate in its satirical cut at the loose-lived gentry and politicians and their ladies in a decade of licentiousness without parallel in our scroll. In Reconstruction Washington, corporate business and industry generally maintained a staff of high-class harlots solely for bedroom lobbying; a shrewd bevy of beauties who made certain their favors were distributed for votes, and accordingly bestowed only upon the "right" Senators or Representatives: those whose infamy could be trusted.

A fantastic instance involving Pauline Markham is pat to this book, for Pauline was a singer of songs of the period, a golden-haired queen of burlesque, a star of *Lydia Thompson's British Blondes*, and the sweetheart of New York for seasons. At the height of her vogue, a political ring, probably with banking background (Jay Cooke would always look the other way), hired her to sleep with the Hon. Robert K. Scott, a gentleman from Ohio who became the carpetbag Governor of South Carolina "by the grace of bayonets," as Bowers says in *The Tragic Era*. Besotted with wine in their room in the St. James Hotel in New York, and in febrile anticipation of satisfied lust, Scott signed hundreds of thousands of dollars in spurious convertible bonds while Pauline, in dishabille, neatly blotted his signature and stacked the worthless securities upon a table.

This is but an essence of the temperament and times. That its manifestation should occur in the songs of the '70s in a manner to meet the Reconstruction's wantonness was inevitable. The songsters of the '70s delighted in pillorying the no-good and, even as the tolerant public, occasionally condoned their actions. The tavern boys, cackling against the silliness of morals while extolling the pleasures they denied, were but a ribald echo of Sodom, D. C., and the Babylon of Boss Tweed. Yet he among us who would cast the first stone should stay his hand. These tavern tunes have their counterparts today in the juke-box platters distributed to nearly every bar and grill in America—songs whose *double entendres* are every bit as brassy as "Little Ball of Yarn" and actually sloppier with sex. Since Patricia Norman's eyebrow-lifting accent of "buck, buck, bucket" as soloist with Eddie Duchin's orchestra in the recording of "Old Man Mose," a succession of disks has been issued with equally mounting innuendos.

Into the bars and grills—our modern taverns—have gone such songs as, "If I Can't Sell It I'm Going to Sit on It Rather Than Give It Away," an innocuous ditty, as it turns out, about a young girl in charge of a shop and her concern for an old chair. "She Had to Go and Lose It at the Astor" piled up nickels in thousands from those who enjoyed the giggle of the tag line—"It" was a fur piece. At this writing, the "Wave" song is at its crest. It tells of a young girl who "got it last night up in Yonkers" from a fellow who was dark and tall and who had told her "because this is your first time, there'll be no charge at all." And it relates the girl's remorse because she hadn't gotten "It" before because "It" was wonderful. "It" in the song is a permanent wave. "It" is the most obscene word in the English language; and to leer, a basic function of man. Let us return to the hymnlike simplicities and naïveté of our tavern tunes for a finale—honest, direct, and with a punch line that fingers no "It":

THE GIRL WHO NEVER WOULD WED

I courted a round-bottomed lass one spring,
The birds were mating free.
The sheep and the goats
Were feeling their oats—
But she would have none of me.
When summer came and fields were filled
With scent of new mown hay,
The weather was hot, but she was not,
For still she said me nay,
For still she said me nay.

The summer went and autumn came,
And when the nights were chill,
We sat beside the fire in
Her house behind the hill.
'Twas then I said,
Two in a bed
Could warm and cozy be.
I pinched her rump, but up she jumped—
Says she, young man you're too free,
Says she, young man you're too free.

When winter came said I, why do
You choose to sleep alone;
And in single bed
Lay like one dead
As cold as any stone?
I offered her my house and lands
And all my worldly pelf
With arms so strong to keep her warm—
Says she, keep your arms to yourself,
Says she, keep your arms to yourself.

For years and years I roamed about
And when I had my fill,
I found this girl a woman grown,
But she refused me still.
Said I, when you are old and gray
And shattery in the knees,
When wintry blast blows round your rump

I hope by Jesus you freeze,
I hope by Jesus you freeze.

The rest is Freud's.

COME, BUSKER! A SONG FOR A TODDY!

THE BUSKERS, who played the taverns almost exclusively, seldom
sang the tavern songs; in fact, seemed studiously to avoid the
bawdy tunes. They virtually made a specialty of the lugubrious
tear jerkers of the day—"See That My Grave's Kept Green,"
or "Lorena," or "I'll Remember You Love in My Prayers"—
dirges that moistened the eyes of the tosspots. True, they may
well have sung "Dick Darlin' the Cobbler," which was so extraordinarily successful that De Marsan published it in his
songs of the period. It is a queer song, apparently of Irish origin
possibly by way of England.

It is astonishing how these old songs got about. They turned
up in the most amazing places in a manner as mysterious as the
migration of birds. Viscount Halifax, British Ambassador to
the United States, made a neat reference to this in an address
at the Berkshire Music Festival in Lenox, Massachusetts, August
15, 1941. He spoke of Cecil Sharp, internationally known
authority on folk tunes, whose collections—traditional words
and melodies gleaned from Great Britain and the United States
—are unsurpassed. "He told me once," said Lord Halifax, "that
he had found in a village in the Catskill Mountains words set
to a traditional English tune which he had sought in vain in
his native country."

"Dick Darlin' " is a typical English busker song, and though
its comedy is a bit macabre, it was undoubtedly in the American
buskers' repertoire. That is the indication in its last verse, and
it is supplemented by De Marsan's American reprint.

Och! my name is Dick Darlin' the cobbler,
My time I served down there in Kent.
Some say I'm an old fornicater,
But now I'm resolved to repent.

My wife she was blinkin' and blearin',
My wife she was humpy and black.
The divvil all over for swearin',
And her tongue it kept goin' click-clack.

But now we are parted foriver—
One mornin' before it was light,
I shoved the ould jade in a river,
And cautiously bid her good night.

My troubles of wedlock bein' over,
This country I thought I would try,
Once more I've become a free rover,
An' single I'll stop till I die.

The buskers were fascinating people, of a character their own. "Busker," English slang, was a term applied to itinerant entertainers in England who appeared on the streets, in pubs, or at summer resorts, or in the smaller towns and villages through which they traveled on foot, playing or singing for throw money—troubadours of the time, descended lineally, if blood-thinned, from those who chanted the "Song of Roland" or the delightful tale of the felicitous lovers, Aucassin and Nicolette, in the palace courtyards of medieval France.

The English buskers worked singly or in pairs, sometimes in groups of seven or eight, these dressing alike for added distinction and identity. The group buskers generally used the concertina and guitar for song accompaniment or instrumental solos. One of the number would circulate among the crowd and politely suggest contributions, waving a long stick, to which was attached a velvet bag. The collector quickly spotted newcomers, and as quickly marked non-paying auditors, whom he shamed by repeated thrusts with his stick and bag. These groups usually canvassed the better neighborhoods and remained on location, as it were, until moved on by a bobby.

The single English buskers were mostly raucoused-voiced singers whose talent was not great enough to gain them even minor music-hall booking. They worked the poor neighborhoods or slums in the larger British cities, collecting occasional pennies tossed from windows. If a beer bottle was flung, or a pail of dirty water—and worse—the busker would curse fluently and obscenely for a few bars, without losing a beat, and then resume the words of his song. Here is the chorus of a veteran busker whose beat was the Whitechapel district in London:

> I'm a bloke wot's done wrong by 'is parents,
> And sadly I wanders about,
> To pick up a few honest coppers,
> Gaw blime but I'm cahst out.

The American busker differed from his British prototype in two important details. He almost always worked alone, and he rode from town to town, obtaining his transportation as best he could by devious methods. He would even pay railroad or coach fare to attend a convention, or fair, or to any assembly where he considered the contributions might be liberal. Most of them worked the saloons and taverns exclusively, but a few had regularly established street locations, worked the ferry-boats, or followed the fairs. No one knew the names of the buskers; they never advertised, received no billing, and were never announced. They were simply referred to as "the old geezer with the dulcimer" (an instrument favored by American buskers) or "the lame fellow who plays the accordion in Franklin Square." Only one authentic name has come down to us—Billy Boyd—and he was known largely because of his brother, who managed a variety hall in Aspen, Colorado, whom Billy continually assailed to anyone who would listen. "I teached him all he knows about show business," Billy would wail, "and now he says I'm a bum. That's what relations do to you." Billy, who worked the saloons in the midwest in the '70s and '80s, had an unusual routine. He had once been a clever performer, but regular engagements irked him because they interfered with his drinking. So he toured the country with a tin whistle, which he played remarkably well. After several showy selections, Billy would announce, "Pop Goes the Weasel, with variations." He played it first in the usual manner, with the whistle n his mouth. Then he stuck it in his nose and played a variation. Next he stuck it in his ear and whistled a strain. Last he stuck t in his backside and played a rousing finale. For the finale he used a rubber tube which ran under his shirt, under the crotch, and out through a hole in the seat of his pants. Billy connected the whistle to the lower end of the tube, turned his back to the audience and blew through the upper end of the tube. It convulsed the drunks.

The singing buskers sobbed out the dolorous ditties previously mentioned. Here is a verse and chorus of

SEE THAT MY GRAVE'S KEPT GREEN

When I'm dead and gone from you, darling,
When I'm laid away in my grave,
When my spirit has roamed to heaven above
To Him who my soul shall save,
When you are happy and gay once more,
Thinking of the days that have been,
There is one little wish I would ask of you—
See that my grave's kept green.

Chorus: For the days will come to you, darling,
When no more on earth I'll be seen.
There is one little wish, darling, grant me,
See that my grave's kept green.

This was lush. The only explanation for these songs in so unruly a period and for their acceptance by so motley a crowd is probably because their bathos had a kind of redemptive quality; it was a sort of painless confessional through sentiment for the blades and bums and political cuckolds who shed for a moment their knavery with their tears.

A few of the buskers, fortunately, were singers of comic songs, and some of these songs are very good indeed. They are indigenous to the period, kin to the tavern songs, but with faces washed and shining—they were never vulgar. A busker known as Jimmy, who was quite popular in the '70s, made much of the following song, which he sang with banjo accompaniment:

ONE HUNDRED YEARS AGO

Now listen while some facts I'll tell, and some will cause you grief
The things that happen nowadays are most beyond belief.
How two old maids were blessed with twins I thought you'd like
　　to know—
We never heard of things like that one hundred years ago.

Old Simpkins' wife died suddenly and she was laid away,
But he went courting a neighbor's gal the very next day.
The men that lived in good old times, you couldn't call them slow
But old bucks now have lots more spunk than a hundred years ago.

How very queer the women dress, it's really not refined—
A wad of cotton up in front, a bustle on behind.
The men they all wear diamond pins, it never before was so;
There were no dollar jewelry stores one hundred years ago.

The last line is a topical scoff at the "Dollar Stores" of the '70s.
These appeared in nearly every large city, although not operated as a chain, and their slogan was, "Nothing over a Dollar."
They were stocked to the ceiling with the most outlandish
junk—earrings, engagement rings, wedding rings, watch chains,
family Bibles, umbrellas, huge boxes of foul candy, family
albums, pints of perfume, silver butter dishes, razors, toilet sets,
cameo pins, oil paintings by some gifted sign painter, fur neck
pieces, etc. etc. For several years they did quite well, but they
were gradually ribbed out of business by the buskers and
variety comics, who used them as the butt of their gags.

A busker who worked the taverns of New England and the
eastern seaboard in the early '70s called himself the Country
Fiddler. He wore overalls stuffed in his boots, a hickory shirt,
a long, colorless coat, and a shapeless felt hat. His hair was long
and ragged, and whiskers of the "rube" type adorned his chin.
He accompanied his songs with a battered old fiddle, which he
held in the hollow of his arm instead of under the chin.

One of his songs, "Old McDonald Had a Farm," is interesting
because, like the tavern songs, it is undoubtedly a throwback
to a folk tune. Here are its lines:

My grandfather had some very fine ducks
In the merry green fields of Ireland.
Quack here, and quack there,
Quack quack here, and quack quack there;
Here a quack and there a quack and quacking everywhere,
In the merry green fields of Ireland.

My grandfather had some very fine sheep
In the merry green fields of Ireland.
Baa here, and baa there,
Baa baa here, and baa baa there,
Quack quack here and quack quack there,
Here a quack and there a quack and quacking everywhere,
In the merry green fields of Ireland.

My grandfather had some very fine hens
In the merry green fields of Ireland.
Cluck here, and cluck there,
Baa here, and baa there,
Baa baa here, and baa baa there,
Here a quack and there a quack and quacking everywhere,
In the merry green fields of Ireland.

My grandfather had some very fine pigs. . . .

And so on, continuing until all the animals of husbandry were included. It has a pleasant nursery quality, and it is unfortunate that the Country Fiddler used sounds to represent the horse and the goat that were extremely vulgar. A final word: the busker must not be confounded with the blind or crippled organ grinder, the street fakir, or the mendicant. The busker sold no merchandise, nor did he solicit alms. He exchanged entertainment of a kind for cash or drinks or both, and on a voluntary basis.

THEY HAD A WINKING LILT

ARTHUR CHAMBERS' free and easy on the west side of Ridge Avenue between Callowhill and Wood Streets, in Philadelphia, was a wonderful place, renowned in the '70s, its atmosphere and character assured through the personality of its owner. Its appointments and settings were typical of the free and easies of the period. The barroom was large. At one end a platform was raised for piano and performers, whose names were scrawled across the bar mirror with soap. No admission was charged; bar revenues supplied the return. The audience was mixed. But the distaff side was, in easy parlance, not nice. They were not whores. The work-a-night trade of the prostitute conflicted with the hours of the free and easies. Girls who attended the free-and-easy performances were of the "easy virtue" type, "out for a good time." To most performers, the free and easy was a "dump," a "slab," or a "honky-tonk." Not Chambers'. It was not only well run; it was unique. Chambers, a noted lightweight champion pugilist of the time, adored pigeons and kept a cote for his prized carriers in the attic. In the basement, Mrs. Chambers raised English bulldogs. The second floor was used for a sparring academy. Chambers had a huge following and in 1882 gained international recognition for promoting a stunt with explosive results in the sporting world.

In that year John L. Sullivan offered $1,000 to anyone who could stay in the ring four rounds with him. Chambers immediately thought of Tug Wilson, a British pugilist, not a great, but an extremely crafty, fighter. He induced Wilson to come over and meet the challenge. And by dodging, ducking, falling down, and otherwise stalling, Wilson kept free of the murderous swings of his opponent and was on his feet at the end of the match. Wilson got his $1,000, and Chambers a gate of $6,700. Songs and gags in relation to that incident are lost— the free-and-easy ditties were as ephemeral as those of the buskers—but many others survive, for Chambers' rendezvous was famous throughout the East.

Eddie Shaw, a veteran singer of topical songs in the '70s, was a frequent and popular performer at Chambers', and his song, "The Five Dollar Note," became a trade-mark for both singer and place. Its doggerel is interesting, extraordinarily topical, and its conclusion, for that time, unusual.

THE FIVE DOLLAR NOTE

One evening after tea, not knowing where to go,
I thought for amusement I'd like to see a show.
I felt in my pockets but I didn't have a groat,
So I borrowed from a friend a five dollar note.

Chorus: Listen now to me,
Your attention please devote,
And I'll tell you how I spent
That five dollar note.

I went to the show and saw a pretty play,
From a very good seat—front row, parquet.
I saw the girl weep and I saw the villain gloat,
And it cost me a dollar of the five dollar note.

The show being over I stepped to the bar
To have a little toddy and enjoy a good cigar.
I met a good friend, I invited him to pote,
And I spent another dollar of the five dollar note.

I strolled to the ferry just to see what I could see.
I watched a fellow juggle with some thimbles and a pea.
I picked the wrong thimble and he jumped aboard the
   boat.
He took along a dollar of the five dollar note.

I went to the park and I sat upon a seat,
It was there that a very pretty girl I chanced to meet.
She sat upon my knee, threw her arms around my throat,
And she soon got a dollar of the five dollar note.

The hour was very late so I started for my home,
I met a poor working man, dejected and alone.
The tears were in his eyes, quite shabby was his coat,
So he got the last dollar of the five dollar note.

The last verse of this song is significant. It was in the '70s
that songs for the first time referred to the condition of labor
and the socially underprivileged. Eddie Shaw's brief reference
and another we shall soon come upon (linked to the notorious

Jim Fisk, of all persons) were forerunners of a song period that took heed of the growing consciousness of the workingman which culminated, in the '80s, in the formation of the American Federation of Labor. The crude stages of the free and easies were actually platforms for the melodic dissemination of social problems, and although the accent of the free and easies' songs was mainly critical and comic, the plight of labor and the poor was never made the butt of jests in song or comedy. Especially after 1877. The railroad strikes that swept the nation that year, with their toll in lives and property damage of millions of dollars, put an effective damper upon such levity. And in the same year the constabulary, spurred by a thoroughly aroused public, moved to halt the murders of the Molly Maguires. This lawless gang of labor guerillas, pledged to keep mine wages up and foreigners from employment in the Pennsylvania coal regions, turned the collieries into a shambles for years, until their leaders were seized by police and hanged.

Songs of the free and easies were essentially topical, because that was the life of the free and easies—for the moment; to the hilt. They lacked the vulgarity and four-letter realism of the tavern ditties, a respectable omission that forfeited punch. But they had a gaiety and abandonment which was alive to the times; an intelligent skepticism, critical and sophisticated, that flayed vogues of the day and thumbed a nose at many a stuffed shirt.

> I'm Mistress Jinks of Madison Square,
> I wear fine clothes and I puff my hair.
> And how the gentlemen at me stare
> While my husband's in the army!
> Where e'er I go I'm talked about,
> I'm talked about
> I'm talked about.
> I wear the latest fashions out
> While the Captain's in the army.
>
> He says he'll get a furlough soon,
> And come back home to stay till June
> Oh! won't I sing a different tune

To my husband in the army!
I'll meet him then with kisses sweet,
With kisses sweet,
With kisses sweet.
I'll hasten out of the door to meet
With the Captain home from the army.

Spoken: Why shouldn't I? Haven't I spent all his money? Owe
arge bills? House rent due? Nothing to wear? Hungry, and——???
Vell . . . I'm Mistress Jinks, etc.

This, a feminine paraphrase of "Captain Jinks of the Horse
Marines," was widely sung throughout the free and easies by
he women performers. It has a winking lilt. The free-and-easy
performers even jibed at "Home, Sweet Home":

When relations come to visit you
There's no place like home.
They bring all their trunks and they stick like glue,
There's no place like home.
When you have to give up the best room you've got
And go and sleep on a tough old cot
With your brother-in-law who is always half-shot—
There's no place like home.

Thus they caroled at Chambers' and at a thousand other free
and easies then in America.

The mother-in-law joke doubtless is of cave-man origin, and
.t may have so much domestic significance in our times that
.t is no longer funny. The '70s thought it was funny, and the
ribbing wives or husbands took at the expense of their maternal
forebears was incessant in gag and song. Gus Williams wrote
perhaps the most popular. Gus was a Dutch comic and vocalist,
and his song, "Keiser, Don't You Want to Buy a Dog?" doggerel
of no merit whatever, nonetheless became through its title a
standard greeting which wags used for several years, much in
the manner of the "Vas you dere, Sharlie?" that Jack Pearl
broadcast to national response in the 1930s. But Gus's mother-
in-law song caught on for its jingle and an acute, if inept,
characterization. It was one of his few songs that is not in dialect.

If you listen a while I will sing you a ditty
About the worst woman that ever I saw.
And when I get through you will say it's a pity
That ever I had such a mother-in-law.
Whatever I do she is always fault finding,
Wherever I go she is sure to be there.
And if I don't do everything that she tells me,
She quick helps herself to a lock of my hair.

Chorus: This world's full of trouble,
    I cannot be happy,
    If I open my mouth
    She will put in her jaw.
    I'd rather be sent
    Off to jail or to Congress
    Than live all my life
    With my mother-in-law.

The lines "I'd rather be sent off to jail or to Congress" com
prise an excellent instance of the topical references with whic
the free-and-easy songs abounded. They had a spontaneou
quality. Yet they were commonplaces of easy acceptance by
public too well aware of the sordid political record of ou
statesmen.

Gus was before the public more than forty years, principall
in vaudeville, although for several seasons he starred in ligh
comedies—*Oh, What a Night, One of the Finest,* and other
under his management. Even today a number of our comic
are hypochondriacs or morose in temperament off stage. Gu
died of melancholia—by his own hand.

The "Personals" in the New York *Herald* were an institution
as much a part of the life of the town as the "agony" column i
the *Times* was to London. The James Gordon Bennetts, fathe
and son, respectively founder and developer of the *Herald* a
an international newspaper, were hell-roaring men, caring no
a fig for sensibilities, reformers, or the blasts from the pro
fessional pulpiteers. It was Bennett, Jr., who inaugurated i
the early 1900s the "cheesecake" form of newspaper art—photo
of girls' legs, limbs crossed, skirts above the knee, and maybe

ι inch or two of thigh showing. They were favorite shipboard
ιots of returning dancers, musical-comedy stars—any girl
ι the news that would so pose—and are still standard art for
ιe picture weeklies, although now regarded as old hat by the
bloids, who lean more to horror stuff.

Bennett, Jr., permitted his Personals column to develop into
ιite a racket, with serious results to himself and its ultimate
imination by the authorities. It was soon found that Mignon,
ιe manicure, offered more than her advertised services. These,
ιd other "announcements," were but screens (some cloaked
ι anagrams whose solutions were obscene) for houses of as-
gnation or definite addresses where work was done on the
remises. The most harmless were flirtatious listening posts in-
iting subsequent rendezvous. Here are a few taken verbatim
:om the New York *Herald* for October, November, and De-
:mber 1875

FRENCH, FORMERLY OF PRATT'S. Would like to see
W.W.F. Address as soon as possible, FRENCH, Herald, Uptown Branch.

Obviously a blind; as was this:

CORA, FORMERLY WITH MRS. SMITH, 32nd. St.—Have
just returned from California. Let me see you. Something important. Address Friend Charlie, Herald Uptown Branch Office.

And this:

ANNIE, I HAVE FOUND A PLACE where we can have
our hair dressed on New Year's either at store or residence
without extra charge at E. L. Ketelas, 411½ Sixth Ave.

The Personals were a haven for the lecherous and sex-starved:

WILL THE LADY WITH BEAUTIFUL DARK EYES who
rode in Atlantic Ave. car last Friday evening from South Ferry
to L—— Place permit gentleman who tried to present her his
card to form her acquaintance? Please address HONOR, Herald Office.

Either the lady did not read, did not read the Herald, or spurne
the advance, for "Honor," a few days later, returned with th
insertion:

> BEAUTIFUL DARK EYES–WHY THIS CRUEL S
> LENCE? Write me anonymous if you wish to say that yo
> decline my acquaintance. I shall then summon my pride t
> assist in effacing those ever to be remembered glances. Addres
> HONOR, Herald Office.

Despite the influence of *Lydia Thompson's British Blondes*, an
of Pauline Markham, who, by the way, was a lovely interlud
in Bennett, Jr.'s, life (and perhaps the other way 'round, fo
the younger Bennett, when sober, was a gracious host and
Croesus spender), most of the ladies attractive to the '70
mashers were brunettes.

> IF LOVELY BRUNETTE, SIXTH AVE. CAR going up
> town, 4 o'clock Friday, dark eyes, dressed in black, dark blu
> veil in hand, umbrella, plain white handle, will permit acquaint
> ance of gentleman of position, address, QUIET BANKER
> Herald Uptown Branch Office.

These were all grist for the topical free and easies, and th
performers made much of them. Many of the references, comi
and in song, were pretty feeble. But one, by an unknow
minnesinger, survives that is worth printing:

THE HERALD PERSONALS

> Of course now you all read the Herald,
> For the topics and news of the day.
> And other affairs interesting;
> Some are sad and some are gay.
> But the subject I wish now to mention,
> Perhaps you have noticed before,
> As you read down the columns each morning,
> And smiled at the things you saw.

Chorus: The Personals in the Herald,
　　　　 Herald! Herald!
　　　　 The Personals in the Herald,
　　　　 The Herald Personals!

If charming brunette in the carriage
Who smiled at the gent in the stage . . .
Perhaps there is millions now in it . . .
If her hand she would like to engage . . .
I'm a first class conductor and puncher,
On the Third Ave. Railroad cars,
And I'm sporting a solitaire diamond,
Much larger than Tweed's ever was.

Charles Henry Augustus; Sweet William,
My darling, I'm yours evermore.
Oh, husband's gone out of the city,
And father will be at the store.
I'm lonely, so lonely without you,
Oh, say, can you meet me at three?
There's boned turkey, champagne and oysters,
Your answer send quickly to me.

Bennett's public-boudoir billets-doux continued until 1906, a considerable source of revenue to the paper and of vast amusement, interest—and gratification—to its readers. William Randolph Hearst, a rival publisher with political ambitions and whose defeat in his campaign for the Governorship in 1906 was largely accomplished, Bennett liked to feel, by the vigorous opposition of the *Herald*, was responsible for the demise of the Personals. Hearst was outraged at his treatment by the *Herald*, and soon after, his manager, S. S. Carvalho, laid the matter of the Personals before the Federal Grand Jury. The *Herald* and Bennett were promptly indicted and thereafter convicted of the publication of information about whores and their locations, for, divested of its legal fustian, that is what the charges amounted to. Bennett paid fines totaling $25,000 and was ordered to cease and desist the publication of his Personals. He was furious and immediately ordered Hearst's name placed on the *Herald's* "Index," which meant that so long as Bennett owned the *Herald*, Hearst's name was never again to appear in its columns. It was a disastrous defeat for Bennett. Don C. Seitz, in his admirable history of the *Herald* and its ownership, *The James Gordon Bennetts*, says precisely that the decline of the newspaper dated from the legal suspension of the Personals.

SAINTS AND SINNERS

BUT THE *cause célèbre* of the '70s, or of any other time in our legal or religious history, began in City Court, Brooklyn, the morning of January 11, 1875, when the clerk of Chief Justice Joseph Neilson's court opened the case of Tilton *vs.* Beecher in a courtroom packed with United States Senators and the *haut monde.* It was Henry Ward Beecher's trial on charges of Theodore Tilton that "the greatest preacher the world has seen since St. Paul preached on Mars Hill" (thus John Hay) had committed adultery with Elizabeth Tilton, his wife. This trial had everything: the animal passions of man and their fructification through hypocrisy and deceit against a time-worn friend in the manner of a libertine and in the person of America's most eminent divine. It ended on July 2, 1875—after 112 days of trial and numerous interruptions because counsel could not cross the icebound East River—with a disagreement by the jury. It is the verdict of scholars in retrospect that Beecher was guilty.

Throughout his career, women had been Beecher's obsession —the dewy-eyed Betty Bates in Indianapolis; Lucy Maria Bowen, the young wife of Beecher's sponsor, Henry C. Bowen, who brought Henry Ward to Plymouth Church in Brooklyn; Martha Sawyer, whose hymnlike voice he never tired of; Rebecca Whitehead, one of the most charming of young Hoosier matrons in the 1830s—and where was the crime? In his hypocrisy and deceit. In his thunderous denunciations of those violators of the Seventh Commandment whom he read out of his pastorates. In his bland, bedside manner, speaking with the tongues of angels spiritual solace for Lib Tilton and Lucy Bowen through the laying on of hands and the passionate ministrations of the flesh. A beautiful, dark-eyed dove, Lib was worthy of more gallant seduction, as was Lucy, who, on her deathbed, left a "terrible confession" that cost Henry Ward his extra-curricular job as editor of Bowen's *Independent* and made European travel for the preacher convenient if not necessary.

But for that busybody, Harriet Beecher Stowe, sister of Henry Ward, it is unlikely that the Beecher-Tilton scandal would ever have risen to foul the furthermost precincts of Christendom. This is the suggestion of the late Paxton Hibben, whose masterly account, *Henry Ward Beecher—an American Portrait,* is not only the most readable, but the sanest of all Beecher's biographies.

On January 11, 1871, the National Woman's Suffrage Association, convening in Washington, listened to an unscheduled address by a woman who had earlier that day completely captivated the House Judiciary Committee, to whom she had presented a statement for the cause of feminine franchise. She was Mrs. Victoria C. Woodhull, whose equally amazing sister was Tennessee Claflin.

The ladies had come on from Ohio, opened a Wall Street brokerage office, and, with the sage counsel of Commodore Vanderbilt, had cleaned up a half-million dollars on the Commodore's baby, the Harlem Railroad. A year before the suffrage convention the sisters began publication of *Woodhull and Claflin's Weekly* as a mouthpiece for their liberal views. They advocated saner divorce laws and birth control, beat a drum for spiritualism, espoused the cause of labor, tucked in refreshing notes of Paris fashions, championed Victoria for President, and supported their weekly ("a much more interesting paper than the *Christian Union*," says Hibben) with advertisements of other brokerage houses. The sisters, attractive hedonists in bobbed, blond curls, were anathema to the hairshirts, who dubbed them free lovers and worse. But they were indefatigable workers for the cause, and they gained the confidence of Elizabeth Cady Stanton, who breathed into Victoria's ear what she knew of the goings on between Henry Ward Beecher and Elizabeth Tilton. For a time Victoria kept her peace, might very well have continued to do so, had not Hattie Stowe and sister Catherine assailed her as a flaming harlot. Hattie Stowe's invective against Lord Byron for his alleged incestuous relationship with his half sister had been unwise. Her tirade against Victoria was sheer stupidity. For Victoria was a skirted tartar, took nothing from anybody, traded punch for punch, and was forever eager for the fray.

On May 22, 1871, Victoria sent an open letter to the New York *Times*. And this, says Hibben, is what she wrote:

I do not intend to be made the scapegoat of sacrifice to be offered as a victim to society, by those who cover the foulness of their lives and the feculence of their thoughts with a hypocritical mantle of a fair profession, diverting public attention from their own iniquity in pointing the finger at me. . . . My judges preach against "free love" openly, and practise it secretly. . . . For example, I know of one man, a public teacher of eminence, who lives in concubinage with the wife of another public teacher of almost equal eminence. All three concur in denouncing offenses against morality. . . . I shall make it my business to analyze some of these lives, and will take my chances in the matter of libel suits.

She made it her business at once to notify Theodore Tilton exactly whom she meant, and she served notice that unless Beecher and his friends kept their big mouths shut, she would crack down upon him with all the force of a woman unjustifiably scorned. Victoria waited, was dissatisfied with their attitude, and in Boston on September 11, at the convention of the American Association of Spiritualists, of which she was president, she told the entire story of Henry Ward's illicit love with Lib. None of the newspapers printed the names, but the whole town wagged tongues with such furious zest that what had happened became known in New York. But Victoria hadn't finished. The following week, *Woodhull and Claflin's Weekly* published the purple story under the heading "The Beecher-Tilton Case." To hell with the libel suits, said Victoria in effect. "I intend that this article shall burst like a bombshell into the ranks of the moralistic social camp," she wrote. A bombshell? It was a panzer-division blitz. And it was met by the Beecher cohorts with a stupidity almost equal to that of Harriet's which precipitated the scandal. General Benjamin F. Tracy, an ardent and important worshiper in Plymouth Church, was also United States Attorney. In a disgraceful usurpation of his office, he at once clapped Victoria and her sister, Tennessee Claflin, into jail for using the United States mail to disseminate obscene literature. They could not meet the prohibitive bail set, and there they languished for six months until freed when the indictment was dismissed. It was stupid because it alienated sympathy from Beecher to his accusers. And because it spurred Tilton's suit for alienation of affection, which bared all.

O rare public morsel!

On March 8, 1887, Beecher yielded up his fantastic life. And in the streets of Brooklyn Heights, when Beecher had been laid to rest, children romping in the bright spring sunshine, chanted, surmised Hibben, in their sidewalk games;

> Beecher, Beecher is my name—
> Beecher till I die!
> I never kissed Mis' Tilton—
> I never told a lie!

But this was almost a fitting dirge compared to the jibes of the vaudeville comics and the free-and-easy songsters. Neglect the scarletry of the Beecher-Tilton scandal? They tossed and bandied the names about in unprintable obscenities and restaged in song and story the sordid love of the unhaloed preacher. Chris Malone, a popular free-and-easy entertainer and a wall-blasting baritone, sang the best of them:

BEECHER'O

> In Brooklyn town there lives a man,
> A celebrated preacher'o,
> Who preached the gospel on an improved plan,
> Did the Rev. Henry Ward Beecher'o.
> In Plymouth Church he used to preach,
> The way to glory he did teach,

Tho' for other men's wives would oftimes reach,
The Rev. Henry Ward Beecher'o.

One of the best members of his flock,
Was a man by the name of Tilton'o,
With faith as solid as a rock,
And a head as classic as Milton'o.
But Beecher, this divine old shark,
Would often go out on a lark,
And preach glad tidings in the dark,
To the wife of Mr. Tilton'o.

Those things went on for many a day,
Till a woman by the name of Woodhull'o,
Made up her mind to give it away,
Did Miss Victoria Woodhull'o.
In a free love paper she spoke of scrapes,
And a funny thing of different shapes,
But it looks very much like sour grapes
In the case of Mrs. Woodhull'o.

There is no one will deny I'm sure,
In the case of Mr. Beecher'o,
But what he is as good in the lady's boudoir
As he is in the church a preacher'o.
They say he is nearly sixty-five;
By the time he is ninety, he'll contrive
To set our country all alive
With little sons of Beecher'os.

How they howled! And Chris, or any other comic, would posit:

Why was Henry Ward Beecher the greatest fireman ever known? Because his hose reached from Brooklyn, N. Y., to Elizabeth.

Another topical medley included:

Henry was a preacher man,
And when to preach he first began
The people walked and rode and ran
To hear what he would say.
Now Henry he was very glib,
He spun a yarn and captured Lib.
But Tilton found out what they did
And there was hell to pay.

Here is the chorus of a "nut" song and dance:

> Oh, my! . . . . . Shoo fly!
> If it ain't the truth I hope to die.
> I was witness in the Beecher-Tilton scandal
> That's the reason why I never told a lie.

Beecher was sixty-two years old at the time of the trial, which "is nearly sixty-five." And the reference to "lies" in the jingle derives from the prevalence of perjury at the trial.

AMOURS, BLACKMAIL, AND MURDER

To STRIKE A SYMBOL for the decade of the '70s, one could well suggest a two-headed coin, Beecher on the reverse side; the swindling, flamboyant, lecherous almsgiver, Colonel James Fisk, Jr., on the obverse. In hypocrisy, greed, lewdness, and double-dealing, these two best epitomize the period. Beecher has been beautifully portrayed by Hibben. But Fisk, "riding the four-in-hand of his riches, packed with courtesans," as William M. Evarts described him, has yet to find an artist. It is astonishing that Fisk, a composite clown and whitefaced Emperor Jones, the most colorful character of the '70s, has thus far eluded the biographers. The late Robert H. Fuller's novelized account is an apologetic survey of a man who was no good. The hand is too loving that weighs Fisk's generosity against the debacle of that Black Friday in September 1869, in the Gold Room in Exchange Place, New York, when Fisk and his clever partner, Jay Gould, ruined hundreds in the gold panic they devised, possibly with the unwitting aid of President Grant. "Where has the money gone?" asked a Congressional committee later of the chesty, paunchy Fisk, a man to mark without his absurd admiral's uniform, or the decorative "colonelcy" he purchased in the Ninth New York Regiment. "Gone where the woodbine twineth," replied Fisk. It is fitting that his birth date was April 1 in 1834. He was a Vermont boy with scanty schooling, a hotel waiter, a ticket man with Van Amberg's circus—boastful, flashy, impudent, yet a likable scoundrel to the day of his murder.

He made money in cotton and lost it, may well have become a nonentity. But he met Dan'l Drew, who soon apprised him how easy, if ill-gotten, were the gains of Wall Street. Able teacher, apt pupil, they arranged a brokerage partnership under the blind of Fisk and Belden. And along came Gould. Fisk, Gould, and Drew—what a trio! They even trimmed the astute Commodore Vanderbilt, wresting from him control of the Erie Railroad. Fisk bought Pike's Opera House at Eighth Avenue and Twenty-third Street, New York; changed its name to the Grand Opera House (it stands at this writing as the RKO-23rd. Street Theater); installed himself in palatial offices there as "Prince of the Erie"; housed the only mistress he ever loved, Josie Mansfield, in a dovecote a few doors west (which the brassy Josie virtually made a public boudoir); and in the theater began the production of *opéra bouffe*, giving personal attention to the female casting.

Thereafter, Fisk's life was about as private as Broadway. His girls, his wine, his parties, his famous clarence (usually packed with blondes), his political connivance with Boss Tweed, his sway over the courts (controlled by Tweed), his blatant public exploitation of President Grant (whom for a time he led by the nose), his vulgar appearances in his uniform as "Admiral of the Fall River and Bristol Lines" were as much a part of New York's daily life as the pages of Bennett's *Herald* and Greeley's *Tribune*. And so to the end, when, aged thirty-eight, he was shot down, January 6, 1872, on the stairs of the Grand Central (now the Broadway Central) Hotel by Ed Stokes, a rattish pimp in lavender pants who had been his longtime friend and whose friendly gesture was to take Josie Mansfield from the bed of Fisk and place her in his own—or rather hers that Fisk had given her.

The Fisk-Mansfield-Stokes triangle, if not the most tragic, is the most dramatic and the most sordid in our amorous annals— a *Police Gazette* epic. Josie, a rumpish tramp, first deceived and then betrayed her benefactor. She had been an indifferent actress, the daughter and foster daughter of would-be blackmailers—a mother and stepfather—who used her in an attempted shakedown of one D. W. Perley, a wealthy Westerner. Josie balked at this. Apparently she had never slept with Perley, and vicarious bedding was beyond her comprehension. To escape, she married an actor, Frank Lawlor, who brought her to New York, where he divorced her because the voluptuous Josie could never say no. (Lawlor, by the way, had a penchant for experienced women. He later married Pauline Markham, whose favors, as we have seen, were at a price.)

Fisk, curiously, never minded Josie's promiscuity; indeed, he lavished presents upon her even after she took up life with Stokes. He loved the woman. He was hurt in heart, but he was not jealous. She showed Stokes a number of Fisk's letters, and the pair promptly sought to blackmail Fisk. They then sued Fisk for libel, but Magistrate B. A. Bixby tossed the case out of court. Fisk, sick at heart, left the courtroom weeping during Josie's testimony. He could no longer endure listening to the hussy he loved perjure herself. This was January 6, 1872. Fisk went at once to the Grand Opera House from Yorkville Court. When Judge Bixby dismissed the suit at the conclusion of testimony, Stokes proceeded to Delmonico's Restaurant, at Broadway and Chambers Street, for luncheon. There he heard that the Grand Jury had indicted him and Josie for attempted blackmail. He went to the Grand Opera House, learned that Fisk had already left for the Grand Central Hotel at Broadway and Third Street. Stokes arrived at the hotel before Fisk. As Fisk came up the staircase through the Ladies' Entrance, Stokes drew his revolver and shot him twice. Fisk died the next day, with Tweed at his deathbed. The pomp of his funeral was as gaudy as his uniform—noisy, gala, a fitting final tribute to a man who had never grown up and whose entire life was as vulgar as an unbuttoned fly. And only Fisk, and Josie, and Stokes, and one or two of Fisk's friends had known all the time that the letters that had brought about the murder were wholly innocuous and could have been read in the public prints by children.

Stokes was arrested and tried, and the jury disagreed. In the second trial he was convicted, but the Court of Appeals set aside the verdict. On his third trial he was convicted of manslaughter and sentenced to six years in Sing Sing prison. He served four. When he was released, the only man who met him at the door of the prison was Cassius M. Reed, who had defrayed Stokes's expenses for his last trial. It cost Reed $60,000.

Reed at that time owned the Hoffman House, a hostelry famous for its magnificent bar, which was hung with nudes by Bouguereau. One, the "Satyr and the Nymphs," was often referred to in the jests of vaudevillians and the comic cartoons of the day. (Picture of a tramp observing the famous painting over the caption: "I've roamed the world over and I never seen a place like that.") Reed put Stokes up at the Hoffman House, resented Delmonico's orders never to let Stokes dine in his restaurants again. He financed a paving company for Stokes. It failed, and Reed sent Stokes to California. There Stokes met John W. Mackay, the mining capitalist, who sold Stokes the Victorine, a prosperous silver mine that Stokes resold in Europe.

After the deal, Reed took in Mackay and Stokes as partners in the Hoffman House. Stokes then cheated Mackay in a telegraph-stock deal. Mackay sued about the time Reed discovered that Stokes was helping himself from the till of the Hoffman House. Reed arranged a different setup in relation to the partnership to protect himself. But Stokes double-crossed him, obtained control, and threw Reed into the street. Reed wound up in the hallroom of a boardinghouse. But death you cannot swindle. Ill of Bright's disease if not in conscience, Stokes, who slept always in a lighted room in fear of Fisk's ghost, sold his holdings, and went off to die, in 1901, in the home of a sister.

Fisk had been a generous man. He probably had never heard of Robin Hood, but he was of that ilk—a one-man Tammany

and Home Relief. He supplied coal and food to the needy,
paid rentals for impoverished tenants, created sinecures for the
halt. When the Chicago fire of October 8, 1871, left thousands
destitute, Fisk sent a trainload of supplies to the stricken city.
And so, as were Beecher and other figures and expressions of
that inglorious decade, he was included in the hymnals of the
free and easies, especially in an inaccurate melodic memorial by
William J. Scanlan, a headline singer and song writer of the
period, in a ballad called

JIM FISK
or
HE NEVER WENT BACK ON THE POOR

If you'll listen a while I'll sing you a song
Of this glorious land of the free.
And the difference I'll show 'twixt the rich and the poor
In a trial by jury, you'll see.
If you've plenty of stamps you may hold up your head
And walk from your own prison door.
But they'll hang you up high if you've no friends or gold—
Let the rich go but hang up the poor.

Chorus: In the trials for murder we have nowadays,
The rich ones get off swift and sure.
With their thousands to pay to both jury and judge
You can bet they'll go back on the poor.

I'll sing of a man who's now dead in his grave,
A good man as ever was born.
Jim Fisk he was called and his money he gave
To the outcast, the poor and forlorn.
We all know he loved both women and wine,
But his heart it was true, I am sure.
He lived like a prince in his palace so fine—
But he never went back on the poor.

Chorus: If a man was in trouble Fisk helped him along
To drive the grim wolf from the door.
He strove to do right though he may have done wrong,
But he never went back on the poor.

Jim Fisk was a man wore his heart on his sleeve,
No matter what people may say.
And he did all his deeds both the good and the bad
In the broad open light of the day.
With his grand four-in-hand on the beach at Long Branch
He cut quite a dash to be sure.
But Chicago's great fire showed the world that Jim Fisk
With his wealth still remembered the poor.

Chorus: When the telegram came that the homeless that night
Were starving to death slow but sure,
The lightning express manned by noble Jim Fisk
Flew to feed all the hungry and poor.

Now what do you think of the trial of Stokes
Who murdered the friend of the poor?
When such men go free is there anyone safe
To step outside their own door?
Is there one law for poor, and one for the rich?
It seems so, at least so I say.
If they hang up the poor then surely the rich
Should hang up the very same way.

Chorus: Don't show any favor to friend or to foe,
The beggar or prince at your door.
The big millionaire you must hand up also—
But never go back on the poor.

Fisk was buried in Brattleboro, Vermont, and its citizens contributed $25,000 for a monument in Italian marble by Larkin Mead. At the four corners of the base of the shaft are the figures of four women. Over the brow of one is a locomotive, symbolic of railroads (the Erie). Another characterized shipping; a third, the stage. The fourth, says Fuller in *Jubilee Jim*, "stands for trade in its broadest sense." Chipped and scarred by souvenir hunters, it is today a forlorn testimonial.

Scanlan's song is unusual. It was one of the first of the class-conscious pieces, not at all the kind of thing at which Scanlan was adept. His most popular song was "Peek-a-Boo," a wretched lyric set to an ordinary tune:

On a cold winter's night when business is done,
And you to your home do retire,
What a pleasure it is to have a bright baby boy,
One that you love and admire.
To kiss and to love and to press to your heart,
What joy to your bosom 'twill bring,
You place him on the carpet and get behind a chair,
To please him you will begin to sing . . .

Chorus: Peek-a-Boo, Peek-a-Boo,
I see you hiding there.
Peek-a-Boo, Peek-a-Boo,
Come from behind that chair—
You little rascal!

We have made the '70s of sterner stuff. But, Jove! there it is. And it was sung for years. Scanlan later starred in light, romantic Irish dramas, and there was always a soft spot in such plays for the intrusion of sentimental ditties. It is, though, a freak; it belongs in the ringlet '80s. Another extraordinarily successful song of the '70s is analogous, with a better story— Matt O'Reardon's "Marriage Bells." Few of the free-and-easy songs were sentimental. "Marriage Bells" was not only sentimental, it was exceptionally popular in the '70s' sporting houses, of all places. While Madam and her girls practiced their most enticing blandishments, the piano player always did his best with "Marriage Bells."

Matt was a striking character. When his free-and-easy audiences—they were an intimate, friendly crowd—learned of his background, he became an outstanding favorite with the bibulous patrons. Irish, he had been an officer in the British Army. But after an unfortunate love affair with a lady of quality (unknown), he was forced to relinquish his commission and come to America, where he drifted and dissipated until, a natural musician, he ended as a free-and-easy entertainer. He was an expert pianist, and he also played the musical glasses. He'd set a tray of glasses on the piano and, while playing the melody of a tune on the glasses with his right hand, he accompanied himself on the piano with the left hand. Only a few could equal his feat of similarly playing the concertina and piano. Matt wrote "Marriage Bells" in the early '70s, and not only was it popular with harlots, it became a standard parlor song and later was adapted for stage orchestras and instrumentalists.

O'Reardon wrote a number of high-class songs, but none ever approached the popularity of "Marriage Bells." He would have gone far as a performer and composer. Drink bottled him in his grave.

MARRIAGE BELLS

Oh marriage bells are ringing,
What a glorious peal for me.
The present hour is bringing
Sweet joy and ecstasy.
For she whom I have loved so long,
Loved dearly as my life,
Will give me ere the hour has gone
The right to call my wife.
My wife—my wife.

Oh marriage bells are ringing,
What a glorious peal to me.
The present hour is bringing, love;
I fondly wait for thee.

Come, my darling, now and haste to me,
Do not tarry love, I wait for thee.
Oh marriage bells are ringing,
What a glorious peal for me!
The present hour is bringing, love
Sweet joy and ecstacy.

O Hymen! O Hymenia!

Wistful virgins, thoughtfully stitching antimacassars, took Matt's paean secretly to their throbbing bosoms. Nor does it pass understanding how it came to be the prostitute's Pervigilium Veneris. To the novitiate, at least, it must have had the ache of wish fulfillment.

But "Marriage Bells" was just a sentimental error for the hard-schooled free and easies. To audience and performer, the mood of love was strictly a commodity, its value determined at sidewalk prices. Best they liked the little red-nose comic in baggy pants and slap shoes, singing:

> Love, it is such a very funny thing
> And it catches the young and the old.
> It's just like a plate of boarding house hash,
> And many a man it has sold.
> It makes you feel like a fresh water eell
> And it causes your head to swell.
> It turns your mind
> For love it is blind
> And it empties your pocketbook as well.

Chorus: Boys keep away from the girls I say,
> And give them lots of room.
> For when you are wed
> They will polish up your head
> With the bald headed end of a broom.

And at this the audience clinked glasses, scuffed their feet, chucked their Mamies and Betsies under their chins and anatomically elsewhere, and shouted, "Another, Mr. Funnyman. Give us 'Her Age It Was Red.'" And the comic highspot of the evening was reached, for the audiences of the decade loved these nonsensical incongruities; the more sordid and bizarre they were, the louder the laughter. And, indeed, it would be difficult to find a more bizarre comedy song than

HER AGE IT WAS RED

> It's a short time ago I remember it well,
> All alone in the poorhouse a maiden did dwell.
> She lived with her father and mother serene,
> Her age it was red and her hair was nineteen.

Chorus: Nineteen—ten and nine—her age—her hair,
> Add it up to suit yourself—nineteen—correct.

> Now she had a lover who close by did dwell,
> He was crosseyed in both feet and humpbacked as well.

Said he, fly with me, by the light of yon star,
For you are the eye of my apple, you are.

Chorus: His eye—his apple.
Her optic—his fruit—her blinkers.

Now when she refused him he knocked down this maid,
And quickly he opened the knife of his blade.
He cut the white throat of this maiden so fair,
And dragged her about by the head of her hair.

Chorus: Her head—her hair—her knob,
Her hirsute appendage;
Her chignon—her wig—poor thing.

Now just at that moment her father appears,
He gazed at his daughter with eyes in his tears.
He grabbed the base villain by the hand with his throat,
And shot him with a horse pistol raised from a colt.

Chorus: With a pistol—a revolver—a gun—a cannon,
A bomb shell—boom boom!—that's all.

THE MINSTREL BOYS

ALL THROUGH this entire period of which we have written, and of much that is still to come, at least through the first decade of the twentieth century, the minstrel show was a distinct and popular form of entertainment, of vast importance in the dissemination of our popular songs. A true minstrel song is precise in its character, but so instinctively so, it is puzzling to analyze. They were jingles, Jim Crow-ish, many with gibberish choruses set to a dance rhythm which the gibberish accented. But, too, others were as topical as any of the free-and-easy songs; often they pictured a condition or mode or expression of their times. But of one topical song you could say, this is not true minstrelsy; and of another, one would recognize at once that it was of the minstrel genre. Such a song is

THE BELL GOES RINGING FOR SARAH

If you please sir I am a domestic,
What some people call servant gal.
My missus she calls me her Sarah,
But others for short call me Sal;
I'm general help round the corner,
My wages are small you'll agree,
I'm slaving from morning till midnight,
And I buys my own sugar and tea.

Patter: Yes sir, if I only sits down for a minute to rest me bones and take a long breath, up I has to jump cause—

Chorus: The bells they go ringing for Sarah,
Sarah—Sarah——
The bells they go ringing for Sarah
From morning until night.

My master he works in the city,
He gets fifteen hundred a year.
They dress like a Duke and a Duchess,
How they do it it isn't quite clear.
They give parties and hold up their noses,
As though they were first in the land.
And often I wait for my wages,
While they go a doing the grand.

Patter: There's the butcher keeps coming for his bill and the baker swears frightful and the grocer threatens awful things and if I open my mouth to talk to them a bit; in a minute they hear—*Chorus*

My missus talks of her connections,
Says her Grandmother's dad was a Judge;
Lady Guff and Lord Muff are her cousins,
Twixt us and the bedpost it's fudge.
She says she was born 'ristocratic,
Of that I can't say to be sure.
But folks for their money keep calling,
And say they won't come any more.

Patter: First I have to dust the parlor, then answer the door then go up three flights to make beds and just as I'm carrying out the chamber—*Chorus*

I'm a lady's maid, housemaid and cook,
And it isn't a matter for joking,
I can't ever look in a book,
For she'll ring if the fire wants poking.
With a book from the library she'll lay,
On a couch in the laziest manner.
Or else for a change she'll sit down
And thump away on the pianner.

Patter: The pianner ain't paid for, the furniture ain't paid for, I hasn't been paid for a fortnight—but if she hears me talking to you— *Chorus*

That is a topical song of the '70s, and a good one too. Its mordant humor of the plight of a domestic serving a snobbish family is a mirror of both unhappy classes. But it is also honest minstrelsy. It may have been occasionally sung in the free and easies, although the writer has never crossed it in that field. Quite possibly it was sung by Tony Pastor, though undoubtedly not in the form given here.

Most minstrel shows of the '70s featured the song in their first parts. Encore verses were worked up with bell-ringing effects, starting with the quartet and followed by the interlocutor. Then a huge bell was produced by one end man, and after the next verse, a large cowbell was sprung by the other end man. The finale was bedlam for Sarah.

Minstrels played to mixed audiences, to children at matinees, but although all ugly references and *double-entendres* were carefully censored, love as a topic was unrestricted, and often the songs were flirtatious, and amazingly specific:

CENTRAL PARK

While strolling through the Central Park
One evening in July,
A maiden fair with golden hair
Came tripping lightly by.
The lustre of her diamond eyes
Shone on me through the dark,
As in a whisper soft, she said,
"Is this the Central Park?"

Chorus: Around her splendid form
I drew the magic circle.
I kissed her—caressed her,
My brain was in a whirl.
Around her splendid form
I drew the magic circle.
I kissed her and I called her
A very pretty girl.

But ever since that fatal night
I haven't seen my queen.
I've since heard tell she ran away
With a great big fat Marine.
If I had the ring I gave that night
I'd not, as you suppose,
Go place it on her lily-white hand
But I'd stick it through her nose.

Minstrelsy has an extensive bibliography, and expansion on this form of blackface entertainment is superfluous here. There were, however, two outstanding minstrel troupes and several important characters specifically identified with popular songs in the '70s that it would be presumptuous to ignore. These were Carncross and Dixey's Minstrels; Lew Simmons, of Simmons and Slocum's Minstrels; Bobby Newcomb; Hughey Dougherty; Billy Sweatnam; Charlie Reynolds; and Mackin and Wilson.

Old-timers today still regard Bobby Newcomb as the greatest of all neat blackface song-and-dance men. He was beautifully proportioned, just the proper height for a dancer—immaculately dressed and wonderfully graceful. He was idolized by audience and professional alike. Newcomb usually wore a perfect-fitting black velvet sack coat with broad lapels and pearl buttons over a ruffled shirt with broad collar that turned over the coat. A loose bow tie, low-cut white vest, lavender satin knee pants, clocked stockings of flesh-colored silk, black dancing shoes with silver buckles, a soft, white felt hat, and a thin silver cane completed his costume. His voice was fair, but his dancing was effortless and his stage presence superb. He played some free-

and-easy time, but his impeccable manners and artistry were out of place among the tosspots, and he soon entered minstrelsy, where the mixed audiences, especially the ladies, adored him.

Bobby featured romantic songs with interpolated dancing, and one of his best—dedicated to the ladies—was "Blue Eyes Peeping into Mine"—rather sugary, but quite effective with a good guitar accompaniment.

> The eve had come, the birds had sung
> Their songs of sweetness,
> And the gentle zephyrs sighed.
> All nature bright with love and light
> That night was peeping,
> And the pale moon lit the skies.
> A fairy form beside me, a tiny hand in mine—
> Oh, yes, she said that we would wed
> And then be happy
> As her eyes peeped into mine.

Chorus: Strolling in the garden
> 'Mong the blushing flowers,
> Telling tales of love
> We passed the happy hours.
> Heeding not our parting,
> Shorter grew the time
> Down among the daisies
> Where the honeysuckles twine.
> Oh, yes, she said that we would wed
> And then be happy,
> Her blue eyes peeping into mine.

Carncross and Dixey's Minstrels, in a bandbox theater in Eleventh Street below Market, in Philadelphia, established an unusual reputation—for forty years they enjoyed the distinction of being the only minstrel show in America that prospered as a permanent organization. J. L. Carncross, the interlocutor, had a light, high tenor voice splendidly adapted to plaintive ballads and "The Low Backed Car," "Blue Alsatian Mountains," and "When the Corn Is Waving" were favorites in his repertoire.

When the corn is waving Annie dear
Oh meet me by the stile,
To hear thy gentle voice again
And greet thy winning smile.
The moon will be at full, love,
The stars will brightly gleam.
Oh come to me tonight, love
And grace the beauteous scene.

Chorus: When the corn is waving Annie dear,
Oh meet me by the stile.
I long to hear thy voice again
And greet thy winning smile.

The bucolic flavor was essentially minstrel, and Carncross an excellent exponent of this type of tender, pastoral song that was still current in the '80s, only to wane in the expanding social and commercial setting of the '90s.

E. F. Dixey occupied the bone end in the first part of their show (the righthand side of the semicircle as the performers face the audience), and his forte was "bone solos"—expert and trick bone playing with two clappers in each hand of bone or ebony. Dixey imitated woodchoppers, barbers, and shoemakers. But his big finale was an interpretation of the race between Dexter and Goldsmith Maid, two famous trotters of the period. Dixey's songs were largely of the domestic type, much favored by the family audiences that attended the minstrels. "Why Don't They Do So Now?" was one of Dixey's best-liked numbers.

Oh when I was a baby
The neighbors used to say,
I was a darling joker
But was always in the way.
The ladies used to pet me
And dance me on their knee,
They tickled me and pinched me
And they wouldn't let me be.
They used to pat my rosy cheeks
And pull my little toes,

> They fondled and caressed me
> And they wiped my little nose.
> They gave me sugar bags to suck
> And cooled my fevered brow;
> They kissed my little tootsies—
> But why don't they do so now?

Dixey always got a big hand for the comedy in this—it was just the right sort of eyebrow-raising, parlor suggestion, which received no more of a reprimand, if carried home to mother, than a tut-tut.

Although most minstrel organizations often shifted their interlocutors, bones, end men, and tambourines continually, Hughey Dougherty was virtually a fixture as tambourine in the Carncross and Dixey show. He was never a singer, but he managed to rasp, crack, and cackle through his tunes in a way that rocked the house. Dougherty enjoyed one of the largest personal followings of any performer in minstrels. The proprietor of the Bingham House, a hotel then on the southeast corner of Eleventh and Market Streets in Philadelphia, inserted a clause in his will that Hughey Dougherty should have free board and lodging as long as Hughey lived. Hughey's songs were comic or they were parodies whose rustic humors he accented with his cackling voice. Outstanding in his repertoire were "Her Front Name Was Hannah" and a parody on "Dear Evelina."

> Her front name was Hannah,
> Her father was a tanner
> She thumped the pianner
> In an artistic manner
> Oh, how she could hammer
> The Star Spangled Banner
> And Eileen Alanna!
> When she fainted we'd fan her

Hughey's "Dear Evelina" is somewhat pigsty for minstrelsy; it has a free-and-easy odor and possibly was recruited from the wine rooms and cleaned—a little.

Way down in our alley that smells like a rose,
The breeze from the tanyard will tickle your nose—
Lives my Evelina, a maiden so sweet;
She walks in the alley all in her bare feet.

Chorus: Dear Evelina, sweet Evelina,
My love for you will never, never die.
Dear Evelina, sweet Evelina,
My love for you will never, never die.

She's thin as a broomstick, she carries no meat.
She never was known to put soap on her cheek.
Her hair is like rope and the color of brass—
But, oh, how I love her, this dear little lass!

It will probably surprise a number of baseball fans that Lew Simmons, the minstrel, and not Connie Mack (Cornelius McGillicudy), was the original manager of the Philadelphia Athletics, the American League baseball team. Indeed, the fact is commemorated by a song called "The Baseball Fever," written by H. Angelo, a song writer of the '6os. Angelo's song was published by Marsh and Bubna, a Philadelphia music house, and was registered in the Eastern District Court of Pennsylvania in 1867. The illustration on the cover presents the national game in one of its earliest forms, with the dedication "To Lew Simmons, Esq." Lew must have loved the "Esq." It presumed a dignity of ownership hardly in keeping with the facts. For these were baseball's sand-lot days and Lew's return was so meager he was forced to dispose of his holdings (which later made millions for John Shibe and Connie Mack) and form a minstrel partnership with Slocum, which they maintained for a number of seasons in a theater at the northwest corner of Arch and Tenth Streets, Philadelphia. Lew was an effective tambourine, Slocum an accomplished interlocutor, and Billy Sweatnam, who afterwards billed himself as Willis P. Sweatnam, was the bone end.

Lew's songs are among the most definitely minstrel we possess—rollicking hobbledehoys with slapstick patter. For example

BAALIM JOHN

I'm driven to desperation since
My true love she has gone,
With a chap who peddled oysters,
And she left me all forlorn.
It really is a sin and shame
How I've been put upon;
This fellow drove a donkey cart,
They called him Baalim John.

Chorus: High O rickety Baalim John,
A-hawkee, hawkee went the donkey.
High O rickety Baalim John,
A hawkee, hawkee haw.

At the repeat of the second chorus, the quartet slipped on large donkey ears and brayed in harmony.

One had a nursery quality:

Monkey married the baboon's sister,
Smacked his lips and then he kissed her.
Kissed so hard he raised a blister;
It began to swell—it began to swell.

What do you think the bride was dressed in?
White silk dress and a green glass breast pin;
White kid shoes so interestin';
Monkey very much pleased—monkey very much pleased.

Sweatnam was a quiet, deliberate worker; a note of seriousness unusual in the minstrel performer. It gave a convincing quality to his act and made him an outstanding player. His songs were topical, lively, and often contained a subtle note of criticism. Here are two with which he was especially identified during his Simmons and Slocum engagement:

HAVE YOU GOT A GINGER JAR?

The troubles I have lately had
Have been enough to drive me mad.
The women are my greatest foes,
They've ruined all my Sunday clothes.

No matter where or what you're at,
They'll steal the lining from your hat.
They never ask you how you are,
But, "Have you got a ginger jar?"

Chorus: How's your nephew, how's your niece?
Will their gabble never cease?
How's your papa, how's your ma?
Have you got a ginger jar?

They steal the buttons from your coat;
They'd steal the whiskers from a goat.
Old Simon keeps a grocery store—
They stole the number from his door.
They never give you any rest,
They'd steal the plaster from your chest.
They stole our new policeman's star—
To paste upon a ginger jar.

This song was a specific jibe at a fad of the period—the ginger jar. It was a squatty, bluish-white jar of Chinese manufacture and held about two quarts of preserved ginger. In some inexplainable manner (comparable to the fad in the early 1900s of decorating ashtrays with cigar bands), a craze developed among women of pasting the ginger jars with pictures, labels, stamps, or affixing to the jar buttons, badges, shells— numberless oddities—until it resembled a fantastic, barnacled urn. Like all fads, it became a nuisance and may well have been laughed out by the popularity of Sweatnam's song.

Another of Sweatnam's songs pictured the plight of many an elder child of the period, perhaps of all times:

TOMMY DON'T WRIGGLE THE BABY

Now I am the oldest one of a family numbering twenty;
At the tender age of one begun my troubles of which I
  had plenty.
The children I had to feed, with an infant's nursery bottle;
Whenever they smiled—I grew so wild—the darlings I'd
  like to throttle!

Chorus: Tommy don't wriggle the baby;
Please don't tickle the baby
Be particular—perpendicular
Always carry the child.

Charlie Reynolds, a member of the Simmons and Slocum
Minstrels, was unique as a performer. He could not sing or
dance and was tone deaf. He never could learn more than
a few words of any song. He could handle neither tambourine
nor bones, and when telling a story he got lost and collapsed
helplessly before reaching its point. But he was irresistibly
funny as an end man. His sway over an audience was complete,
compensating for an erratic temperament that almost cost him
his engagement time and again. Often he'd leave a performance
flat and be found later contentedly smoking a pipe on the
porch of some farmhouse, entirely oblivious of his obligation.
He extemporized continually; it was virtually impossible for
a straight man to work with him in an interlude or afterpiece.
But he was always funny. Here are the straight lines of a
song called

GOODBY LIZA JANE

The time has come I do declare;
I must have a lock of my gal's hair.
Walk dad Lew, oh, Mr. Lew, he he he, hear me now.
I'se goin' trav'lin' very far,
With a bottle of gin and a big cigar.
Walk dad Lew, oh, Mr. Lew, he he he, hear me now.

Chorus: I'se goin' away to leave you, goodby, goodby,
I'se goin' away to leave you, goodby Liza Jane.
I'se goin' away to leave you, tell every one goodby.
I'se goin' away down Lynchburg town,
Goodby Liza Jane.

Behind a hen roost on my knees,
Thought I heard a chicken sneeze.
Walk dad Lew, oh, Mr. Lew, he he he, hear me now.
It was only a rooster sayin' his prayers;
'Most broke his leg gittin' upstairs.
Walk dad Lew, oh, Mr. Lew, he he he, hear me now.

To the best of Jack Murphy's recollection, Reynolds' performing version of this popular minstrel song was like this:

Oh, the time has come I do declare, I do declare, I do declare
Da da da diddle, da da da . . . (*pats tambourine clumsily*)
Oh, the time has come I do declare . .
I think I said so once before . . .
Da da da diddle da. . . .
It's a pretty little song, just a simple little thing. You don't have
to bother about the words. It just goes right along . . .
(*Quartet then sings the chorus while Reynolds sits down and
beams at the audience.*)
INTERLOCUTOR. Well, we are waiting.
REYNOLDS (*surprised*). Oh, are we waiting? Well, while we are
waiting let's all go home.
INTERLOCUTOR. No, no. We are waiting for the second verse.
REYNOLDS. The second verse? The one immediately following the
first verse? Yes, yes. Do you think I could be trusted with another
verse? When I once get started I'm all right.
INTERLOCUTOR (*in a loud whisper*). Behind the hen roost . . .
REYNOLDS. Once again, please.
INTERLOCUTOR (*louder*). Behind the hen roost!
REYNOLDS. Behind the hen roost on my knees,
          Right on my knees, down on my knees,
          Da da diddle. . . .
(*And chorus by quartet as before.*)
INTERLOCUTOR. Well?
REYNOLDS. Oh, yes, yes. Let's see. Where was I? I was still behind
the hen roost when last heard from. It was very nice of you gen-
tlemen to help me out in the chorus. It adds, it adds, to the addition.
The tambourine helps out, too. I play a number of instruments but
of course not as good as I play this one. . . .

And thus on and on for a number of encores, until Reynolds
would stop the applause to tell a story and make a ridiculous
botch of it.

Mackin and Wilson often appeared with Simmons and
Slocum's Minstrels. They were a blackface song-and-dance team
and when playing the variety beer halls later were what was
known as a "rival" act—*i.e.*, a song and dance in which both
appeared as suitors for the hand of the same girl. Few, probably,

will recognize the Wilson referred to here. He was Francis
Wilson, who, on the death of Jimmy Mackin, entered the
legitimate theater as a comedian and became a famous star.
Wilson, of Quaker origin, was a forceful man of great principle.
He led the actors in 1919 in the drive that resulted in the forma-
tion of Actors Equity and became the union's first president.

When Simmons dissolved his partnership with Slocum, he
leased Concordia Hall in Philadelphia and presented a number
of dramatic productions there, among them *Shenandoah*, a
popular war play. Later he teamed with Frank White, a blackface comic, and toured the variety halls in a blended version
of two old acts, "Ghosts in a Pawnshop" and the "Three O'Clock
Train." Simmons and White were both married to non-professional women. White's wife traveled with the act and so,
thought Mrs. Simmons, would she. About the time Mrs. Simmons joined her husband, Mrs. White became stage-struck
and insisted she be permitted to play the ghost in the act. She
did, and Mrs. Simmons promptly pronounced her performance
ham and asserted she could play the role better. To keep the
peace, the women were allowed to alternate in the role for a
time, until the dissension between them became so great that
both "ghosts" had to be sent home. Simmons' wife went to
New York and in due course wrote Lew that she had opened
a boardinghouse, giving a glowing report of her splendid
ménage in a high-class neighborhood. Lew, she said, could
come to a real home at last when his season ended. When Lew
finally completed his tour and came on, he was quartered in a
corner of the parlor, where a ragged screen masked a cot. The
rest of the room was occupied by nondescript lodgers, cots,
pots, and broken chairs.

Lew didn't complain. He was one of the friendliest and
best-liked men in the profession. The humor of any situation
was the first thing he saw, even if the joke was on him. He
was born in Reading, Pennsylvania, and there he died upon
a visit—struck down and killed by a beer truck. Lew probably
drew a celestial chuckle out of that. He was a great guzzler.

GET THEE GONE, GIRL!

SOCIAL CLUBS, those informal associations of crafts solely for amateur self-entertainment—"get-together" is their own term—even today prevail. They flourished in the '70s, some under misleading names. The deception was pointless; the boys just liked the sound of the titles. For example, the Riverside Boat Club was largely justified by the hiring of occasional rowboats for an outing on the water. Others were the Silver Star Social Club, the Acme Pleasure Club, the Harmony Social Club, etc. The latter was aptly named, for most of these organizations assembled mainly for beer and song to while away a Saturday night after a week of ten-hour-a-day toil.

The membership was composed largely of young mechanics, paperhangers, tinsmiths, hucksters, gas-meter inspectors, icemen, house painters, cab drivers, nail-and-brass finishers, candy pullers —the gamut of labor. They were by no means rowdy assemblies; their affairs were noisy, but the members were not quarrelsome. They met usually over a saloon, in a large room which they furnished with pool table, card tables, chairs, racks for beer kegs, a broad shelf for glasses, and always a secondhand piano, which was invariably played by ear by some talented member. Good voices were by no means rare. It was not uncommon for some burly, red-whiskered iceman to oblige, in a light, high tenor, with

> My pretty red rose, my pretty red rose;
> 'Tis a sweet little token, my pretty red rose.
> While lonely I sigh for my darling's bright eye,
> Of my pretty red rose I will sing.

Some of the social club songs were a bit rough, but on the whole they were an agreeable medley indicating a wholesome regard for family amenities and sentiment. The clubs were a social expression of considerable interest in the '70s, reflected the period's gregarious tendencies, and were by no means unimportant as disseminators of popular songs. So robust a membership naturally would lean to such songs as "Nobody Knows" and "Finnegan's Wake"—rollicking, uncouth ballads of the when-you-see-a-head-hit-it type—but in no manner akin to the bawdy tavern tunes.

"Nobody Knows" relates the story of a brawl between "a Dutchman, a Scotchman, a Nigger and a Mick" and how it all started when somebody called Johnny McIntyre a bum. "Finnegan's Wake" is just as gory and has an added Amazonian touch, surprising even in the '70s, when few holds were barred. Finnegan, a hod carrier, cracked his skull when, drunk, he fell from a ladder. Here are two of its most belligerent verses:

> His friends assembled at the wake.
> Miss Finnegan called out for the lunch.
> First they laid in tay and cakes,
> Then pipes, tobaccy, and whisky punch.
> Then Biddy O'Brien began to cry—
> "Such a fine boy I never did see;
> Och, now, Tim, why did ye die?"
> "Hold your gab," says Judy Magee.

> Then Peggy O'Connor took up the job.
> "Arra, Judy," says she, "you're wrong, I'm sure."
> But Judy then hit her such a belt in the gob
> It laid her sprawlin' on the flure.
> Each side did then in war engage—
> 'Twas woman to woman and man to man.
> Shillalah law was all the rage,
> And a rousing ruction soon began.

Yet, after this free-for-all, they would listen with respect and liking as some member rendered the tender

NORA O'NEILL

> I'm lonely tonight, love, without you,
> And I sigh for one glance of your eye.
> For sure there's a charm, love, about you,
> Whenever I know you are nigh.

Like the beam of the star when 'tis shining
Is the glance which your eye can't conceal.
And your voice is so sweet and beguiling,
That I love you sweet Nora O'Neill.

Chorus: Oh don't think that I'll ever doubt you,
My love I will never conceal.
I'm lonely tonight, love, without you,
My darling sweet Nora O'Neill.

With these sentiments duly expressed, the boys would then
shift to their bare-knuckle ballads. Some of these were gustatory,
of the style of the earlier "Simon Johnson's Ball," and one
such was

I HAD BUT FIFTY CENTS

I took my girl to a fancy ball it was a social hop.
We stayed 'till all the folks went home and the music it did stop.
We went into a restaurant, the finest in the street,
She said she wasn't hungry but you ought to see her eat.
Some oysters raw, a plate of slaw, a chicken and a roast.
Some sparrow grass and apple sass, a soft shell crab on toast.
A big box stew and crackers too, her appetite was immense.
She called for pie but I thought I'd die for I had but fifty cents.

She said she wasn't hungry, she didn't care to eat,
But I've got money in my clothes to bet she can't be beat.
She took it in so easy, she had an awful tank,
She said she wasn't thirsty, but this is what she drank:
A whiskey skin, a glass of gin which made me shake with fear,
A ginger pop with rum on top, a schooner then of beer,
A glass of ale, a gin cocktail, her appetite was immense,
She called for more but I fell on the floor; I had but fifty cents.

You can bet I wasn't hungry, I didn't care to eat;
Expecting every minute to be pitched into the street.
She said she'd bring her family 'round some day and have some fun.
I gave the man the fifty cents and this is what was done:
He tore my clothes he smashed my nose with me he swept the floor.
He gave me a prize, he blacked both eyes, he nearly broke my jaw.
He caught me where my pants hung loose and pitched me over the
    fence.
Take my advice, don't try it twice, when you have but fifty cents.

But the striking song of the social clubs was "Get Thee Gone, Girl!" Here is a macabre theme unique in the popular song genre. Nowhere has the writer seen anything quite like its story of "a fair blushing maiden with a face full of scars" and of her murderous haunting of "the driver of the city horse cars." It is as though the chill irony of Heine had been visited upon some talented coal heaver who, morose and sodden in the back room of a Bucket of Blood, for a fleeting hour immersed himself in a graveyard spell.

GET THEE GONE, GIRL!

A horrible story of late I've been told,
Makes my heart cease to pulsate, my blood chills and cold.
Of a fair blushing maiden with a face full of scars
Who was stuck on the driver of the city horse cars.
Now the driver was wealthy, but he worked in disguise.
And the girl was a villain, though blue were her eyes.
And whenever she'd go near him he'd yelp loud and strong—
"Get thee gone, girl! Get thee gone, girl!"
But the girl wouldn't get thee gone.

She followed him daily and hung on like glue;
He wasted away till his clothes he fell through.
Then he hired him a yard and he slept in a shed,
But the maiden hung on till his reason had fled.
She'd crawl through a knot hole and roost by his side;
With a piece of blue ribbon his ankle she tied.
He'd awake from his slumber and in tragic voice say,
"Get away, girl! Get away, girl!"
But the girl wouldn't get away.

She followed him up 'til one morning he died;
He opened his mouth, and his breath he let slide.
In an alley way they laid him to sleep his last sleep,
Where the Thomas cats fight and the oyster cans weep.
She dressed herself up in her new ulster coat;
With a toothpick his age on a shovel she wrote.
Now she gets bilin' full, and a voice to her shouts—
"Get thee out, girl! Get thee out, girl!"
But the girl won't get thee out.

The arresting juxtaposition of the bizarre line: "And the girl was a villain, though blue were her eyes" is amazing in its economy of characterization. The loose threads of the narrative fret a student like strands from a straitjacket. "Now the driver was wealthy, but he worked in disguise." The relation is as abstract as the allusions in Rossetti's ballads—and as fecund in phrase. "With a toothpick his age on a shovel she wrote." What grinning, semi-literate death's head is here making sport? And through it all is the poignant hint that the haunt was justified; ghostly retribution for an unnamed wrong. The song defies analysis. What an epitaph for an era the poetic Bowers sugars with the adjectival "Tragic!"

A VIOLET FROM MOTHER'S GRAVE
and
A HOT TIME IN THE OLD TOWN WITH BABE

THE INELEGANT EIGHTIES

A PSEUDO SELF-CONSCIOUS righteousness suffused the social and cultural expression of the 1880s. It was largely a hangover from the debauch of the preceding decade. Yet it is a mistake to call the '80s drab; egregious is more nearly the word. It was the era of great mistakes, of blind groping, of blundering effort to recover from the debacle of the '70s. It was the era of expansion, the winning of the Western empire. To the West sped our men to mine and ranch, to lay ties for the railroads that were to obviate frontiers, to amass fortunes (ill gotten or gained through intelligence and energy), leaving a woman's world in the East, and a bewildering and decadent culture. No decade in our history is so enmeshed in inconsistencies, incongruities, baffling contrasts. How truly the lowly pop tunes picture the early years of the period! Banal, crude, uncouth, or dripping in sentiment, most of them possessed not even the essence of clabber:

> I wish I had a glass of water—
> I will tell you the reason why:
> While I am drinking, I am thinking
> Of my true love with a sigh.
>
> *Chorus:* Sweet Maggie Gordon, you are my bride.
> Come and sit thee on my knee,
> And tell to me the reason
> Why I am slighted so by thee.

A yellowed cutting from the New York *Herald* for November 9, 1884, refers to this song in an interview with a penny broadside seller in Chatham Square.

"That song," the article quotes the sidewalk merchant, "had a tremendous run among the shop girls of this city." It does not absolve the more opulent and supposedly intelligent middle class, behind whose portieres bustled dames in ringlets gathered about the piano to sob:

EMPTY IS THE CRADLE, BABY'S GONE

Little empty cradle, treasured now with care,
Though thy precious burden it has fled;
How we miss the locks of curly golden hair,
Peeping from thy tiny snowwhite bed.
When the dimpled cheeks and little laughing eyes
From the rumpled pillow shone, then I gazed with gladness.
Now I look and sigh;
Empty is the cradle, baby's gone.

Chorus: Baby left her cradle,
For the golden shore,
O'er the silvery waters she has flown.
Gone to join the angels,
Peaceful evermore;
Empty is the cradle, baby's gone.

And of this, the same penny broadside seller in the *Herald's* interview observed: "It had a fine run, but it stopped suddenly, and I took the pains to investigate the cause of its current unpopularity. I found that there were so many houses that were emptied by death that the song generally called up unpleasant memories. We used to sell a great many songs about men who were hanged. But so many people are hanged nowadays that we can't keep up with the mortality, and so we have abandoned that class of song." The penny broadside seller's conclusion appears facetious. Few of the songs of the '80s were so rigorous as hanging.

The acme of the lugubrious note, however, is the dubious distinction of J. P. Skelly, whose masterpiece, "Why Did They Dig Ma's Grave So Deep?" was keened for several years in saloon, parlor and variety hall.

Poor little Nellie is weeping tonight,
Thinking of days that were full of delight.
Lonely she sits by the old kitchen grate,
Sighing for Mother, but now 'tis too late.
Under the daisies now covered with snow,
Rests the fond mother away from life's woe.
Nellie is left now to murmur and weep—
Why did they dig Ma's grave so deep?

Chorus: Why did they dig Ma's grave so deep,
Down in the clay so deep?
Why did they leave me here to weep?
Why did they dig Ma's grave so deep?

Skelly—Edward B. Marks says in his delightful reminiscences of his experience as a song publisher, *They All Sang*—was a Bible House plumber and the author of some 400 ditties. One of these was "Take This Little Rosebud," a song more distinguished for its back cover advertisements:

Madame Larcher, 38 W. 14th St., Manicure, Chiropodist.
Nail-biting positively cured. From Paris—Parlor Office.

Tiffany & Co., Jewelers, 11-13-15 Union Sq., N. Y.

Enoch Morgan & Sons. Sapolio. Price 10 cents per cake.
Send for our card about the terracotta statuette—Ange Dechu.

During the '80s, and in the '90s too, songs were often used for commercial exploitation. "Murphy's Head," or "After Kelly's Party," by Henri Le Verne, vaunted the remedy of the Emerson Drug Co. as sovereign for hangover.

Melodic testimony to the enigma of the era are its contrasting comic and topical songs. There was much drunkenness—a partial escape, perhaps, from the red plush. Odd, rather than quaint, songs celebrated the saloons and the alcoholics; they were mainly morose moralizations, lacking the jolt of the tavern tunes. In the '80s, too, the hobo and bandit were heroized in lyrics along with abundant uncouth comic songs—a striking metronomic swing from the sentimentality with which the ballads dripped.

With the East left to the women, the sectional feminine influence became pronounced in the '80s. Women virtually dominated the literary output. In his scholarly examination of the decline of our Eastern culture—*New England: Indian Summer*—Van Wyck Brooks supports this conclusion with a quotation from William Dean Howells' *Literature and Life*.

The man of letters must make up his mind that in the United States the fate of a book is in the hands of the women. It is the women with us who have the most leisure, and they read the most books. They are far better educated, for the most part, than our men, and their tastes, if not their minds, are more cultivated. Our men read the newspapers, but our women read the books.

Alert observers, the popular song composers, their ears reacting as a seismograph to the social expression, recognized the advancing feminine culture. Less intellectual, possibly, than Howells, but equally as aware, was Frank Dumont. Dumont was a sprightly writer of skits and lyrics. He wrote *The Book Agent*, a filthy vaudeville afterpiece that slopped around the dumps and slabs like stale beer. From it Charles Hoyt devised the immensely successful family farce, *The Parlor Match*, that was to earn Evans and Hoey, who played its leads, close to $400,000. Dumont wrote, too, the amazing song called "The Aesthetic Girl; or Too Utterly Utter"—amazing not only because it is one of the extremely few satirical songs of the '80s, but also because it is clever—qualities rare in the '80s in whatever activity. To music composed by W. S. Mulally, Dumont wrote:

> I represent one of the latest
> Whims that arise in our day;
> At a glance you will see by my actions
> I've a touch of the aesthetic craze.
> I go in for genuine culture,
> I sigh, and I silently mutter,
> If anything chances to please me,
> For I'm too—yes, too—utterly utter.

> *Chorus:* Over sunflowers yellow as butter,
> I linger in aesthetic flutter,
> And I lisp with a sort of a stutter,
> For I'm too—yes, too—utterly utter.

I never attend any dances,
For I should certainly die
If I sought to display rapid motion,
I'm so languid I never could try.
But give me a party of culture,
I'll put them all into a flutter;
I'll crawl and I'll drawl 'round the parlor,
For I'm too—yes, too—utterly utter.

I love to admire china dishes,
Broken and battered with age,
And flowers that possess faintest odors,
And my poems I'm sure are the rage.
Each movement of mine is a study,
And a picture of all that is utter:
For I walk and I talk sort of dreamy,
For I'm too—yes, too—utterly utter.

Only Howells' phrase: "and their tastes . . . are more cultivated" may be questioned. Already women ruled the home, and their social expression became assertive, with what devastating effect one may experience in the recoil from the horrific pages of the costume books of the period and the portrayals of the interiors of middle-class homes. Cosmetics and face make-ups for women (deemed "fast" even in the '70s) were introduced, a synthetic scent that enhanced the era's meretriciousness. True, these were simple: powder and rouge and a soft lead pencil for eyebrows (sparingly used) were the adorning aids. But a deal of attention was given the hair, which was worn long and piled on top of the head. Against the sides of this structure a number of false curls, or puffs, were pinned, which at least gave the hirsute pylon an architectural stability. The girls also modified the "waterfall," that enmeshed bag of hair attached to the back of the head and a mode of the '70s, to the size of a boxing glove.

Dressing the hair of the women of the '80s was a feat. The first duty of a young woman in expected attendance at a reception or party was to repair to the hairdresser, who curled, oiled, crimped, and perfumed her locks before piling it, and then added the curls and ringlets from his own stock. Sprinkling this creation with gold, silver, or diamond dust was the final touch. Gold dust was gold leaf ground to fine flakes, silver dust was ground tinfoil, and diamond dust was mica. For his masterpiece, the hairdresser usually charged seventy-five cents or one dollar.

One of the comic songs of the '80s clinched the fanatical feminine interest in hair-dos. It was written by Charles R. Fisher, and his lines run:

HAIR-DYEING GREASE

I'm a weak, troubled youth, and disturbed in my mind,
Three months have I courted a lass quite refined.
But taking her close you'll find covering her head,
A vast prairie of red hair, and a visage like lead.
A schoolmate of mine told me a short time ago,
That he knew what would knock all redheads quite low;
He gave me a card, at it I did stare,
And found 'twas an ad of Dr. Le Clair.

Chorus: Dr. Le Clair, Dr. Le Clair,
Your hair-dyeing grease works so charming and fair.
I'm sure 'twill be soon that her hair will decrease,
If my girl keeps on using her hair-dyeing grease.

I bought her a box and gave it to her,
Her hair she informed me would turn soft as fur.
I earnestly hoped that her words would prove right,
For whenever I travelled her hair caused a sight.
For over a year she had the hair grease,
Till at last she resembled a large porky piece.
I'd dare not to press her for fear she would boil,
And "run over" some day and my clothes surely soil.

Skirts were exceptionally long. They trailed the ground; and for protection, rows of brush braid were sewed to the edges, excellent catchalls for straws, horsehair, splinters, and humus.

The diamond splurge came in the '90s. Most of the jewelry of the 1880s consisted of amethysts and semi-precious stones, such as garnet, carnelian, sardonyx, moss agate, topaz, blood-stone, cat's-eye, and cameo. A favorite gift of a swain to his lass was a "Regard" ring. This was a thin gold ring in which were set six stones in typographical series to spell "Regard," the initial of each jewel forming the word. Thus:

Ruby	Emerald	Garnet	Amethyst	Ruby	Diamond
R	E	G	A	R	D

The stones were tiny, but the sentiment was large, and it gave the favored girl quite an edge over her friends.

The uncommon diamond was occasionally worn by men, in cluster pins of small stones for the shirt front. One end of a thin chain was fastened to the cluster, while the other end was pinned to the shirt front under the right arm. Indeed, watch chains for men were often made to hang around the neck, drape over the vest, push through a buttonhole, and loop over to a lower vest pocket. They were made of all manner of materials: gold, silver, bamboo, slabs of onyx, cherry-stone links—even braided human hair.

The souvenir sentiment of the '80s was pronounced. It was attached to almost anything. A number of songs dismally testify to the whimpers of the period. Flowers were especially esteemed:

> Only a pansy blossom;
> Only a withered flower.
> Still to me far dearer
> Than any earthly bower.
> Bringing me back to the springtime,
> And memories of long ago—
> The happiest, merriest springtime
> That ever I did know.

This was caroled in hall and minstrel shows and played through-out American cities wherever a hand organ creaked. So was J. F. Leonard's song

A LITTLE FADED ROSEBUD IN OUR BIBLE

'Tis a little faded rosebud in our Bible,
A memory, and, to us it's ever dear.
'Twas placed there by our loving angel mother,
And has remained as placed so many years.
Our token is a little faded rosebud—
A rosebud that we've long since laid away;
We miss it ever fondly in our old home—
A rosebud that has long went to decay.

Chorus: A rosebud—a rosebud in our Bible,
Only a rosebud that's decayed.
Though its ever-loving sweet remembrance
Will bring back the happy years that's passed away.

Equally maudlin was "A Flower From My Angel Mother's Grave." This was written by Harry Kennedy, a ventriloquist and a remarkably versatile song writer whose work ranged from the aforementioned "Empty Is the Cradle, Baby's Gone" and the graveyard flower above to "I Owe Ten Dollars to O'Grady," "My Sweetheart's Family," and "Her Father Was a Plumber." (Those '80s!) Kennedy published his "Flower From My Angel Mother's Grave" in 1878, but its popularity was achieved in the '80s—an interesting illustration of how precise and dated are our sentiments. In the '80s it drew commensurate sobs; in the late '70s and in the '90s—as today—it was —and is—a wail:

I've a casket at home that is filled with precious gems,
I have pictures of friends dear to me.
And I've trinkets so rare, that came many years ago
From my far distant home across the sea.
But there's one sweet little treasure that I'll ever dearly
prize,
Better far than all the wealth beneath the wave;
Though a small, faded flow'ret, that I placed in childhood's
days—
'Tis a flower from my angel mother's grave.

Chorus: Treasured in my memory like a happy dream,
Are the loving words she gave.

And my heart fondly cleaves
To the dry and withered leaves—
'Tis a flower from my angel mother's grave.

In the quiet country churchyard they laid her down to
 sleep,
Close beside the old home she's at rest.
And the low sacred mound is enshrined within my heart,
By the sweet ties of love forever blest.
In the still and silent night I often dream of home again,
And the vision ever tells me to be brave.
For the last link that binds me to the place I love so well
Is the flower from my angel mother's grave.

Many an eye moistened and let fall a tear on the crazy quilts the old ladies were making in the '80s as they listened while a favorite niece intoned this lament at the piano during a quilting bee in a neighbor's home. The sewing of carpet rags in the '60s and '70s had given over to the quilt. It was a social diversion. Six or eight women met at one another's homes, and as needles jabbed at the patches on a huge pattern stretched over a frame, tongues wagged and tunes were hummed. When dusk timed the close of the afternoon, they draped themselves demurely and gracefully upon the heavy red or brown plush furniture which had replaced, with no added comfort, the horsehair upholstering of the '60s, and tea was served.

The old melodeon had been discarded; pianos were more frequently seen, and heard, in practice. And the banjo, and its player, were absolved of all iniquities and given a place of warrant in the home or the concert. The recognition of an instrument previously socially despised was largely due to the important manufacturers—Dobson, Mosher, Clark, Rickett, and Stewart. The latter, S. S. Stewart, did much to improve the quality and appearance of the banjo and supported his work with an expensive—and remunerative, as it turned out—advertising campaign in which he extolled the instrument as "The Banjo as an Art."

Stewart was the first to introduce steel strings, as he was the first to publish comprehensive and practical instruction books. He wrote with authority. He was an expert player himself and gave frequent recitals on the instrument. High-class entertainments they were, too, in which he often astonished his auditors with full chords and chromatic runs encompassing three octaves. He asked $75 for a Stewart Concert Model Banjo —and got it. It seems little enough against prevailing prices. Today $275 is the average price of a modern banjo. But in the '80s, when $15 per week was a foreman's salary in most trades, $75 was no small item in the family budget.

Although they were a nuisance, coins were favored over paper money (probably a continuance of the distaste for the "shinplaster," the twenty-five-cent paper currency of the '60s), and workmen were frequently paid in pennies, half dimes, and dimes rolled in newspaper cartons containing one, two, or five dollars each. In the '80s, illuminating gas was in general use, and gasfitting became a specialized trade distinct from plumbing. But gas appliances for cooking were not common. In summer, many families cooked meals on charcoal stoves in the yard to avoid heating the house.

Steam heat for winter had not yet appeared on the scene. Comfort was obtained from stoves, open grates, and Baltimore heaters, a glorified, coal-burning heating stove. It was fitted neatly into the fireplace and had a large, convex front with many mica doors. This appliance featured the parlor, or "best room," and an attachment of pipe and sheet-iron drum was supposed to heat the room on the floor above, which it did not do.

OL' MASSA—AND THE WATERY GRAVE

HERE IN THE BEST ROOM was the piano, and here were sung the "parlor" songs. Memories of the Civil War still clung, but were softer. The plight of the South in defeat and the subsequent humiliation of the Reconstruction were regretted by gentle folk in the North, and the expression is often found in the numerous "slave" songs that were a part of the '8os' musical culture. The lyrics were similar in trend and invariably portrayed the character as a feeble, lame, rheumatic, and homesick octogenarian traveling on foot to the deep South from far Northern points. Characteristic and popular was

THE OLD SLAVE'S DREAM

While wandering all alone, and thinking of my home
And the friends I used to know before the war,
I sat beside a stream, and fell asleep to dream—
I thought I saw the cotton fields once more.
Ol' massa was as big as life, the darkies in the corn,
Singing happy songs so merry, light and gay.
I saw my dear ol' Mammy sittin' by the cotton gin,
And by her side the pickaninnies at play.

Chorus: But it's no use—it's no use—
Still I'm sighin' for the good ol' times I've seen.
And my home in Lou'sianny on the Mississippi shore,
I long to see if only in a dream.

I felt the gentle breeze, heard the rustle of the trees,
And the birds with sweetest music filled the air.
The flowers in the lane were blooming just the same
As when I was a boy and wandered there.
Then my brothers and my sisters gathered round my cabin
door,
And they sang the same old songs I used to know
When I was on the old plantation long before the 'mancipation
When the darkies from their homes were forced to go.

Occasionally the "slave" songs summoned up an old love, enhancing the plaintive quality of plantation memories. The popular "Darling Chloe" was one of these:

In the South Ca'lina state where I was bred and born
And the pickaninny darky learns to hoe,
There is one I long to see, she was always dear to me,
But I left her many, many years ago.

Mid the cotton and the corn, there we both were bred and
　　born
And together in the fields we used to sow;
But it's twenty years or more since I left the cabin door,
And I'm going back to see my darling Chloe.

Chorus: Darling Chloe, darling Chloe,
　　　　Then your sweet face I soon will see I know.
　　　　Where the sunny southern breeze
　　　　Fans the old palmetto trees,
　　　　I'm a-goin' back to see my darling Chloe.

In that dear old sunny clime where the sweetest blossoms
　　grow,
And the birds make sweetest music all the day,
There I'm bound to see my Chloe, she'll be waitin' for
　　her Joe,
But I know like mine her hair has turned to gray.
Oh the cornfield is no more and the day of toil is o'er
For she's creepin' mighty close to eighty-three.
But she'll wait till I come back by the coon and 'possum
　　track,
For I haven't seen her since we all were free.

The slave songs were the most authentic of the '80s' pop
tunes. They clung to the old genre of straight melody fashioned
to a lyric of at least understandable sentiment and, as in the
foregoing songs, often added an underlying political sympathy
that was decent. That they became moribund in the latter half
of the decade is further evidence of the period's uncertainty.

The '80s had reached an impasse—were midway between the
old-style tunes and the ragtime and hobbledehoy of the cham-
pagne-and-ruffled-drawers of the '90s. The social historian would
do well to bring his lancet pen to the '80s, remove the veneer
of Edith Wharton, and expose the plush-covered dust. The
sneer of Thomas Beer at the rollicking '90s is anachronistic
pique.

Mainly, the burghers of the '80s interrupted their casino
games (euchre was becoming passé—family games of the decade
besides casino were checkers, parchesi, dominoes, authors, and

jackstraws) for the lamentations of J. K. Emmet, a popular yodeler who had forsaken the beer halls of the variety circuit for the "Fritz" comedies of the legitimate stage. In 1882, the John Church Co. published Emmet's "Sweet Violets," a song from his play, *Fritz among the Gypsies*, and immediately they took root in the hearts of simple folk:

> Sweet violets, sweeter than all the roses,
> Laden with fragrance, sparkling with dew.
> Sweet violets, from mossy dell and rivulet,
> Zillah, darling one, I plucked them
> And brought them to you.
> Oh, Zillah, stay, go not away,
> Violets are blooming, love for you alone.
> Oh, sweet violets, sweeter than all the roses,
> Zillah, darling one, I plucked them
> And brought them to you.

Then Emmet yodeled.

His lullaby, published in 1878, became one of the really immense songs of the '80s, crooned and hummed in parlor and nursery in a surfeit that must have been maddening. It was also known as "Brother's Lullaby," because in the play from which it was taken, *Fritz, Our Cousin German*, a brother sings the song to his sister:

> Close your eyes Lena, my darling,
> While I sing your lullaby.
> Fear thou no danger, Lena,
> Move not, dear Lena, my darling,
> For your brother watches nigh.
> Watches nigh you, Lena dear,
> Angels guard thee, Lena dear.
> My darling, nothing can come near.
> Brightest flowers bloom for thee,
> Darling sister, dear to me.
> Go to sleep, go to sleep my baby,
> My baby, my baby, go to sleep my baby,
> Baby, oh bye, go to sleep, Lena sleep.

Against these, the popular "I'm Just Going Down to the Gate," a song of Gus Williams' (to music by Plumber Skelly of a few pages back), represents a high degree of sophistication:

> My sweetheart's a sly little fairy,
> Her age is just seventeen.
> Her parents think that she's too airy,
> But a sweeter girl never was seen.
> At night she steals out from the cottage,
> Her mother cries after her, "Kate!"
> She answers, "Dear Ma, I'm not going far,
> I'm just going down to the gate."

> *Chorus:* "I'm just going down to the gate, dear Ma,
> Just down to the old garden gate.
> The moon is so bright,
> And it's such a nice night—
> I'll just go as far as the gate."

A curious phase of the sentimental ditties of the later '80s is their "if" character, a sort of skepticism in the love-and-mother ballads that is inexplainable and can only be charged off as another of the period's incongruities: Maybe the sweetheart will be true; possibly the lover will come back; let us hope Daddy will mend his errant ways; you say you'll always love me, but; I hope you will always be happy—that kind of thing.

One of the most popular songs of this type was written by Jack Mitchell, which is understandable enough when you consider the kind of life he led—insolvent, hopeless, leading to death in the free ward of a New York hospital, destroyed by dissipation. As a song writer he was extraordinarily successful and his song referred to, "Say Will He Ever Return?" enjoyed a remarkable vogue:

> Say will he ever return?
> Where can the wanderer be?
> Ne'er will my heart cease to yearn,
> Be roving on land or o'er sea.
> If my tears and my prayers can bring you
> From far off foreign shore,
> Oh, bring back my boy,

My pride and my joy,
To your home and your mother once more.

As a pop-tune lyric, this is good. Indeed, and here is another indefinable substance: almost all of these skeptical or frustrated themes were marked by much better writing than the drool of the parlor songs. They have a quality of realism which makes for sense, and possibly that is the reason. A writer with that mental approach surely would scorn Ma's deep grave in the clay; nor would he idle his tears on faded flowers, however angelic his dead mother. The finest lyric of the '8os written by a contemporary is an admirable illustration of love among the aloes. Thus:

THE DAY WHEN YOU'LL FORGET ME

You call me sweet and tender names,
And softly smooth my tresses;
And all the while my happy heart
Beats time to your caresses.
You love me in your tender way,
I answer as you let me.
But oh, there comes another day,
The day when you'll forget me—
The day when you'll forget me.

I know each ever fleeting hour,
Some unseen joy may bring you.
I know there dwells a subtle power
In those sweet songs I sing you.
I do not fear the darkest way
With those dear arms about me;
Oh, no, I only dread the day
When you can live without me—
When you can live without me.

De Marsan's *Singer's Journal* gives the author of this only as "Morgan"—using the quotes. It was probably a gracious gesture by the actual writer to the girl who popularized the song, Jennie Morgan, a sweet songstress of the halls. The composer (and a pretty melody it is), was J. R. Thomas, the composer also of "Bonny Eloise," ("The Belle of Mohawk Vale,") and "Eileen Alanna."

Not anywhere near so good, but more in the pop-tune vein is:

THE LETTER THAT NEVER CAME

Any letter here for me? was the question that he asked
Of the mailman at the closing of the day.
He turned sadly with a sigh, and a tear stood in his eye
As he bowed his head and slowly walked away.
Then he said, "How can it be? Will it never come to me?"
He had waited all those many years in vain.
But from early morning light, he would wait till late at
    night,
For the letter, but alas, it never came.

Chorus: Was it from a grayhaired mother,
A sister or a brother,
Had he waited all those many years in vain?
Yet from early morning light
He would wait with spirits bright
But the letter that he longed for never came.

An interesting phase of this song is its mystery. Pop tunes invariably kiss and tell. Yet the chap in the letter song winds up a corpse on the beach:

His poor soul it had gone out with the tide.
In his hands they found a note with the last words he had
    wrote,
"Should a letter come please place it by my side."

But the letter that he longed for never came, nor is it disclosed from whom he expected the note, a striking violation of the rules.

Quite a number of the '80s' sobbers were of the sea and its precarious following. America's foreign trade was developing, new inventions in marine engineering were being manufactured, and our ports were busy with ships and sailors—of widespread economic influence, for Jack ashore is a sprightly seeker of spirits and entertainment and, as the world's song literature melodiously substantiates, a leading inspirer of tunes.

HI, HO, I LONG FOR YOU MAGGIE

NATURALLY, the doleful '80s wept copiously over him, and in the variety halls, as about the parlor piano, "A Picture of Her Boy" choked every throat.

A mother kissed her boy goodby, the time had come to part,
The good ship sailed that day across the main.
The tears were streaming down her cheeks,
She clasped him to her heart,
She knew not if they'd ever meet again.
Long years she waited patiently as slowly on went time,
For tidings of her comfort and her joy.
One day there came a letter from a far off distant clime,
And with it came a picture of her boy.

Chorus: Only a picture, only a picture,
Only an image of her boy.
For he was her pride,
And e'er by her side;
Only a picture of her boy.

A celebrated ballad with a lyric more restrained in its emotion is "The Ship That Never Returned." The tune is the same as that used currently for the "Wreck of the Old Ninety-seven."

On a summer day when the sea was rippling
In a soft and gentle breeze,
Did a ship set sail with her cargo laden
For a port beyond the seas.
The wind was fair and her sails were shining
In the early morning light,
As she left her port for a far off country
And went sailing out of sight.

Chorus: Did she ever return?
No, she never returned.
And her fate is still unlearned.
And for years and years
There are fond hearts waiting
For the ship that never returned.

"Just one more trip," said the gallant captain,
As he kissed his weeping wife.
"Just one more sack of the golden treasure
That will last us all through life.
Then we'll settle down in a cosy cottage
And enjoy the rest we've earned."
Oh, alas, poor man, that kind commander
Of the ship that never returned.

Most popular of all was "White Wings," which is also interesting because of its contentious origin and influence. In the early '80s, Banks Winter, a minstrel tenor, bought the song from another minstrel tenor, Joseph Gulick, for $20. Some publishers still contend that Winter did not write the song. Their belief varies from that of old performers. Jack Murphy says it is true Winter bought the song.

But Murphy says he (Winter) was impressed only with the title and that he rewrote the words and music. Winter submitted his version to a number of publishers, but none would consider it, a curious reaction, for, although it had promise and cheer, it was in the vein of the '80s' contemporary sentiment, as Winter, quite unwittingly, subsequently proved. At first, Winter, a singer of importance, was afraid to try it in any place of importance because of a suspected unfavorable professional response. But when he joined Primrose and West's Minstrels, he decided to take a chance and used it for his solo number in the first part. What happened is history. "White Wings" was sung, whistled, warbled, hummed, tootled, ground out on hurdy-gurdies, and banged on pianos and every other conceivable instrument and remained a request number for Winter as long as he lived.

WHITE WINGS

Sail home as straight as an arrow;
My yacht shoots along on the crest of the sea.
Sail home to sweet Maggie Darrow;
In her little white cot she is waiting for me.
High up where the cliffs they are craggy—
There's where the girl of my heart waits for me.

Hi ho, I long for you Maggie,
I'll spread out my white wings
And sail home to thee.
Yo ho, how we go. Oh, how the winds blow.

Chorus: White wings they never grow weary.
They carry me cheerily over the sea.
Night comes—I long for my dearie.
I'll spread out my white wings
And sail home to thee.

Winter was a popular performer, liked by the public and his colleagues. In later years he quit minstrelsy and went into vaudeville with his daughter, Winona. After a spell of this trouping, he retired, settled on the West Coast, and died a few years ago in Los Angeles. He probably never knew that his song set a new style—ended the graveyard keening that had been the parlor and variety type of pop tune for the first half of the decade.

Indeed, the drift toward the frolic of the '90s' tunes occurred almost immediately after his "White Wings" became intrenched in the '80s' song culture, around 1885. Here is an instance:

I'LL MEET HER WHEN THE SUN GOES DOWN

In an ivy-covered little cot
About a mile-and-a-half from town,
Dwells a maiden that I dearly love—
I'll meet her when the sun goes down.
Her cheeks are like the red, red rose,
And her hair is a beautiful brown,
She's the darling of my heart, she is,
I'll meet her when the sun goes down.

Chorus: Oh, how I love,
Pretty little Mary,
The keeper of the dairy.
You're my turtle dove—
I'll meet her when the sun goes down.

Of course, this isn't within a B-flat of Lottie Collins' "Ta-Ra-Ra-Boom-Der-É" in the '90s (and a song we shall have fun with when we get to it), but it is a leap from the dolors of the '8os' parlor stuff, as is "Treat My Daughter Kindly," a song so quaint and naïve that it is unbelievable it was popular in the middle '8os.

> I once did know a farmer,
> A good and kindly soul,
> Who used to work upon his farm
> Around his cottage home.
> He had an only daughter,
> To win her I did try.
> And when I asked him for her hand,
> This was his reply:

Chorus: Treat my daughter kindly,
> And say you'll do no harm.
> And when I die I'll leave to you
> This little house and farm;
> My stock, my plough,
> My sheep, and cow,
> And everything I own.
> And all those little chickens in the garden.

SHABBY GENTEEL

JACK MURPHY tells of an unusual street faker who appeared in Pueblo, Colorado, during the middle '8os. He was a tall, handsome man about fifty-five years old, with long gray hair and a Vandyke beard. He wore a neat gray Prince Albert suit and soft felt hat. Nothing about him suggested the mountebank. He worked on a small platform and sold automatic clothesline reels at $1.75 each, and he sold plenty of them. His sales talk was not blatant. He used no form of con, not even long con, which is slow, deliberate, expert persuasion. (Short con is quick, snappy, aggressive jollying; bull con is rapid-fire insistence accompanied by elbow shoving and intimidation.) It was refined, dignified, almost paternal. He had a fine baritone voice and he attracted his customers by singing old ballads to his own accompaniment on a small but loud portable organ. As many women as men paused to listen to him, unusual in a street faker's crowd. Murphy says the most effective song in his repertoire was, "Papa, What Would You Take for Me?" It is of unknown origin, and Murphy heard it nowhere else in fifty years of trouping vaudeville in America, on the Continent, in England, and in South Africa.

The faker never worked at night, only afternoons. His evenings were devoted to distributing the day's receipts among the gambling saloons, and sometimes he was lucky. One night at a faro game he had extraordinary luck. As the game proceeded and his chips piled up, he drank a great deal of whisky. Except for making him rather gloomy, it had no effect on him, and the house slipped him a "special." To the astonishment of the house man, he brightened at once, played a little while longer, winning, then cashed in his chips and strolled out singing. It was afterwards discovered that he was a laudanum drinker, and the knockout drops only exhilarated him. One morning he was found dead on a slag dump back of one of the smelters. His name was never known.

PAPA, WHAT WOULD YOU TAKE FOR ME?

She was ready for sleep and she laid in my arms
In her little frilled cap so fine.
With her golden curls peeping out from its edge
Like a circle of bright sunshine.
And I hummed her the tune of Banbury Cross,
And the Three Men Who Put Out to Sea.
When she sleepily said as she closed her blue eyes,
"Papa, what would you take for me?"

Not the treasures of earth or its palaces,
Or its temples and stores of art,
Would I take for one smile from my darling's bright eyes,
Or one throb of that dear one's heart.
And the fire burned low and dim in the grate
To the tune of the Three Men at Sea.
And she sleepily said as she closed her blue eyes,
"Papa, what would you take for me?"

So I rocked my baby and rocked away,
She was tired and weary with play.
And I held her warm in my strong arms
At the closing of that long day.
Her cheeks were flushed by the embers' bright glow,
And I prayed that from harm she'd be free.
And she murmured so low as she dropped off to sleep,
"Papa, what would you take for me?"

The song sounds like a recitation, an Ella Wilcoxian effort set to music. Certainly it is not in the pop-tune genre, and obviously no pattern of the mid-'80s. Banks Winter's "White Wings," published in 1882, had already given a fillip to the ditties of the day, a snowballing influence that at the halfway mark of the decade was pronounced. It did not dry up the tear jerkers, but it put an effective brake upon them, and the songs of the '80s, toward the close of the period, moaned less, became more topical, and, in some examples, recognized life in spade-calling lines, as in "We Never Speak as We Pass By," which is a daring tribute to an adulterous wife by a husband willing to forgive.

The spell is past, the dream is o'er,
And tho' we meet we love no more.
One heart is crushed to droop and die,
And for relief must heav'nward fly.
The once bright smile has faded—gone—
And given way to looks forlorn.
Despite her grandeur's wicked flame,
She stoops to blush beneath her shame.

Chorus: We never speak as we pass by,
Altho' a tear bedims her eye.
I know she thinks of her past life,
When we were loving man and wife.

The song, in ballad style, then relates how "she became my virtuous bride" and how happy were the young couple in the purity of a union blest by sun and fields and flowers, "Until the tempter came to Nell." The final stanza:

In gilded hall, midst wealth she dwells,
How her heart aches her sad face tells!
She fain would smile, seem bright and gay;
But conscience steals her peace away.
And when the flatt'rer casts aside
My fallen and dishonored bride,
I'll close her eyes in death—forgive!
And in my heart her name shall live.

Certainly this continues the stress of the song themes of the '80s, which were love, death, and blighted romance. But its lines are braver and better than the penny-whistle dirges previously cited, and, if you will recall your latest neighborhood movie, its morality (sin must be punished before the benison of forgiveness) is undated.

The people of the '80s were serious folk who lived circumscribed lives, and the men busily engaged in the vast commercial and industrial movement then at the beginning of its geyserish expression. They had neither the time nor the mentality for satire. The improvement in masculine attire is an earnest of those earnest times. A favorite with the successful businessman of the '80s, and of his ambitious junior clerk, was the Prince Albert, the cutaway, or Chesterfield. Ulster overcoats were popular. They were very long, double-breasted, topped with an immense collar, bound with a four-inch belt with metal buckle, and were trimmed with slanting breast pockets:

Chorus: Oh the world may wag, but I can brag
I am free from care and labor.
I am quite sedate with my large ulster,
And I like to love my neighbor.
The ladies fair I do declare,
Upon me they all dote.
You can hear them sigh as they cast their eye
On Neddy with the Ulster coat.

So runs a jingle of the '80s.

Silk hats were worn by businessmen, professional men, book agents, song-and-dance men, street fakers, hack drivers, pugilists, young men, old men, equestrians, and equestriennes. And they were not cheap. A fashionable block cost $5.00 (about $20 in our economic scale), but there were silk hats known to the trade as "skinners" that could be had for $2.50 or $3.00. They were rather dull and had a stove-polish finish, but they were all right after dark.

Low-cut patent-leather shoes with large, silver-plated buckles were often worn, and many were made with "Scotch" soles. These extended a full half inch beyond the uppers and were stitched with bright yellow thread. Sideburned oldsters who raged at THAT MAN Cleveland and sighed for the good old days of Chester A. Arthur and James A. Garfield shod themselves in Congress gaiters, which came well up over the ankle and had rubber-cloth sides instead of lacing or buttons. It was a neat-enough shoe, until the rubber slackened.

The Paisley muffler was faddish in the '80s. It was a large, Paisley-pattern kerchief which was folded and worn round the neck and under a low-cut vest, with about an inch of the muffler showing. A wing collar, a bow tie, and an amethyst pin in the shirt front completed the setting. Everyone thought well of himself; it is not strange that there are almost no songs at all of any value that satirized the raiment, masculine or feminine. The hoot of the '70s was faint at last.

There is an interesting exception. Joe Sullivan was a blackface song-and-dance man in the '80s, and, according to his own story, he lived with his parents on the outskirts of Brooklyn one season while laying off between dates. Rummaging through the attic one day in search of something suitable for eccentric make-up, he found an old-fashioned plug hat. The hat was unusually tall, Sullivan was short and plump. It was a comic combination, but to test its certainty, Sullivan wore it on the street. He had hardly reached the sidewalk before he was forced to grab his hat and run to save himself—and the hat—from a gang of urchins who raced after him pelting him with stones and screaming, "Where did you get that hat?" Sullivan finally escaped, returned home, and celebrated the incident with a celebrated song. "Where Did You Get That Hat?" was sung by everybody, played by all bands, and wheezed by all hurdy-gurdies for thirty years, and it still is heard occasionally over the networks.

> How I came to get this hat is neither strange or funny;
> My granddad died and left to me his property and money.
> And when the will was read to me they told me plain and
> > flat,
> If I would have his money I must always wear this hat.

Chorus: Where did you get that hat?
> Where did you get that tile?
> Isn't it a nobby one
> And just the latest style?
> I should like to have one
> Just the same as that.
> Wherever I go they shout, "Hello!
> Where did you get that hat?"

> If I attended the opera, in the opera season,
> Some one sure will shout at me without the slightest reason.
> If I go to a chowder club to have a jolly spell,
> There's some one in the party who is always sure to yell . . .

There was, though, a sort of reverse Alger-ian note, a riches-to-rags theme, which was quite prevalent. The downtrodden-outcast-with-noble-principles thing occurred in plots of many plays, a number of them modeled on the "poor old bum" who turned out to be a young millionaire in the last act. The counter-part of all this in the pop tune is expressed in "Poor, but a Gentleman Still," which was the best of this, the "shabby genteel" type of song. It had a catchy 3/4 melody and always got a big hand.

> Don't think by my dress that I came here to beg
> Though the sharp pangs of hunger I feel.
> The cup of misfortune I've drained to the dregs,
> If I'm poor, I am shabby genteel.
> The time was when snobs who would meet me would say,
> "Ah, Harry, dear boy, come and dine."
> But now when they meet me they look 'tother way,
> My company now they decline.

Chorus: Though poverty daily looks in at my door,
I'm hungry, I'm footsore and ill.
I can look the whole world in the face and I'll say,
If I'm poor I'm a gentleman still.

Last week I was up to the end of the town,
And while wandering sadly along,
I picked up a purse that a lady had dropped,
The temptation to keep it was strong.
My pockets were empty but firmly I said,
She shall have her own come what will.
She looked at my dress as I gave it and said,
"If you're poor you're a gentleman still."

Last week I defended a poor homeless girl
Whom a swell was insulting I found.
My strength for the moment seemed something immense
As I hurled the great brute to the ground.
He cried out, "You beggar, don't meddle with me
Or you'll very soon get a pill."
But I said, "Lay a hand on that girl and you'll find
If I'm poor I'm a gentleman still."

Even the love songs brightened up:

SANDY HAIRED MARY

I board with Mrs. Dooley,
I have an attic room.
There's a little Irish lady,
She sweeps it with a broom.
Her name is Mary Daly
And when the supper's ate,
She's titivated gaily down
Beside the area gate.

Chorus: She's a duck, she's a dove,
She's the only girl I love,
She's a jewel, she's a lily, she's a fairy.
A pet, you can bet
She'll be Mrs. Grogan yet,
Fair sandy haired Mary in our area.

Then the song takes a surprising turn. Mary is a flirt, visiting her blandishments upon the policeman on his beat, has an eye for the milkman, tête-à-têtes with the fat German grocer who lugs her heavy basket "to the area gate." And Mr. Grogan wails:

> The iceman and the butcher,
> The baker with his bread,
> The plumber and the glazier
> Have nearly turned my head.
> The dreamy undertaker
> Has finished me complete.
> He marries her next Sunday
> And they'll close the area gate.

Indeed, the comic aspect appears in a number of love songs of the mid-'80s, and it continued to the close of the decade. It wasn't emphasized, nor do any of the songs have the vitality and nose thumbing of the '70s. It was about like this:

BEAUTIFUL LOVE

> Oh, love, beautiful love,
> Love it is makes a man feel so peculiar.
> Oh, love, who does not love
> A Susan, Matilda, a Jane or a Julia?
> Love it is, and love alone
> That makes this world go round and round.
> Love is certain to be known
> Wherever a woman can be found.
> When one gets his first attack,
> It's like raspberry jam running down his back.

Chorus: Oh, love! Beautiful love,
> Love it is makes a man feel so peculiar.
> Love, love, beautiful love;
> A man's but a fool when he first falls in love.

As the '80s moved not so sedately toward the frolic of the '90s, the comic element reached a point that, in some instances, was almost macabre, and the topical note of previous reference became pronounced, especially in relation to drunkenness. Here again is a variant from the '70s, whose songs, as we have seen, were often downright justifications of tippling, relished by the rummers with unashamed delight. Some of the '80s' songs flung high the glass to Bacchus: mostly they were moralizations.

PUBS—AND WENCHING

ALMOST, the '80s could be called the saloon age. Pubs were everywhere, and liquor was cheap. A sizable snort of rye or bourbon could be had for ten cents in the most flamboyant emporium, and the universal price for beer was five cents in a goblet the size of a goldfish globe. In the "barrel houses," whisky sold for a nickel and was drawn from a barrel and nothing else, which explains the dubbing.

The taste of the middle class ran to fancy drinks, many of which are now forgotten—brandy smash, cherry cobbler, whisky skin, egg flip, rum and gum, whisky sling, ale sangaree, and porter sangaree. The latter were either ale or porter mixed with sugar and water and a flip of nutmeg on top. The old peat-bog saw, "The rich they ride in chaises, the poor they walk be Jasus," was not entirely applicable to the '80s. Any modest income could afford a carriage. A good horse and buggy, harness, halter, flynet, blanket, lap robe, whip, and canvas water bucket could be purchased for about $125. Board for the horse and storage for the buggy cost from $3.00 to $3.50 a week. This meant hay, grain, straw for bedding, and grooming. The farmers hauled immense loads of timothy and clover hay into town to service the stables. Many of them used oxen and walked beside them the entire distance, controlling the teams with guide rope and gad, which they could not do riding atop the heavy loads. At journey's end they repaired, of course, to the saloons, rubbing elbows with the gentry, as was the custom in the taverns of the '70s.

The moralizing drunk songs of the '80s had a wide range from the specific, unredemptive sot to the sad chiding of young brides at the periodic tippling of their husbands. "I See You've Been Drinking Again" was one of these and is the best in its lesson and unconscious humor ("When you stumbled and fell in the hallway, I knew you'd been drinking again") the writer has examined.

Just one year ago we were married,
And the happiest moment in life,
Was the day when to church we both wandered,
And you made me forever your wife.
Your eyes were as bright as the day, love,
When fondly you called me your own,
And promised me faithful and truly
That you would let liquor alone.

Chorus: You promised tonight you'd come sober,
And spare all my sorrow and pain.
But alas, my fond hopes are all over,
For I see you've been drinking again.

Last night I awaited your coming
As fondly as ever before.
I sat by the fireside thinking,
And heard when you opened the door.
But I heard that your step was unsteady,
I knew my fond hopes were in vain,
When you stumbled and fell in the hallway
I knew you'd been drinking again.

Sometimes the moralizing took the queer slant of parody,
which nearly made the message ironic. Willie Wildwave, pseudonym of William Delaney, a wonderful character who published the Delaney song books of the '90s and to whom we
shall devote some space when we get to that period—the acme
of his expression—wrote and published a parody on Harry
Kennedy's sobber, "Empty Is the Cradle, Baby's Gone," turning it into a temperance lecture of dubious effect. Delaney
called his parody,

EMPTY IS THE BOTTLE, FATHER'S TIGHT

Oh! thou empty bottle, standing all alone,
What miseries to many you unfold!
Oh! thou dreadful tempter, causing many a moan,
From the hearts of both the young and the old.
When your baneful shadow casts its glance on me,
Bright day seems turned to bitter night;
Then I glance in sadness, and behold, I see—
Empty is the bottle, father's tight.

Chorus: Oh! that dreadful monster, ever causing woe,
Oh! that thou were banished from my sight!
Then would peace and gladness cast its warming glow,
Empty is the bottle, father's tight.

Oh! the desolation by the curse of rum!
Oh! that you would lose your wicked sway!
Causing ruin and squalor, striking people dumb,
Filling convict prisons day by day.
When your dreaded sceptre is torn from thy grasp,
Then rejoicing and delight
Will fill the world with gladness,
Dear old hands will clasp—
Empty is the bottle, father's tight.

This was too much for the bottle brigade, and one Tommy Tucker, who may have been a beer-hall performer, quickly responded with

BOTTLE'S EMPTY, WHISKY'S GONE

Little empty bottle you would tell a tale,
If once your mouth could only speak.
Yes, for you I've often had to go to jail,
And the judge would send me up Salt Creek.
Up on Blackwell's Island, I would almost cry,
When the spirits from you had all flown.
Sitting in my cell, there, I could only sigh—
Empty is the bottle, whisky's gone.

Chorus: Little empty bottle, drained till not a sup
In the bottom of it can be shown.
How I'd like a horn to keep my spirits up—
Empty is the bottle, whisky's gone.

Forthright aid to Delaney's well-meant morality was immediate through the effort of a gentleman possibly identified as William H. Trimble. The song, which appears under Trimble's name in a beer-hall sketch in an '80s' song book called *Dr. James L. Thayer's Laugh and Grow Fat Clown Songster*, wastes no time on hyperbolical clichés but immediately lives up to its title:

THE OLD MAN'S DRUNK AGAIN

You've no doubt heard the song
Called father dear come home.
And the fate of hungry little Ben
Who sent for him to come.
How the old man used to smile
And cause his family pain.
He'd let up for a little while,
And then get drunk again.

Chorus: We've given him up for gone.
He's lying in the lane.
And almost everybody knows
The old man's drunk again.

Oh father, dear, come home.
Quit drinking like a sow.
You've drank away the bed and stove,
Don't swallow up the cow.
Why must you be a bum,
And sleep out in the rain?
The neighbors sigh as they pass by
The old man's drunk again.

The use of "smile" in the fifth line of the first verse was slang of the period. It meant to tipple, to partake of a snort, snifter, or eye opener.

And again the bottle brigade, incensed at the temperance note, held forth for their rum. An odd song of the '8os (De Marsan does not name the author), in celebration of champagne, even ignores that wine's horrific hangovers.

FIZZ, FIZZ, GLORIOUS FIZZ

Where am I Mister Lamp Post? Don't dance in the air,
I—recollect, now that I've been, to a glorious party,
A full dress affair.
And now I'm going home all serene.
The spread was delightful, the wines were all right,
But the fact of the matter now is,
That we have imbibed to our hearts' full delight,
And got screwed on glorious fizz.

Chorus: Fizz, fizz, glorious fizz,
       I own it with meekness,
       I've got a strong weakness,
       For fizz, fizz, nothing there is,
       To equal the flavor of glorious fizz.

       When supper was over I danced with Miss Brown,
       And she was the belle of the ball,
       But we hadn't stood up long, before we both fell down,
       To the gratification of all.
       But in picking her up, I unfortunately asked,
       "Where did you hurt yourself, Liz?"
       Said she, "That's no business of yours,
       But I see that you've had a deal too much fizz."

       We filled up each glass for the fortieth time,
       And the jolly good health we did drink,
       Of our host and our hostess, in language sublime,
       With musical honors, I think.
       Then at the suggestion of old Tommy Jones,
       Who is reckoned a bit of a quiz,
       I sang them a song in most sweet, husky tones,
       Brought on through the last glass of fizz.

       I've just shaken hands with the pump, I believe,
       Which has caused me a bit of a spill,
       But for such slight accidents I'll never grieve,
       Though I wish the lamp post would keep still.
       My head is beginning to spin round and round,
       And I fancy that this isn't "bizz,"
       So I'll wish you good evening, for I'm homeward bound,
       To sleep and dream still of fizz.

"Fizz" is a sprightly song for the '80s, and although it appears in De Marsan's *Singer's Journal* for that period, it is definitely '70s in lilt and attitude and may well have been written in those earlier days. The copyright date is not given. It must have been popular in the '80s, however, else De Marsan would not have printed it. And it illustrates rather well the drift from the early dirges of the '80s.

Old grads, and perhaps contemporary classmen, surely will remember "Son of a Gambolier," an archetype of drinking song, meet for the flagon and echoed in taprooms throughout the nation in the '80s—even as Stevenson sang, in exquisite diction and unrivaled facility—when, on a metrical lark, he set down his experiment (for Horatio F. Brown) in English alcaics:

> Brave lads in olden musical centuries
> Sang, night by night, adorable choruses,
> Sat late by alehouse doors in April
> Chaunting in joy as the moon was rising:

Well, the sentiment is the same in the "Son of a Gambolier," if it has not the finesse of a master spirit. The lyric, which became a collegiate bacchanal, seems Western in origin; certainly there it was first "chaunted." From Texas to Canada, from Kansas to the Pacific Coast, it was shouted from well-oiled throats as beaker upon beaker was downed. It had many verses, which varied according to regional preference. The melody is rollicking, of easy range, was readily memorized, and permitted roaring in unison by a saloon crowd or solo rendition by the street-corner busker in tamer versions.

As the miners and cattlemen sang it in frontier dives, it is a broad song, full of nuts and bolts and smelling of leather and whores. It is the most vigorous ballad of the '80s, and may well have been launched in the previous decade. Tavern tosspots of the '70s would have wetted it down with rounds of noisy delight, and probably did. Songs lasted long in those days, are best appraised during their periods of popularity rather than from their copyright dates. The "Gambolier's" specific references to lusty professional intimacies, however, were no social incongruity in the '80s, whose plush often cluttered parlors far from decorous.

SON OF A GAMBOLIER

I'm a rambling rake of poverty, from Tippery Town I
    came,
'Twas poverty first compelled me to sleep out in the rain.
In every sort of weather be it wet or be it dry,
I'm bound to get my livelihood or know the reason why.

Chorus: Listen to my ditty, for Tippery Town I steer,
Like all good honest fellows I like my lager beer.
Like all good honest fellows I take my whisky clear.
I'm a rambling rake of poverty, a son of a gambolier.

I've seen my ups and downs in life but manage to keep
on top.
This coat of mine so rusty I bought in an old Jew shop.
This hat I got from a sailor lad some eighteen years ago;
My shoes I picked up on the dump that everyone else
let go.

I'm known throughout the nation, I've a rag on every bush.
I never ride the brake rods, I always sit on plush.
My luggage in a paper bag, a bottle on my hip;
I ride from Maine to Frisco and I never give a tip.

When I arrived in Deadwood City the tarts all cried for
joy;
One handed me a bottle, and said, "My darling boy."
One handed me a bottle, and another one gave me a glass;
Said they, "My right good royal nobs, you've struck the
town for ass."

For stud or for the faro game I always have a stake;
My luck is always with me but the bank I never break,
I spend my money freely, as free as all outdoors;
The envy of the sporting men, the pet of forty whores.

There was a good deal of wenching as the decade declined.
Sporting houses, especially in the Eastern cities, were everywhere, often in respectable neighborhoods. They were not
segregated. Invariably there was one in the middle of a block
of workingmen's homes, the Madam a neighborhood character
who, as good Mrs. Smith just up the street, passed the time of
day at the counter as she obtained her daily foodstuffs at the
corner grocery. As long as the houses were quietly run and
reasonably circumspect, they continued in the same locales for
years. Indeed, the sporting houses were considered good in-
vestments. The renting agent was not only pretty sure of his
money, the rent was higher. The Madam charged the girls high
rates for room and board, and the girls did the best they could.

Most of the sporting houses in the '8os played to popular prices—one dollar top. Of course, there were slum and red-light districts where the accommodations and risk were meaner, cheaper, and dangerous. But there were also high-class assignation and bed houses in good residential sections which catered to selective trade. The lone worker who had a room of her own listed a few regular subscribers who preferred to deal with a conservative firm without risk of meeting their employees or the teacher of the Bible class.

There are no specific hymns to prostitution in the '8os; at least none has been found by the writer. But there are some borderline ditties, tonal hints that the custom of boy beds girl was not unpopular then either. For instance:

> If a kiss be delightful, so tempting my lips,
> That a thousand soft wishes beset you;
> I vow by the nectar that Jupiter sips,
> On certain conditions—I'll let you.

Although De Marsan prints this in his second volume of the '8os' popular songs, the lyric is far too good to be germane to that genre. Again, it may be a recitation and probably was. De Marsan, maddening in his neglect of essential data, gives no author and no date. The "certain conditions" were eternal fidelity, an unsullied affection. But throughout the song (if it is a song) is a sly suggestion that the maiden's exactions were not inexorable.

The super hedonism of "Oysters and Wine at 2 A.M." is a better illustration of the latter-day '8os' feminine looseness, if less facile.

> I'm a maiden who never refuses
> The pleasures that come in my way:
> For now is the time to be merry,
> To be bashful is but to delay.
> When the stars far above us are shining,
> With a party of friends, but a few,
> Quick the night passes by and we finish
> With oysters and wine at 2.

Chorus: Oysters and wine at 2 A.M., 2A.M., 2A.M.,
Oysters and wine at 2 A.M., oysters and wine at 2.

Now a journey to Long Branch is pleasant,
Oh, yes, 'tis delightful to me!
We stroll on the beach in the moonlight,
When the wild waves are roaring with glee.
Oh! but give me a partner for dancing,
And sweet music to liven us, too,
While we whisper "Good night," and then finish
With oysters and wine at 2.

This is a fair lyric. And note again how, when realism creeps into the songs of the '60s, '70s, and '80s, or any other period for that matter, the lines are invariably better. The epigrammatic "To be bashful is but to delay" slogans an entire philosophy; may be bravely interpreted without a leer.

Almost as adroit is "Flirting on Our Block." And for this song Mrs. Pauline Lieder, who apparently took over De Marsan's publishing interests in the '80s (nothing is known of either person), gives the author as Dr. T. D. C. Miller and the composer as W. W. Bentley, and nothing is known of them either; at least, as far as our research extended. It is a good song, amazing for that period in its characterization, and its *double entendre* in the third stanza is, well, hardly bland. We have observed before that "It" is the most obscene word in our language. Then to't:

FLIRTING ON OUR BLOCK

It's nice, they say, but naughty,
As all good folks can tell.
The way our maidens do it,
As sly as a gazelle.
They drop their glove demurely;
Just fancy such a shock;
And then with some dear fellows
Are flirting on our block.

Chorus: I look from out my window,
And fancy what a shock

To see such pretty maidens
A-flirting on our block.

They put on paint and powder,
And false curls by the score.
Then dress in silks and satins
And love hats, "*à Lenore!*"
And then these flattered darlings
Whose fathers delve in stock,
Go to meet nice fellows,
And flirt upon our block.

In handkerchief flirtations
They pass the hours away.
In female charms so winning
Are what the boys call gay.
They smile so sweet when walking
It gives our nerves a shock.
But all the girls will "do it,"
When flirting on our block.

One may scarcely be called evil-minded in deriving from this the hint that these fizgigs were poaching in professional fields. It is not curious that the embraceable references in this type of song were either sly or frank—that, at least, was a part of the life when those were the times. We have been able to find but one moralization in the '80s' semi-risqué girly songs, and that a maudlin ballad whose theme is mocked by a surprising critique of misunderstanding parents. "She Died on the Street" is the name of the song, and it was written and sung by P. J. Downey, an entertainer of the '80s.

Dark was the night and the snow it was falling,
Streets all deserted, the wind bleak and chill.
Those who were happy were silently sleeping,
Death in its mantle could not be more still.
Hark to a noise—Heavens!, some one is crying!
Some one tonight is suffering, I fear.
"Help me, oh, help me! O, Lord, I am dying!
Must I die friendless, is nobody near?"

Chorus: Starving and crying, friendless and dying,
Wandering about, but no friend could she meet.

Cold winds a-teasing, her poor heart a-freezing;
Heaven relieved her, she died on the street.

Once I was young and as pure as a dewdrop,
Often my parents were asked for my hand.
Oh! No—never, they could not part with me;
Mother thought I was the best in the land.
When they were dying for me they were praying;
Heaven have mercy, I cannot help cry.
I sent them both to their grave brokenhearted—
Now on the streets a poor outcast I lie.

But the accent on pubs and prostitutes that enlivened the declining decade appears at its best, perhaps, in the song of Frank Lum, who was as well known for his topical songs as he was for the so-called "motto" songs which began in the late '80s and reached their zenith during the early '90s: "A Boy's Best Friend Is His Mother"—that sort of song. Although Lum was no better or worse than his colleagues in the matter of inept rhymes and faulty construction, he was an astute observer, and in his tours as a singer in the variety halls, all that touched him was grist for his creaking mill. His topical song that depicts the pub-and-wench expression of the period is "Chicago in Slices," but 'twill serve as a print of the general hellishness in any key city of the times.

CHICAGO IN SLICES

I have been to the North and been to the South,
In traveling a man may a-far go,
To the jumping off place before you will find
A city to compare with Chicago.
If you never have altered your name in your life,
Or never did up to a bar go,
Or never run away with another man's wife,
They won't let you live in Chicago.

Some folks send by Adams express,
And other put faith in old Fargo.
But if you want to go to the devil direct
Just enter yourself for Chicago.

The city with fast gals and gay gamboliers,
Is as full as a ship with a cargo.
And it is truthfully said that the very best men
Fight chickens and dogs in Chicago.

The infants they feed on whisky direct,
And for liquor they to their Ma go.
And the muly cows give, as some might expect
Whisky punch in the town of Chicago.
They won't let the ministers live in the town,
For on him they will put an embargo—
Unless he drinks wine with all his young friends,
And then he may stay in Chicago.

THE GRACEFUL, CHARMING SPIELERS

FOOD WAS STILL CHEAP and plentiful in the '80s, and so were amusements. Summer recreation was quite varied: picnics, the circus, baseball, fairs, archery, boat trips, croquet, riding, driving, open-air platform dances, and a diversion peculiar to the period—the watermelon party. These were usually held out-of-doors, on grounds illuminated by hollowed-out watermelons with candles inside. They looked like enormous, green jack-o'-lanterns. The watermelon parties were carefully planned fetes. Splendid melons could be had from some near-by farmer for $5.00 a hundred, and, upon arrangement, the farmer would keep them in spring water throughout the day. At night the boys and girls would hire an immense omnibus drawn by four horses to carry them to the farmer's grove. The expense, about $10 in all, was shared by the boys. An ancient who recalls these merry times told the writer of his own delight in the watermelon fetes. They were extraordinarily popular, and it is surprising that no songs commemorate them; exactly as it is not surprising that no songs of the '80s relate to tennis or golf. Few played at these sports; neither had been popularized. Indeed, tennis was considered rather sissy even in the '90s.

But there are plenty of singing reminders of the other recreations. Scores of songs hymn the interest in roller skating, picnics, boat trips, and excursions; especially the open-air platform dances, which were as popular as the watermelon fetes. Groups of girls made a point of attending them unescorted, and these, forerunners of our taxi dancers, were called "spielers." It is an interesting word. It took on the verb form in the '90s, and well into the first decade of the twentieth century "to spiel" meant to dance. The word still lives, but it no longer has that connotation. In United States slang, according to Webster, it means to play and is "applied to almost any action or thing, especially a talk, speech, story, etc."

There is a song of the '80s actually called "The Spielers," celebrating these girls—"Mary Ann and Sarah Jane, Maggie, Nell and Kate"—and although "They work in stores and shops," they were always ready for tonight's dance, albeit in style and rhythm a nostalgic contrast to the antics of our jitterbugs. "The Spielers" was written by J. L. Feeney, probably a variety performer, to the air of an old-time ballad, "Sweet Forget-Me-Not." Here are two verses and chorus:

> I'll sing about some nobby girls,
> I met the other night,
> Who are very fond of dancing,
> In it they take delight.
> They go to parties and soirees,
> And almost every ball;
> You're sure to find the "spielers" there
> Who take the shine of all.

Chorus: Graceful and so charming,
> They glide along so neat,
> Enchanted by the music,
> They time their busy feet.
> Their merry, ringing laughter,
> Their faces with pleasure beam;
> While dancing in the mazy waltz
> The "spielers" reign supreme.

> They dance the lanciers and glide waltz,
> Mazourka and quadrille,

Polka and Virginia reel,
It seems they can't keep still.
They're on the floor at every dance,
All night they're sure to stay,
And when the dawn comes peeping in
They go home at break of day.

Murphy and Mack, a well-known variety team of the '80s,
used a song more specifically identified with the platform
dances. This was "The Dance at Battery Park," and though its
lines are unpolished, it gives a hearty picture of the period's
open-air dancing.

THE DANCE AT BATTERY PARK

For fun, for sport and merriment,
After working hard all day,
Go down to the Battery, that's the place
To drive dull care away.
They have a band of music there,
Where the boys and girls have a lark;
It's better than Newport or Long Branch,
The dance at Battery Park.

Chorus: You'd split your sides a-laughing,
To hear Crook's concert band;
The boys play concertinas,
And the girls they look so grand.
They dance around like fairies,
And then commence to spark.
It's better than Newport or Long Branch,
The dance at Battery Park.

You never saw such a happier lot
In the course of all your life,
Young men of twenty with their girls,
The workingman and his wife.
They're happy as if they were kings and queens,
They're bound to have a lark;
Would set you wild, the music would,
The dance at Battery Park.

All classes are represented there,
Every Tuesday and Friday night,
The best of order is maintained,
And not a single fight.
It is always crowded, yes,
From six till after dark,
The pivoters and spielers are always there,
To dance at Battery Park.

Well, the Battery (if minus its Aquarium, the old Castle Garden)—its approaches and ventilators to the Brooklyn tunnel, stark monuments to engineering feats undreamed of sixty years ago, and softened by its colonnade of trees—is now become another streamlined arboreal unit in the vast schemes of that ruthless crusader for civic beauty, Park Commissioner Robert Moses of New York. Yet Mr. Moses is mindful of the rhythm of the city. In summer, on the Mall in Central Park, our boys and "spielers" of the 1940s swing and sway to the beat of music our grandfathers would have stopped their ears against, and it may be that the Battery again will echo to tapping feet even as it did when Murphy and Mack enlivened the variety halls of the '80s with their topical ditty.

One of New York's most popular picnic resorts was Jones' Wood, now a teeming section of tenements, brownstones, and expensive apartment houses north of East Seventieth Street, in a section known as Yorkville. It was part of a ninety-acre farm originally owned by Samuel Provoost, the first Protestant Episcopal Bishop of New York and who doubtless smarted at the dubious distinction of being cousin to David Provoost, a notorious smuggler. But a mashie shot from the corner of East Seventy-first Street, where the beautiful building of the New York Hospital stands now, was Provoost's cache for his contraband, and for years his landing place on the Manhattan shore of the East River was known as Smuggler's Cave. In the 1850s, Jones' Wood was seriously considered for New York's largest municipal park, but authorities with other minds eventually selected the present site of Central Park.

The same Feeney who extolled the spielers did as well by Jones' Wood in a song of unbuttoned humors and beery flirtations.

UP AT JONES' WOOD

Myself and Lizzie Rodgers,
Who is my steady company,
Attended a moonlight picnic,
Of the Peerless Coterie.
The girls with smiling faces
Were in a happy mood,
And every one went in for fun,
Up at Jones' Wood.

Chorus: We danced and waltzed together,
And Lizzie was so good,
I kissed her and caressed her,
Up at Jones' Wood.

The girls were captivating,
You could not keep still.
They danced the merry lanciers,
Also the gay quadrille.
To please the charming creatures
The boys did all they could.
But they got on their ear a-drinkin' beer
Up at Jones' Wood.

Excursions, picnics, watermelon fetes, as one may derive from the songs, were but flirtatious rendezvous where easy camaraderie of the sexes was explicit. Yet the soft glances and hand holdings were of no marked inspirational benefit to the song writers of the '80s, and although the period abounds in songs relating to recreations, not one is exceptional. Apparently amours, realized or anticipated, were too emotional to embalm in type. It is surprising that they are such drivel. The hallowed aspect of woman as the purest creature on God's green earth, with man unfit to touch the hem of her garment, an attitude supposedly prevailing in the '80s, is a false cliché in relation at least to the latter half of the decade. It certainly is not true of what were then known as the working classes. We have

seen in numerous songs that men and maids were not only
quite aware of each other, but that there was, too, a suggested
sexual expectancy sociologists today would call a normal reaction. One bowed reverently in the presence of ladies who
were always chaste—in the pages of Horatio Alger (an ardent
chippy chaser in Paris), and Edith Wharton. But for Sarah,
the seamstress, Millie, the milliner, the Mary Anns, Maggies,
Nells, and Kates, spieling (and flirting) delightedly with new-
found companions, it was no age of innocence, and they romped
knowingly and unashamed, if not with boudoir abandon. Frank
Lum, that astute observer who wrote "Chicago in Slices," jelled
it neatly in a song of considerable popularity called "My Girl
in Kalamazoo"; girls are girls, here or there, is the point of
Lum's song. She was Matilda, charming, fair, redheaded (according to Lum, who also refers to her "thick lips," an egregious
term, but at least a variant from "rosebud," "cherry," etc.),
who wore her insouciance on her sleeve. A verse of "My Girl
in Kalamazoo":

> Oh! you ought to see Matilda,
> When she's walking down the street,
> Dressed to death in all her best
> She looks most wonderful sweet.
> She's always looking at the boys
> And flirting with them, too.
> I'll tell you she's right on the mash
> Is this girl from Kalamazoo.

This is not an isolated illustration of our argument. From
the mid-'80s to the death of the decade the songs were full
of light o' loves and spontaneous affection. Bennett was still
running his man-wishes-to-meet-girl "Personals," even as the
boys and girls in the still sporadic and unorganized popular-
song industry. A silly, yet quite popular, "flirt" song of the
'80s was written by a woman, Annie St. Clair, another obscurity. (It is a pity so many of these humble minnesingers
died with their songs. Like the dime novelists, mostly they were
known only to their colleagues, who carried their memories of

one another to their graves.) The song of Miss St. Clair, who may have been a performer, is "Sailing Up the Hudson on a Moonlight Night," and it is chiefly distinguished for a round-heeled "heroine," who was probably the easiest pushover in popular-song history. We must give this song in full in Miss St. Clair's own lines, for to retell it in paraphrase gives a touch of sense to it that erases its wide-eyed naïveté. Very well, then:

> Sailing up the Hudson on a moonlight night,
> I saw my fancy's queen.
> Form so perfect, such rare beauty,
> I ne'er before had seen.
> The moon shown down with radiant splendor,
> Throwing its mantel 'round;
> The fairest maiden I've e'er looked on—
> My fancy's queen I'd found!

Chorus: Sailing up the Hudson on a moonlight night,
> Is awfully grand, romantic quite.
> When holding a pretty little hand so tight;
> Sailing up the Hudson in the moonlight.

> Just a little flirting and I gained her side;
> Just how I could not say.
> But we soon became quite social in the usual way;
> Time passed quickly, chatting gaily,
> Nonsense to be sure:
> She said her pa and ma were traveling,
> Making a summer tour.

> Charming little beauty, I loved her so,
> And that I quickly told.
> As the time was passing quickly I became quite bold,
> When I asked her, there in the moonlight,
> Could I call her mine?
> The answer came so soft and sweetly—
> "Yes, forever thine!"

This is a horrible example; most of the flirt songs were livelier, as in the manner of Lum's lass from Kalamazoo. In them there is none of the sprightliness of the early '90s, whose harps were strummed to the same theme. But they did much, these later-'80s flirtation songs, and the absurdly comic ditties that followed them (and which we shall presently examine), to dispel partially the pall of plush that still hovered over the period despite the sunny influence of Banks Winter and his "White Wings."

Fumbling they were, and labored and low-class; but they were loose and sinewy—unshackled by the conventions that later were exacted of the song writers when the publishers began the mushroom development that in the early 1900s was to become Tin Pan Alley, the label of an industry immense in its mass dissemination of ordinary songs for the ordinary public. These later publishers were not fools; their aim was to sell as many songs as they could. In the fields of industry, he makes the most who satisfies the most. This axiom the publishers never forgot (it holds today for Hollywood, radio, and the slick magazines), and in keeping it uppermost they graded the pop tune (one might almost say degraded) to a standardization that carried no affront—and little authority. But we have that socio-commercial bridge to cross; we are still in the lumbering, awkward '80s—crude, slobbering, sometimes vulgar, but unhampered in expression.

It may seem odd that one of the most prolific of the '80s' comic song writers was Harry Kennedy. We have met him as the author of those grief-stricken dirges, "Empty Is the Cradle, Baby's Gone" and "A Flower from My Angel Mother's Grave." But Kennedy was like that, a man of startling contrasts. It is surprising that his stuff was not macabre, it would have been a natural inheritance. Marks, in his book, *They All Sang*, tells a fantastic story of Kennedy that was related to him by Frank Harding, one of the early pop-tune publishers, whose shop at 229 Bowery was a rendezvous for song writers. Harding had published a number of Kennedy's hits, among them "Molly and I and the Baby," and "Patsy Brannigan," and one afternoon he went over to Brooklyn to see Kennedy on business. Kennedy's mother answered the doorbell, with testiness, for she disliked Harding, whose influence on her son she suspected was not for good. "Harry's upstairs," she said, "go ahead up."

Harding did, opened the bedroom door, and discovered Kennedy laid out in his coffin.

As a ventriloquist, Kennedy worked with two figures, a boy and a girl, and though he played usually to stag audiences, his stuff was never risqué. He published a ten-cent songster, as many of the other performers did, and he wrote numerous songs, some of them extremely popular. Yet he always protested that song writing was a sideline. He had a pleasing personality and was rather shy. Unlike his noisier colleagues, he never boasted of his inspirations nor of the great things he was going to do. Except for occasional sessions at poker, he appears to have been a "loner," in Broadway patois a man who prefers his own company.

Nearly all Kennedy's comic songs were topical; his most popular, "I Had Fifteen Dollars in My Inside Pocket," was a political cartoon of Tammany Hall, as understandable today as in 1885, when it was published.

> I'm an Irishman, now don't mind that,
> For you can't play tag with Paddy Flynn.
> In the Fourteenth Ward I claim my hold,
> But the gang they played me for a skin.
> They said that they'd make me Alderman,
> Then they took me 'round to see Red Bill.
> We were drinking rye and rock, till from four o'clock,
> And they made me pony up for all the swill.

> *Chorus:* I had fifteen dollars in my inside pocket,
> Don't you see to me it is a warning.
> Saturday night I made a call
> On a friend of Tammany Hall,
> And the divvil a cent I had on Sunday morning.

> Oh, the gang they hung around the bar
> Like a swarm of educated mice.
> Oh, they made me drink a claret punch
> And a whisky sangaree on ice.
> They stood me on my head when my wealth gave out,
> Then they hung me on a fence to dry.
> In the early morning light, forninst Judge White
> These words to him I plaintively did cry. (*Repeat chorus.*)

Another of Kennedy's popular topical comics was "I Owe Ten Dollars to O'Grady," a song that recites the occasional difficulty in meeting installment payments, a commercial plan then (1887) being rapidly developed.

> I lost my situation twelve months ago today,
> The divvil a stroke I've done from then till now.
> They had me on half wages, I struck for better pay,
> They fired me out before I raised a row.
> A brand new suit I'd ordered from a tailor on our block,
> I bought it on the new instalment plan.
> I paid him just five dollars, that left me owing ten,
> Pat O'Grady was the little tailor man.

> *Chorus:* I owe ten dollars to O'Grady,
> You'd think he had a mortgage on my life.
> He calls me early every morning,
> At night he sends his wife.
> He tried to have me pawn my girl's piano.
> I think O'Grady has a dreadful gall.
> Unless he wants to wait,
> I'll rub it off the slate,
> And divvil a cent he'll ever get at all.

The difficulties of a suitor for the hand of a girl in a large family whose parents are anxious to marry her off is the universal theme of Kennedy's "My Sweetheart's Family, or Her Father Is a Plumber."

> My sweetheart's family's very large,
> And when on her I call,
> Each makes a run to be the one
> To meet me in the hall.
> The sister takes my coat and hat,
> The brother grabs my cane,
> And they lead me in the parlor
> For to see dear Jane.

> *Chorus:* Her father is a plumber,
> Her brother is a drummer,
> And her uncle sold,
> So I've been told,

> Hot waffles on a tray.
> Her sister's fond of candy,
> With taffy she's a dandy,
> And the family occupy a flat on Avenue A.

His prospective in-laws frighten off the suitor in Kennedy's song.

> They listen to each word I say,
> And Mary with a grin,
> Expects a breach of promise case
> To scoop me in.

Thus sighs the suitor. Somewhere in the song Kennedy makes it clear that the girl's full name is Mary Jane; he uses both names interchangeably to preserve his meter, which makes him virtually a purist as a pop-tune writer.

For a brief time in 1884, Kennedy achieved nation-wide publicity with his song "Liberty." In this year only fifteen feet of masonry had been raised to erect the pedestal for Bartholdi's statue of Liberty Enlightening the World (a hostess, as she was to prove, welcoming more troubled hearts than any other lady in the world). In France, through the efforts of the historian Edouard Laboulaye, one million francs had been raised by popular subscription, and the statue was formally presented to the United States in Paris, July 4, 1884. Americans, unfortunately, displayed an apathy that was as ill mannered as it was a denial of our birthright, and Joseph Pulitzer of the New York *World* lashed out daily in editorials blistering the nation for its failure to subscribe to the fund for its installation on Bedloe's Island in New York Harbor.

Kennedy, deeply stirred by the *World's* crusade, contributed a song as his donation to the cause. It was called "Liberty" and it sold for fifty cents a copy, the proceeds going to the Statue of Liberty fund. Here are two verses and chorus—and how tragically pertinent they are at this writing!

> When Liberty first saw the light of day,
> She burst from the tyrant's chain,

And soared up aloft to the heaven's bright dome
To search for a home on the main.
She looked to the North, to the South and East,
Then flew to the western sea.
And there 'neath the glow of the red setting sun
She first saw the land of the free.

Chorus: Henceforth my land shall ever be,
The sacred land of freedom!
Guided by right, strong in its might!
Thine be the praise for all.
And faithful hearts inspire
The patriotic fire!
Creator of the universe inspire
With patriotic fire:
Creator of the universe endow
With peace and plenty
Land of freedom's choice—America!

An eagle she called of the swiftest wing,
And to every land on earth,
She bade him proclaim to all patriots' hearts
The dawn of a great nation's birth.
Then gathered the Saxon, the Celt and the Gaul,
The Negro, the Dane and the Moor,
And she charged them defend to their last dying breath
The land that all patriots adore.

One of Kennedy's last songs, and perhaps his most popular, was "Say Au Revoir, but Not Good-bye."

Say "Au revoir," but not "Good-bye,"
Tho' past is dead love cannot die.
'Twere better far we had not met—
I loved you then, I love you yet.

Kennedy died of tuberculosis. Popular in the craft and widely known on the variety circuits, his funeral drew hundreds of mourners who, says Burton B. Fagan, son of the minstrel and song writer, Barney Fagan, uncovered and sang "Say Au Revoir, but Not Good-bye" at the services.

PADDY AND MOE AND GUS

AN UNUSUAL SONG called "A Starry Night for a Ramble" was popularized by a variety singer named Dick Gorman, a performer as curious as his song. Proficient in all dialects, a clever character actor, excellent at punching home his comic topical songs, yet he never reached the heights because of his peculiar personality. He was a remarkable entertainer of children and a confirmed misogynist. His blasphemy often blued the air, but he was a voracious reader of good poetry. He would lend an acquaintance $50 and bridle at a ten-cent fee. Season after season (and Gorman lasted well into the 1900s) he began with first-class engagements, then, for some imaginary grievance, he would quit the company to play a honky-tonk beer hall, where he would remain as long as the manager could stand him. "A Starry Night for a Ramble" would seem a silly song; and yet, in its contrasts and conflictions, its awareness of the social life of the times, it may be logically interpreted as a critique with an eyebrow-raising sex angle to it that the naïve Kennedy would never have noticed and would have been appalled at if he had.

> I like a game of croquet or bowling on the green,
> I like a little boating to pull against the stream.
> But of all the games I love best that fill me with delight,
> I love to take a ramble upon a starry night.

> *Chorus:* A starry night for a ramble,
> In the flowery dell;
> Through the bush and bramble—
> Kiss, but never tell.

> Talk about your bathing or strolling on the sands,
> Or some unseen veranda where the evening zephyr fans,
> Or rolling home in the morning, very nearly tight, (they)
> Could never beat a ramble upon a starry night.

> Some will take the horse cars and some will take a drive,
> And some will sit at home and mope, half dead and half
> alive.

> While some will choose a steamboat and others even fight;
> I still enjoy a ramble upon a starry night.

Gorman, with the exact inflection and accompanying facial work, could make his ramble extremely suggestive.

Most of Gorman's songs were heady, forthright topicals. They had an uncommon puissance. The conjecture is not unreasonable that they influenced other writers and singers. And they had a strong racial flavor. Immigration bars were still down, Europe's hordes seeking freedom and opportunity in the New World were arriving in boatloads, an influx the song writers did not ignore. The later '8os are replete with Irish, German dialect, and Italian pop tunes. Nor were the Jews forgotten. One of Gorman's most popular songs was "The Men That Came Over from Ireland." Here are two verses:

> Now one St. Patrick's Day as they marched down the street,
> The men that came over from Ireland,
> They passed an Italian with organ so sweet—
> The men that came over from Ireland.
> As they passed the Italian so blithe and so gay—
> It was God Save the Queen the old organ did play.
> But the Dago was buried that very same day
> By the men that came over from Ireland.

> Now a Dutchman and Irishman once had a fight
> On a ship coming over from Ireland.
> And the Dutchman succeeded in landing his right
> On the man coming over from Ireland.
> "I'll get square with the Dutchman," said Pat. Sure as sin,
> When six months in this country the Dutchman had been,
> For selling beer Sunday sure he was run in
> By the man that came over from Ireland.

There were almost as many Jewish pop songs as Irish in the late '8os. Many of them were critical, and not always in good humor. Generally they were messy and without character. A fairish Hebrew topical song celebrated the exploits of a drummer and was introduced in a comedy of the '8os called *Samuel of Posen*, whose plot was built around an Austrian Jew, a commercial traveler. The song bore the title of the play, and it was

written by Isaac Scholem to music by Roger Putnam. A verse
and chorus:

> The happiest man you ever met
> Is the drummer on the road.
> His words are gay to all, you bet;
> In spinning yarns he's great.
> He sweetly smiles, "Good day, sir,"
> And offers a cigar.
> But when that part is over,
> Oh, then begins the war.
>
> *Chorus:* Machovis he has plenty,
> And lots of stuff that's bad.
> But if you speak against his goods
> Oh, don't he then get mad!

"Samuel of Posen" was one of the first of the Jewish popular
songs, and they became a vogue throughout the '8os, undoubtedly because of the popularity of Frank Bush, eccentric
Jewish comedian who often sang his own songs in a sort of
bastard Yiddish. Here is one of his first; no doubt a jargon of his
own invention:

> Oh, my name is Solomon Moses, I'm a bully Sheeny man,
> I always treat my customers the very best what I can.
> I keep a clothing store 'way down on Baxter St.,
> Where you can get your clothing now, I sell so awful
> cheap.
>
> *Chorus:* Solomon, Solomon Moses,
> Hast du gesehen der clotheses?
> Hast du gesehen der kleiner kinder,
> Und der sox iss in der vinder?
> I sell to you for viertel dollar,
> You will say was cheap,
> Oskaploka overcoats
> For fimpf sehn dollar and half.
> My name is Isaac Levy Solomon Moses,
> Hast du gesacht?

Bush wrote another song, a parody on Harrigan and Hart's
"Babies on Our Block," called "Sheenies in the Sand." It was

popular around New York because its allusions were understood and relished.

> If you want some recreation during the heated spell,
> Come down to Coney Island, to Corbin's big hotel.
> He owns the bathing houses, the balloon and Gilmore's
>   band,
> Where Israel's represented by the Sheenies in the sand.
> There's the Oppenheims, and the Pappenheims, and the
>   dealer in old clo's,
> And all the glass-put-in men a-sittin' in a row.
> The Isaacs and the Levys and the Steins, a jolly band,
> Singing with Austin Corbin, for the Sheenies in the sand.

Chorus: Little cornet Levy a-blowing with all his might,
> All the tribes with noses around him every night,
> Toot, toot, Levy, toot, drown the blasts of Gilmore's
>   band,
> And play as once at Jericho for the Sheenies in the sand.

> Of a warm day in the summer, when the Island you will
>   reach,
> One hundred thousand Sheenies may be seen upon the
>   beach,
> They come from Corbin's building, with their babies hand
>   in hand,
> Oh! what a show of noses, among the Sheenies in the sand.
> There's the Rubensteins and the Hildebeins from the Tem-
>   ple Emanuel,
> And Moses and his family, from Corbin's big hotel,
> All the tribes of Benjamin, likewise old Aaron's band,
> With the B'nai B'rith and Ahawad Chesed, 'mong the
>   Sheenies in the sand.

The ol' clo's man, with his street cry, "I cash clothes," and the put-in-glass man, a comparable streethawker who repaired windowpanes, were familiar New York types as recent as twenty years ago, when "Umbrellas to mend" and "Scissors to grind" still echoed from the sidewalks of New York. Bush's reference to "little cornet Levy" was to Jules Levy, the great cornetist whose triple-tongue polka drew salvos at all of Gilmore's concerts whenever Jules was the soloist. It was even more personal to Bush, this reference. A highly esteemed performer, Bush, as an encore for his own act, often obliged with tin-whistle solo in which he imitated Levy's famous triple-tonguing. Bush was actually an expert on the tin whistle, and, an eccentric, between shows would make a pitch on the street (often near the theater, to the management's embarrassment) and sell tin whistles. With a satchel full of them dangling from his neck, he'd mount a soapbox and, when the crowd collected, call for tunes: "No trouble to play it, gents. Give me a tune. Look—it's easy——" With his gentle con and friendly personality, he sold thousands at a dime apiece, no small addition to his performer's salary.

Nearly all of the racial comics in the vaudeville of the '80s were faithful in the burlesque of their types, but most of their songs were woeful adaptations, and especially is this true of the Jewish songs. Harry Thompson's "Let Us Go to the Sheeny Wedding," for example, appears to be merely a substitution for an Irish comic song.

> Let us go to the Sheeny wedding,
> All the Sheenies will be there,
> Such a dancing and such singing,
> It will be a grand affair.
> All the hightone Hebrew people,
> Will be there from every town,
> Such a fun and such beauty
> Will be at the Sheeny wedding.

> *Chorus:* All the Sheenies will be there,
> Now Solinsky curl your hair;
> Bring along your Sarah quick
> To the Sheeny wedding.
> Won't we have a jolly time,
> Eating motzers (sic) and drinking wine,
> All the hightone Hebrews will
> Be at the Sheeny wedding.

Thompson concludes his song with a fight in the manner of an Irish brawl. It is a pointless ditty, and its popularity is inexplainable. A number of the Jewish popular songs, as well as the

Jewish comic acts, many of them sung and portrayed by performers who were Hebrews themselves, were critical of the Jew's alleged foibles. A patient race, there was no open resentment, probably because no malice was intended.

Indeed, it was the Irish who were sensitive. Paddy and Ella Murphy, a vaudeville team of the '80s, exploited their own indignation at the characterization of the Irish on the stage and in the pop tunes of the day with:

THE TRUE IRISH GENTS

It's a shame on the stage how they mimic our race,
In a style that's a mystery to me.
How the people in front will stand such insults,
Receiving such blockheads with glee.
If they went to ould Ireland they'd find their mis-
take,
For our boys and our girls are well dressed,
In manners as well, to you I will tell,
For they stand in the land with the best.

Chorus: For in singing and dancing, and all kinds of sport,
And if ever to Ireland you went,
From their heads to their toes,
They all wear decent clothes—
I speak of a true Irish gent.

The Irish led all nationalities in immigration to our shores. Next were the Germans. This was the relative rating in popular-song references. There were many more songs of Hans und Fritz und Gus, *mit der schwesters*, than Jewish songs. Most of the German pop tunes were sung in dialect; it is easy to imitate, and the public took to the songs quickly. The popular "Walking Down Broadway" is an illustration:

De sweetest ting in life, vat odder peoples say,
Iss Samstag afternoon, a-walkin' down Broadway.
Mein schwester in der lager beer saloon vill stay.
But I should always make a valk
Right down dot pretty Broadway.

Chorus: I valk dot Broadway down,
I valk dot Broadway down.

Der nicest ting as neffer vas
Iss valk dot Broadway down.
Der fellows vink der eyes,
Und ven I look around,
Der ain't no harm I take his arm
Und valk dot Broadway down.

The infiltration of races gave an exotic fling to the social expression as well as an odd comic twist to the songs. The expansion of America, the broadening of entertainment, the larger scope of things generally loosened apron strings and broke home ties. It sent the people—women as well as men—to the vaudeville shows, for Tony Pastor had douched his acts, insisted on clean comedy and songs, and was presenting (at his bandbox theater in Fourteenth Street, adjoining Tammany Hall) antisepticized bills—a policy Keith and Albee soon followed. There was no night life in the sense of Fifty-second Street today; anyone out after midnight in the '80s was a rounder. But folks did go out more; the accent, as the '80s moved toward the ultimate decade of the nineteenth century, was no longer on the home; it was on business and outside pleasure. Commercial expansion was immense, and new hotels, restaurants, and theaters that were opened, prospered. Our popular songs reacted accordingly, with a liveliness and drive that reflected the upsweep of the times, often with astonishing mockery; occasionally, as in the boarding-house, hobo, and bandit songs, with saloon vulgarity.

BUMS, HASH, AND BANDITS

THE ITINERANT MENDICANT has been a character in history and fiction since the Ptolemys. From him derives the picaresque tale in which he is sometimes pleasantly, sometimes grimly portrayed as a rogue. He tweaked the burghers' noses, he pinched the maidens' rumps, filched here, begged there—a likable knave whose apotheosis was Eulenspiegel's. Renaissance Europe is full of him, and he lasted longer than kings of ancient lineage; until, in fact, the death of the American hobo, his blooded counterpart. He of the rods, the handout, the jungle, that is; not the dime-fer-a-cup-o'-cawfee moocher. As a symbol in American life, the ubiquitous tramp has gone. Well into the first World War he filled our comic strips, peopled our vaudeville stages, decorated our humorous magazines. All that is left of him of the true genre of any consequence now is Denys Wortman's delightful "Mopey Dick and the Duke," superb creations by an admirable artist. The American tramp was unmatched as a modern character (historically speaking). Almost, it seems as though the railroads were built for him. Certainly he was made for them. The rhythm of his songs beats to the click of the rails. And as the '8os were the railroad days, so were they the hobo's. His songs were many in the '8os, and they have the quality of honesty. Each was a stern analysis; none pulled a poor mouth except as an act. To hell with life as well as work, sang the tramp. They were always in character—rough, tough, and rowdy. One of the most popular was "The Great American Bum." The song had many variations. Here is the version most favored:

> Come all you American bummers and listen while I hum,
> For I'm going to sing a song about the American bum.
> We are three bums, three jolly good chums
> And we live like royal Turks.
> We have good luck at bumming our chuck,
> To hell with the man that works.
> Tra la la la lee boys, la de de da di de da.

Chorus: We are three bums, three jolly good chums
> And we live like royal Turks.
> We have good luck at bumming our chuck,
> To hell with the man that works.

> Oh, it's early in the morning when the dew is on the
> ground
> The bum arises from his couch and pipes him all around.
> He spies a cozy cottage, 'way up in yonder path,
> The way the gilly pipes it off it makes the farmer laugh.
> Sleeping 'neath the rosies, tra la la la la la lee,
> Smoking butts and stogies, tra la la la la la lee.

Oh, mister will you be so kind as to give me a bite to eat,
A piece of bread and jelly with a nice cold slice of meat?
A little pie and pudding to ease my appetite?
For I'm so tired and hungry I don't know where I'll sleep
    tonight.
Sleeping out at night, boys, tra la la la la la lee.
Smoking butts and stogies, tra la la la la la lee.

A man once asked me to work for him as I never had done
    before.
I asked him what the business was, he said 'twas digging
    ore.
Said I, "What are the wages paid?"—A dollar-and-a-half a
    ton.
"Get out," said I, "you son-of-a-bitch, I'd a damned sight
    sooner bum."
Clothing right in style, boys, tra la la la la la lee,
Fits within a mile, boys, tra, la la la la la lee.

This is abandonment arm in arm with the son of the Gambolier. Thus did the tramp reply to the epithets "maladjusted," and "antisocial" hurled at him to his final handout and now reserved for his degraded half brother, the criminal.

There is a slight whine in Billy Stanford's "The Pennsylvania Tramp" (which became even more popular than "The Great American Bum"), but it is resolved in a raucous guffaw at society if one interprets it conscientiously.

Here I am a lonely stranger
All the way from Pennsylvania.
When I work my life's in danger;
Ladies please come pity me.
I have traveled this world over,
In my pockets not a stamp.
My name's a terror to this nation,
I am the Pennsylvania Tramp.

Chorus: Counting ties's my occupation,
    Hunger gives me many a cramp.
    Sleeping at all railway stations—
    Hooray for the Pennsylvania Tramp.

From New Haven to Weehawken,
That's the road, boys, no use talkin'.
I'm the gent that fears no walkin',
I'm an old professional.
When the summer time is over
And the weather's cold and damp,
Robbing hen roosts, that's my racket—
I'm the Pennsylvania Tramp.

Stanford, a seasoned trouper, did a song-and-dance tramp act for years. He had a novel entrance, a bit of business that anticipated Olsen and Johnson's *Hellzapoppin* and *Sons o' Fun* by almost sixty years. In tramp make-up, baggy pants, slapshoes, unshaven face, and fright wig, he planted himself in the rear of the house he was playing and waited for the stage manager to announce, "Due to illness, the next act will be unable to appear." At this, Stanford engaged the stage manager. "I can give a better show than the other fellow," Stanford would shout as he walked toward the stage. "All right, come on up and try," the stage manager would reply. Whereupon Stanford would mount to the stage and go into his specialty.

Once Stanford was amusingly—and damagingly—frustrated. In the late '80s, a combination museum (mostly side-show freaks) and vaudeville show opened with a matinee in Butler, Pennsylvania. It was a venture for the town, and a special officer, unfamiliar with Stanford's entrance, was assigned to maintain order. He considered it a disturbance, and when Stanford persisted in trying to go through with his act, knocked him out, hurting him so badly that he was unable to appear for the evening performance. When the night show opened, the stage manager's announcement, this time unfortunately correct, was answered by a real hobo who volunteered to take Stanford's place. He went up on the stage, played some tunes on a trick cigar-box fiddle he carried under his coat, told a few jokes of the road, and made his exit. Nobody ever saw him again, and Stanford never learned who his substitute was.

The tramp songs really were of the road. Except for "The

Pennsylvania Tramp," no one knew who wrote them. And usually they were sung to the tunes of other songs. "The Hobo's Dream," a popular tramp song of the '80s, was sung to the melody of "The Old Oaken Bucket."

Unlovely, unwashed, unwanted, yet there was a stoical quality about the early 'bo that was alleviating if not redemptive. He made his own misfortunes, was quite aware of it—indeed, accepted it with a philosophy others in kindlier circumstances might well envy if not admire. The tramp song, "The Poor Old Bum," catches this flavor:

Oh, once I was a dashing swell when I was in my prime,
I used bank notes to light cigars but now I haven't a dime.
In swell hotels in summer time I once had many a lark,
But now in summer time I sleep on a bench in Central Park.

Chorus: I used to walk up and down the street
And I thought that I was some.
I used to smoke twenty-five cent cigars
And drink up the very best rum.
But now my clothes are all worn out
And my shoes won't cover up my toes,
And the rim of my hat goes flippety-flap—
And look at my rum-blue nose.

I used to drive a tandem rig, and pass them on the road,
But now, sometimes I can hardly walk—when I have on a load.
When winter comes I take my leave—give all my kind regards;
My apartment is a swell box car in the Pennsylvania yards.

The later '80s were prosperous times. The barometers of industry and business were not to crash till 1893. And as in the mid 1920s, until that fatal October of 1929, the '80s, too, enjoyed their financial fling. And what has this to do with hoboes? Little, except that they mark the other end of the sweep of the pendulum and that the loose stridency so characteristic of their songs is an earnest of the abandonment that accompanies all needled prosperity like a camp follower. The brassy roars of the hoboes were but another manifestation of the general cacophony that was marked in other expressions of song by eccentric, Bunyanized ballads, hash-house ditties with slop-jar lines, macabre mockeries of love, and eulogies to dead bandits almost as heroic as the celluloid epitaphs of Hollywood. Oddest of the first group was:

THE HUNGRY MAN FROM KANSAS

There was a man in our town,
His hair was red, his name was Brown.
He'd eat up everything he found,
His appetite was scandalous.
His stomach he could never fill,
A barrel of whisky he could swill,
His jaws worked like a rolling mill,
This hungry man from Kansas.

Chorus: He went to a farm house and asked for some bread,
He tackled the farmer and chewed off his head.
He ate all the dogs and the kittens and cat,
He killed the old hog and bit into the fat.
He swallowed the woodpile, the hatchet and saw,
The stovepipe and chimney went into his maw.
He swallowed a mule team in excellent style,
And he raced the driver half a mile,
This hungry man from Kansas.

This man could never sleep at night,
He prowled around till broad daylight,
To hunt for something he could bite
To satisfy his hunger.
For grub of all kinds he would claw,
He'd swallow either hay or straw,
And lots of folks have seen him chaw
A wagon load of lumber.

Second One day he went to get a drink,
Chorus: He felt quite dry, so what do you think?
He drank all the water up out of the well,
He drained it so dry that to pieces it fell.
He swallowed the bucket, the rope and the frame,
He nibbled the oxen, the yoke and the chain.

He went down a cellar to nibble some glue,
The cellar caved in, but he ate his way through.
He ate the old horse and he licked up the marrow,
He swallowed the harness, the plow and the harrow.
He went to the river, the water was high,
He stood on the bottom and drank it up dry.
He swallowed a cow with her halter and bell,
It stuck in his throat, his throat it did swell.
It choked him to death, on the prairie he fell,
And he's trying to eat his way up out of —— the cemetery;
This hungry man from Kansas.

This pot-walloper from the plains, one may suspect, was a
'70s' song, and he would be right. It was. It was also the longest-
lived of the barrel-house ballads, and it is introduced in this section because, like so many songs that originated in the West in
the bite-the-dust days (presumably; we have been unable to
trace its origin), it hung on there until achieving its greatest
sway in the '80s. Indeed, it was going well in the '90s. Curiously,
too, for it is not an easy song to memorize. But its air is lively,
its rhythm fetching, and it was rattled off by many robustos on
and off the stage.

In Kansas City, during the '80s, a variety honky-tonk known
as Hank Clark's was visited occasionally by Jesse James. But as
background you should have the original words of

BABY MINE

I've a letter from your sire, Baby mine, Baby mine,
I could read and never tire, Baby mine, Baby mine.
He is sailing on the sea, he is coming back to me,
He is coming back to thee, Baby mine, Baby mine,
He is coming back to Mama, Baby mine.

I'm so glad I cannot sleep, Baby mine, Baby mine,
I'm so happy I could weep, Baby mine, Baby mine.
Like a rose of May in bloom,
Like a star amid the gloom,
Like the sunshine in the room, Baby mine, Baby mine,
He is coming back to thee, Baby mine.

Deep-chested, able-bodied contraltos leaned on this heavily during the '80s (a fair song it is, too), and like all immensely popular songs, it soon faced a hundred parodies. Well, one evening in Hank Clark's an obscure performer sang this parody:

> I've a letter from Maria, Baby mine;
> She is like a house afire, Baby mine.
> Oh, she says I'm such a dub,
> And she'll hit me with a club
> If I don't run up an alley, Baby mine.
>
> I'm a rang-a-tang-tang tavvy, Baby mine;
> I'm the gent the girls all savvy, Baby mine,
> And if Jesse James was here,
> And he wouldn't buy the beer,
> Then he'd walk out on his ear, Baby mine.

At his exit, one of the girls in the show took his arm. "Psst—that's him in the box," she said. "Who's in the box?" asked the performer. "Jesse James," replied the girl, and the performer went right away from there—in fact, to Texas, where he stayed. But not for long. In 1882, Jesse was living in St. Joseph, Missouri, under the name of Howard, when his supposed young friend, Robert Ford, while Jesse's back was turned, drilled him through the head.

This was rich song material, and a few years later somebody responded with

JESSE JAMES

> It was on a Wednesday night,
> The moon was shining bright.
> They robbed the Glendale train,
> And the people they did say
> For many miles away,
> It was the outlaws, Frank and Jesse James.

> *Chorus:* Jesse had a wife he honored all his life,
> His children they were brave.
> But a dirty little coward shot Mr. Howard
> And he laid Jesse James in his grave.

> Oh, it was Robert Ford,
> The dirty little coward,
> And how did he behave?
> He ate Jesse's bread,
> And slept in Jesse's bed,
> Then he laid Jesse James in his grave.

Thereby, one might add, performing a public service and creating, if unwittingly, another tale for Hollywood to garble.

That other great and more authentic American institution, the boardinghouse, is one with the hobo—gone and forgotten. Proletariat America now lunches at the corner drugstore and dines, if not at home, in a bar and grill or a roadside tavern. The motley assemblies at the boardinghouse dinner table were true cross sections of the social life of the '70s, '80s, and '90s: the speculation, *sub rosa*, on the new blonde on the second floor rear; the vacant chair at the place of Mr. Plumkin, furniture salesman at Wanamaker's—"I saw him last night with that girl. They were having a soda in Hudnut's. Really, I don't understand what he sees in her . . ."; the widower and star boarder, patronizingly to the bank clerk at his right—"I tell you, sir, Cleveland is the poor man's champion . . ."; the schoolteacher, faded and a bit forlorn, yet brightening a bit this evening as she hastens through dinner. She has a ticket to see the new star, E. H. Southern, in the play, *The Highest Bidder*, and there to forget an old blighted romance.

> He said he would always remember,
> But alas! he didn't mean her.

Album leaves, now—chromos to the comics, professional and parlor, of the '80s. The boardinghouses in the '80s (the '90s too) were the butt of jokes, the grist for scurvy songs. This was received with uproarious acclaim:

THE ALL GO HUNGRY HASH HOUSE

> There's a boardinghouse where we stay
> That is turning my hair gray,
> And the landlord is always full of beer.
> All the beds the bugs have rented

And the rooms are sweetly scented
By an old fashioned tanyard in the rear.
The sausage is pock-marked,
You can see it in the dark.
We kneel and pray before we go to grub.
And if ever you get a breeze
From that antiquated cheese
You will think that some one struck you with a club.

Chorus: The molasses looks like paint,
If you smell it you will faint.
Beef steak, you couldn't cut it with a sword.
But the minute they open the gates
We rush in on roller skates
To that all go hungry hash house where we board.

Second Oh, the bread's made out of wood,
Chorus: And it isn't any good,
The butter is served up in a gourd.
Yesterday we all were tryin'
To get a skeleton for a sign
For that all go hungry hash house where we board.

Inmates, as well as food, came in for the general ribbing:

OUR BOARDINGHOUSE

I rented a room in a boardinghouse, a shame and a disgrace,
I'd pack my trunk and leave it if I could find another place.
I never saw such sights since the day that I was born,
A lot of tramps came yesterday and more will come this morn.
There's a couple up above who are always making love,
Next door to me they fight like cat and dog.
Next room to me but one there's fiddler and his son
Teaching two old maids to dance a clog.

One night when I was sound asleep and dreaming of a dance,
They broke into my room and stole my only coat and pants.
They even took the bed clothes, and crept away like mice,
When I awoke I thought I was a solid cake of ice.
There were two tramps on the floor, a pig behind the door.
In the corner was a dirty chicken coop.
There were insects in the air, in the butter old red hair,
And the baby had both feet stuck in the soup.

The decade of the '80s was an age of Literal Lymans. They were not given to subtlety, and although most humor is sadistic, that fashioned for the risibles of the unimaginative must be broad as a sidewalk banana peel. Mark Twain, a literary wonder in any period, stands as phenomena in the '80s, whose people accepted him—if with an eye on their watches. How he appraised their reactions! Someone had dared write a novel in which the word "navel" was mentioned. "Obscene!" observed a douce, pedestrian-minded guest to Mark at a party. "Haven't you got one?" asked Mark. Simplicity is the Excalibur with which to slay censors.

Thus the decade closed—in its songs (not all of its songs, but those quoted are the essence of its expression)—on a note not honest enough to be obscene, but on a pitch of verisimilitude, which is vulgar. Its folk were rapturous over

TOO RAL LI OO RAL LI A

You have heard many stories of love and deceit,
And sometimes quite sad they'll appear.
But the one I'll relate is a hard one to beat,
And it happened in April last year.
When I met a fair maid of Italian descent;
Through the day she sold apples and pears.
She moved every month for she never paid rent,
And she lived in an attic upstairs.

Chorus: She sang too ral li oodle li oodle um,
Too ral li oodle li a.
Too ral li oodle li oodle um,
Lum tum ti addy ti a.

The name of the maiden was Angeline Squibbs,
The fairest that ever was seen.
And she was my darling, my own ducky doo;
But she died at the age of sixteen.
In the nasty cold clay they have laid her away
By the light of the silvery moon.
And my poor heart is broken and busted with grief,
As sweetly I sing by her tomb.

Her nose it was red and her breath was dark blue,
And green was the shade of her eyes.
And, oh, how I loved her there's none ever knew—
The boys called her gooseberry Lize.
They buried her deep where the whats-a-names weep
Close by where the thing-a-ma-doots will bloom.
And the bumble bee bumbles his soft mellow notes
From 'way before breakfast 'til noon.

There were dozens of this type of song in the late '80s— macabre burlesque; at least they were an unaimed blow at the cemetery sentimentalities with which the period opened, possibly an unconscious release from those dirges. The author of the foregoing is as unknown as his purpose. But the purpose of Ned Oliver, who wrote "It Takes A Girl to Fool You Every Time," is known—a deliberate flout of the love songs of that sugared period. Oliver was one of the cleverest of the banjo entertainers of the decade. He wrote his own songs, fashioned his own accompaniments, and, like most of the banjoists of the period, was self-taught. He had a wide vein of caustic humor, and his "Girl" song is characteristic.

Some say that married life is milk and honey—
If you listen I will give you some advice.
My experience was anything but funny,
I tried it once, I'll never try it twice.
I met a girl I thought a charming creature,
I hung around and acted like a loon.
We packed our bags and hunted up a preacher.
Then off we started on our honeymoon.

Chorus: Oh, my!—Mind your eye!
Or else the girls will fool you every time.
They'll make you think you're lord of all creation,
Then skin you 'til you haven't got a dime.

At night when we retired to our chamber,
I closed the door and softly turned the key.
Then I saw a sight I always will remember—
For I'd married half a woman, half a tree.

Her glass eye and teeth were in a tumbler,
Her waterfall and curls hung on a peg.
You may judge of my surprise and consternation,
When I saw her unstrap a wooden leg.

Good enough. Oliver was an uncommon writer. Although successful throughout the variety circuits, he tired and quit to manage one of the largest and best medicine shows then faking the country. He was billed, "Nevada Ned, The King of Gold."

So the period that began with plush and the bleat of phony grief ended with clumsy mockery, a yahoo nose-thumbing accompanied by the guffaws of an overgrown yokel. Ned Oliver's song guides us nicely over the bridge to the '90s. His lines have spin and dash, if his situation is crude and extravagant. The '90s veneered this, disowned the decade it succeeded, and speedily harked back to rejuvenate and refine the '70s. It trotted out its girls with the same vivacity, but ruffled their drawers to make 'em naughtier, and nicer. It was the roué era of *joie de vivre* expressed in a curious juxtaposition of naïveté and sophistication. "Ta-Ra-Ra-Boom-Der-É," caroled Lottie Collins. This was the cry of the pack—and, waiter, chill that wine.

SOMETIMES SCARLET—BUT MAUVE? NEVER!

It is difficult to write of the 1890s. Those who remember its champagne and the lilt of Victor Herbert grow too heady with memories. That garter with the embroidered rose the "Girl in Blue" flung at grandfather on a night at the Gaiety. Where is it now? Gone with the kiss that it won. The fur-collared Hamlets of Herald Square are one with the moths, their Knox toppers gangrened relics on the attic shelf. Thus the gaffers prattle of a decade, forgetting its dregs are dust. The indignant roar of Dr. Parkhurst comes not even faintly across the years. Yet what was it the old hairshirt challenged? Fun. What was it Comstock, the smutty researches of his mind beating him on, flailed at? Fun.

Except to the party-liners who can see no one but Altgeld and Debs; except to Thomas Beer, whose Johnsonese *Mauve Decade* fatuously scored this most romantic of our periods for its absence of realism—the '90s were a happy time. True, the feeling against labor was at first bitter, and then murderous. But the bloodshed in the Homestead steel strike in 1892, and in the Chicago railroad strike in 1894, was spilled for a social ideal engendered in that time. It was a time of sacrifice, and of an awakening too. Even the '90s could produce an Altgeld Roland for a Pullman Oliver. Nor did Debs languish in jail in vain.

Beer, in his diatribe, apparently sought not among the lay expressions for a humanistic picture. Indeed, throughout this decade of song he could find but three lines of a ditty:

> In room two hundred and two,
> The walls keep talking to you.
> Shall I tell you what they said? . . .

Here are two verses (one apparently a rowdy vaudeville version not in the original song) and the complete chorus:

> The hotel clerk said, "press the button once if you want
>   ice,
> "And if you want a maid, you'll have to press it twice."
> The fellow really wanted ice but got the number wrong;
> And so he pressed the button twice the whole night long.

Chorus: In room two hundred and two,
> The walls keep talking to you.
> Shall I tell you what they said
> Or put out the light and go to bed?

> A fellow woke his wife up on a windy night,
> He said an open window gave him such a fright.
> "I want another blanket, dear, I'm getting cold."
> She said, "The breeze don't strike you, you are getting
>   old."[1]

Beer gives the lines some import by tying them to the suicide of a famous unnamed soubrette during the Chicago World's Fair in 1893; supposedly she had taken poison in room 202 of a

[1] By permission of the copyright proprietor, Mills Music, Inc.

hotel. But no research of the writer supports this. And Andy Gardener, of the Three Gardeners, who used the song extensively with topical, local, and political verses added, says that it was not written until long after 1893. He is right. The song was written in 1919 by Edgar Leslie, Bert Kalmar, and Dave Harris. It is unimportant except that in the mild sting of their lines there is a lack of prudery, an awareness Beer continually denies throughout the '90s. Curious anachronism!

What is important is that among the humble jongleurs of the '90s we sing of in this chronicle, labor had its champions who recited, with apparent relish, robust chants in behalf of the workingmen's effort for betterment. Especially good were those of J. W. Kelly, a natural humorist who was one with the "pee-pul" and whose grist came from their hearts and his. A native of Philadelphia, he removed to Chicago in his early twenties and there obtained employment in a rolling mill, the source of his sobriquet and subsequent variety billing as "The Rolling Mill Man." Having the knack of rhyme, and himself a born story-teller, he soon began fashioning verses and inventing tunes for them which he tried out on the mill hands, to their delight and his advance. Lew Hawkins, a blackface comic of the '70s, induced him to appear professionally. After touring with Hawkins, Kelly went out on his own and became a headliner. In the early '90s Tony Pastor consented to book him for a week. He stayed a year. Kelly pleased all classes of patrons (none loved him more than Governor Alfred E. Smith of New York), and he became so big a feature in New York that he made his home there and seldom left town. He didn't have to. He could fill all his playing time in that city.

During his early appearances at Pastor's, the shambles at Homestead occurred. This was the strike of the Amalgamated Association of Iron and Steel Workers in 1892 against a reduction in wages at the Carnegie Steel Company, which was to become the important unit in the United States Steel Corporation on its organization in 1901. The Carnegie plant was at Homestead, a milltown on the Monongahela River, near Pitts-

burgh. The strike began June 30, and Henry Clay Frick, a
pronounced antagonist of labor, at once hired a band of Pinkerton men to protect his plant and his assembled strikebreakers.
The strikers had been informed of the coming of the Pinkertons, who were to arrive by boat from Pittsburgh. The strikers
met them. Who fired the first shot still is not known, but seven
persons were killed and a number wounded. The Pinkertons
finally surrendered and were returned to Pittsburgh. But the
workers lost the strike. Kelly commemorated the tragic event
with a vigorous and characteristic song:

A FIGHT FOR HOME AND HONOR
(Sometimes called "The Homestead Strike")

We are asking one another as we pass the time of day,
Why men must have recourse to arms to get their proper
  pay;
And why the labor unions now must not be recognized,
While the actions of a syndicate must not be criticised.
The trouble down at Homestead was brought about this
  way,
When a grasping corporation had the audacity to say;
You must all renounce your unions and forswear your
  liberty,
And we'll promise you a chance to live and die in slavery.

Chorus: For the man that fights for honor, none can blame him;
  May luck attend wherever he may roam;
  And no song of his will ever live to shame him
  While liberty and honor rule his home.

When a crowd of well armed ruffians came without
  authority,
Like thieves at night, while decent men were sleeping
  peacefully,
Can you wonder why all honest men with indignation
  burn,
Why the slimy worm that crawls the earth when trod
  upon will turn?
When the locked out men at Homestead saw they were
  face to face

With a lot of paid detectives then they knew it was their
     place
To protect their homes and families and that was nobly
     done,
And the angels will applaud them for the victory they
     won.

See that sturdy band of working men start at the break of
     day,
Determination in their eyes that surely meant to say;
No men can drive us from our homes for which we've
     toiled so long,
No men shall take our places now for here's where we be-
     long.
A woman with a rifle saw her husband in a crowd;
She handed him the weapon and they cheered her long and
     loud.
He kissed her and said, "Mary, you go home 'til we are
     through."
She answered, "No, if you must fight, my place is here
     with you."

However you reason, there was nothing wrong with Kelly's
facts. They were substantiated (except for the wife who fought
by her husband's side, which is justifiable fiction; it could have
happened, and perhaps did) in a survey made by Margaret F.
Byington and published in 1910 by the Russell Sage Foundation.
    Another effective song of the Homestead strike was written
by Willy Wildwave, whom we have already met as William
W. Delaney, publisher of the Delaney song books, which, by
the way, are the most accurate and complete annals of the songs
of the 1890s and 1900s. (They bring stiff prices today because,
printed on the cheapest of paper, they have been almost thumbed
out of existence. It is doubtful if there are more than three
complete sets of Delaney's eighty-nine numbers in the United
States. The only two the writer knows are in the Grosvenor
Library in Buffalo and in the collection of Elliott Shapiro. They
were published at ten—later fifteen—cents each at 117 Park Row,
New York, and each contained from one hundred and sixty to

one hundred and sixty-five songs, a total of more than fifteen thousand.) Delaney's song was

FATHER WAS KILLED BY THE PINKERTON MEN

'Twas in a Pennsylvania town not very long ago,
Men struck against reduction of their pay.
Their millionaire employer, with philanthropic show,
Had closed the works till starved they would obey.
They fought for home and right to live where they had
  toiled so long,
But e'er the sun had set some were laid low.
There're hearts now sadly grieving by that sad and bitter
  wrong,
God help them! for it was a cruel blow.

Chorus: God help them tonight in their hour of affliction,
Praying for him whom they'll ne'er see again.
Hear the poor orphans tell their sad story:
"Father was killed by the Pinkerton men!"

Ye prating politicians who boast protection's creed,
Go to Homestead and stop the orphan's cry.
Protection for the rich man—ye pander to his greed,
His workmen they are cattle and may die.
The freedom of the city in Scotland far away,
'Tis presented to the millionaire suave.
But here in free America, with protection in full sway,
His workmen get the freedom of the grave.

Here again, the facts are correct, even to the reference to millionaire Andrew Carnegie civically feted in his native Scotland. But the song is a rabble rouser foreign to the expression, if not belief, of the gentle Delaney, who was a beloved character among the sheet-music publishers for years. Delaney published only the words of the songs, and these he obtained from the sheet-music publishers, usually for a pittance or, in later years, for nothing at all when, seedy in an overcoat green with age, buttonless, and tied together with string, he prowled through their shelves, helping himself to the songs whose lyrics he thought would sell. A printer, he set his own stuff; where his hat was, there was his office. Once a sheet-music publisher, indignant at Delaney's use of his song, started legal action against Delaney. When the sheet-music publishers heard of their colleague's move, they threatened him with commercial boycott, and the suit was withdrawn. Home-loving America owes Delaney a tribute for preserving its otherwise forgotten lore of inconsequential songs, which, however unpretentious and ephemeral, were the massed hearts of our folk—simple, often genuine, and that "caught the living manners as they rise."

McCLOSKEY, THE BARROOM DELIGHT

IN HIS SMALL WAY, Delaney was a humanist too—of the tribe of Kelly, whom we left suspended to introduce Delaney's Pinkerton-Homestead number. Kelly's contribution to our pop-tune literature was by no means limited to his topical songs. He wrote also "Slide, Kelly, Slide," which in the early '90s almost equaled the popularity of that greatest of baseball classics, "Casey at the Bat," which was a recitation, however, not a song, immortalized by the countless renditions of De Wolf Hopper. Most popular of Kelly's songs, though, and still remembered, was (one might almost say is) "Throw Him Down McCloskey." He wrote it specifically for Maggie Cline, stentorian queen of the '90s' variety halls, and Maggie took title with roaring might. Her performance was an informal Kilkenny which staged the brawl of the song in correct crescendo. No one who ever heard Maggie sing it will ever lose its memory, and they do say on faint nights, in theaters long since darkened, it comes hurtling, like some terrible banshee, across what once were footlights.

THROW HIM DOWN McCLOSKEY

'Twas down at Dan McDevitt's at the corner of this street,
There was to be a prize fight and both parties were to
    meet

To make all the arrangements and see everything was
   right
McCloskey and a naygur were to have a finish fight.
The rules were London Prize Ring and McCloskey said
   he'd try
To bate the naygur in one punch or in the ring he'd die;
The odds were on McCloskey though the betting it was
   small,
'Twas on McCloskey ten to one, on the naygur none at all.

Chorus: "Throw him down McCloskey" was to be the battle cry—
   "Throw him down McCloskey you can lick him if you
      try,"
   And future generations, with wonder and delight,
   Will read on history's pages of the great McCloskey fight.

The fighters were to start in at a quarter after eight
But the naygur didn't show up and the hour was getting
   late;
He sent around a messenger who then went on to say
That the Irish crowd would jump him and he couldn't get
   fair play.
Then up steps Pete McCracken and said that he would
   fight
Stand up or rough and tumble if McCloskey didn't bite.
McCloskey said "I'll go you" then the seconds got in place,
And the fighters started in to decorate each other's face.

They fought like two hyenas 'til the forty seventh round,
They scattered blood enough around by gosh to paint the
   town,
McCloskey got a mouthful of poor McCracken's jowl,
McCracken hollered murder and his seconds hollered foul.
The friends of both the fighters, that instant did begin
To fight and eat each other the whole party started in.
You couldn't tell the difference in the fighters if you'd
   try;
McCracken lost an upper lip, McCloskey lost an eye.

Maggie Cline was unique as an entertainer. She was a large,
plain-faced woman with a huge toss of auburn hair and a voice
that would blast out the walls of a theater. She was wonderfully

effective in the rougher type of ballads, and of these, "Mary Ann Kehoe" was a favorite, esteemed by some above the riotous "McCloskey."

> *Chorus:* For she's a great, big, stout lump
> Of an agricultural Irish girl.
> She neither paints nor powders,
> And her figure is all her own.
> But she can strike that hard
> That you'd think you'd been
> Hit by the kick of a mule—
> The full of the house of Irish love
> Is Mary Ann Kehoe.

John L. Sullivan said that she was the greatest singer on the American stage. As Jack Murphy says, "No one cared to contradict John L., so his statement stood."

Supposedly, the McCloskey song derives from an actual brawl Kelly once witnessed in a saloon—no holds barred and footwork not necessarily confined to Queensberry rules. It is possible Kelly himself occasionally sang it, but there is no reference to his rendition anywhere in his career. Kelly, in his act, worked without make-up of any sort. He appeared in a rather rusty Prince Albert coat, a silk hat, with old-fashioned spectacles dangling from the end of his nose. He based his monologue on human traits and peculiarities: the man who risks his life crossing the street and then turns 'round and watches the vehicles pass for ten minutes. That was his type of material. He died of Bright's disease, aged thirty-eight, in 1896.

Yes, the expression of the '90s, despite the economic upheavals (understandable in a period that was trying to right itself) was mainly happy. It was often silly; nor was it always gay, or even too naughty—a fusion of the labels perhaps. And "mauve" is scurrilous. For every Puritan who objected to the word "whore" in print, his '90s' antagonist had the solace of a Babe Connors whose imitation, if not peer, was available in every community. (Beer says "whore" was printed "w——"

and that the children were told it meant "where," but the children didn't believe it. Any psychologist could have told Beer that children are always realists.)

In the '90s, most people made enough money to enjoy themselves according to caste. Europe was a holiday for the comfortable, and "my trip abroad" supplanted operations as table talk in such homes. Those less fortunate unenviously accepted the "Family Entrance" or five-cent "suds" across the bars as magic casements. Folks stepped out: the theaters, music halls, concerts—all available at nominal admissions. Home entertainment of the old sort was waning. Only grandma and her cronies persisted at euchre. And a man was old at fifty.

The fads and crazes of the '90s were youthful. The "skirt" dance and its successor, the "serpentine" dance, were insane swirlings, albeit not to the distemper of the then unimaginable swing music. All the girls had a fling at the skirt dance, regardless of bone structure, muscle development, or heart action. It was really no dance at all, but a series of kicks, twists, and hitches which agitated a full-pleated skirt extending well below the ankles. The skirt permitted vast expansion, and because of its fullness, kicks and whirls could be made without exposing the limbs. The "dancing" was done in 4/4 time, with the accent, or phrasing, of the old-fashioned schottische, and any number of persons could participate. The serpentine dance was a simple waltz movement featured by a voluminous gown. This was made of thin white silk, with yardage enough for a side-show tent. Buggy whips were fastened vertically along the right and left sides of the gown, and by means of these "whips" the gown could be spread, whirled, funneled, or twisted into innumerable rapidly changing shapes. When it was performed professionally, the dancer wore white trunks against a darkened stage, and colored lights were projected, which followed her movements. It was daring, and the blades were delighted, perhaps humming merrily W. R. Williams' song, "That Girl in the Serpentine Dance," which Will Rossiter (who was W. R. Williams) published in 1892.

The latest sensation we've got in the town,
She lives next to us on the street.
Reporters of dailies are writing her up,
To see her it is a great treat.
She's not a prizefighter from Australia's shore,
Or ballet girl over from France.
With her newfangled style she's knocked them all cold,
Has this girl in the serpentine dance.

Chorus: She's graceful and neat, such curves she makes,
A man if he's sober would think he had snakes.
She's startled the town, they seem in a trance
With her latest sensation, the serpentine dance.

In this great creation she dresses like Eve,
Her clothes they are usually white.
The first thing they do is to turn out the gas,
Of course, that makes her "out of sight."
Then up starts the music, you see a dark form,
While lime lights quite prettily rise,
Then she lifts up her dress, that's simply immense,
That you'll hardly believe your own eyes.

The amethyst, moss agate, sardonyx, and cameo so dear to the '80s now gleamed only at Aunt Nettie's throat. And mother's "R-E-G-A-R-D" ring Maybelle considered frightfully funny in comparison with the flashing brilliance of the diamond Fred had given her at plighting their troth. Indeed, the '90s' swain who failed to give his fiancée a diamond risked chances of dispelling the romance. (Maybelle: The '90s liked affected spellings. But it was still twenty years from the Kathryns and Berenices of the poetic Ziegfeld, who, in the '90s, had Sandow, the strong man, on his mind.) Anyway, Maybelle, comforted as much by her stylish diamond as by her emotional concern for her sweetheart, carefully turned out the gas (the Welsbach mantles after the protective coating had been burned off were fragile) and trotted off with Fred to the trolley-car party, which may have been—that night in 1891—say, to Elizabethport or Coney Island, at either place to enjoy ice cream, watermelon, and dancing.

If Maybelle was a "dare" girl, relishing with blushing co-

quetry an inane song made risqué by a naughty glance or flip of
hip, perhaps Fred took her to Koster and Bial's—on Thirty-
fourth Street, of course. No nice girl, however daring, would
have attended the partners' music hall at Sixth Avenue and
Twenty-third Street, which was a "drop in" place, a dive you
walked out of on your knees. But on August 28, 1893, aided
by a $500,000 deal with Oscar Hammerstein, Koster and Bial
opened their Thirty-fourth Street hall, which ran through to
Thirty-fifth Street, where the rear end of Macy's department
store is now. Its policy was Continental and its acts mainly
foreign. Bial was a good showman and booked some of the
greatest variety and music-hall talent the world has known.
Anna Held, Lottie Collins, Marie Lloyd, Yvette Guilbert, Eu-
genie Fougere, and Albert Chevalier made their American de-
buts at Koster and Bali's—artists of the very first rank. And
about one of them—Lottie Collins—is woven the fantastic story
of one of America's most popular songs of the '90s, "Ta-Ra-Ra-
Boom-Der-É." When it was published in 1891 by Willis Woodward at 842 Broadway, New York, no one cared except Woodward and Henry J. Sayers, whose name appears on the copy as
the composer. Neither New York nor the nation would have
anything to do with its senseless, naughtyish lines or its silly,
repetitious melody, and Woodward restacked his copies on the
top shelf and tried to forget. Gladly he and Sayers gave Lottie
Collins permission to sing it in the London halls—and overnight,
it seemed, the song became a sensation. London unconsciously
accepted it for what it was—a rollicking, hoydenish rhythm
that sealed the '90s' insouciance in a strain that epitomized
volumes of social analysis. The song, and then its story:

> A sweet Tuxedo girl you see,
> Queen of a swell society.
> Fond of fun as fond can be
> When it's on the strict Q.T.
> I'm not too young, I'm not too old,
> Not too timid, not too bold.
> Just the kind you'd like to hold,
> Just the kind for sport I'm told.

Chorus: Ta-ra-ra-boom-der-é,
Ta-ra-ra-boom-der-é.
Ta-ra-ra-boom-der-é,
Ta-ra-ra-boom-der-é.[1]

Lottie sang it in London in 1892, and on February 28 of that year the New York *Herald's* correspondent cabled:

London has gone stark mad over the refrain. It has become a hideous nightmare everywhere from Belgravia and Mayfair to Houndsditch and Whitechapel.

In drawing-rooms and hovels one hears "Ta-Ra-Ra-Boom-Der-É" and there is hardly a theatre in London in which the refrain is not alluded to at least once during the night. Even at the ultra-fashionable performance of Mr. Oscar Wilde's play at the St. James Theatre the other night [it was *Lady Windermere's Fan*] one of the actors who could not resist the craze cried out, "Ta-Ra-Ra-Boom-Der-É" and convulsed the audience. If you go to the House of Commons lobby it is probably the first thing that greets your ear, and one expects no other reply from bus driver, newsboys, hawkers and policemen. Influenza and fogs sink into insignificance beside the refrain, for which Miss Lottie Collins, who is known on the American stage, is responsible.

It took a curious turn before Lottie brought it back to America. She gave it over to two British song writers, Angelo A. Asher and Richard Morton, who respectively rearranged its words and music. Their version was published in London by Charles Sheard, and so great was its success that Sheard was able to sell it at four shillings a copy (about $1.00), although London then was driven nearly crazy by its doggerel.

Then another publisher brought out an edition, also rearranged, for a penny (two cents) a copy. Sheard brought suit but lost, Mr. Justice Stirling ruling that Sheard's version was bastard. The court did, however, enjoin the defendant publisher from reproducing Lottie's picture on his cover. But the penny sales ruined its popularity, and the song later (in London) was given gratis with packages of tea and soap.

When Lottie returned to America and introduced it at

[1]Copyright, Edward B. Marks Music Corp., RCA Building, Radio City, N. Y. Used by permission.

Koster and Bial's, the audiences, primed by the furore of London, hailed it as eagerly and writhed to its rhythm with all the fervor of the British. Presumably Lottie used here the American version. And this, the tune, that is, was as bastard as the British arrangement. Sayers, to his friends, never contended that he wrote the melody; was frank in telling its origin— Babe Connors' famous St. Louis brothel. There it was sung originally, if not composed, by Babe's Negro songstress and entertainer—the fabulous Mama Lou, who, it is said, originated, or sang versions of, the immensely popular '90s' tunes "There'll Be a Hot Time in the Old Town Tonight," May Irwin's "Bully Song," "Who Stole the Lock Off the Henhouse Door," and heaven knows how many others, including "Honey on My Lip, God Damn," which, although scarcely a parlor number, was a widely rendered brothel ballad.

PADEREWSKI, BABE, AND MAMA LOU

IN HIS DELIGHTFUL reminiscenses of his father (who was the late George S. Johns, the editor of the St. Louis *Post-Dispatch*), *The Time of Our Lives—My Father and I*, Orrick Johns refers to a specific night in the '90s when Johns, *père*, Ignace Paderewski, and the famous pianist-composer's manager dined at Tony Faust's, a nationally known St. Louis restaurant. Paderewski apparently had just concluded a recital and sought diversion.

"Tell me," asked the composer, "is there anything novel, anything out of the ordinary, a trifle bizarre, to be seen in St. Louis tonight?" "Yes, there is Babe Connors," said Johns. "Everybody sees Babe Connors, sooner or later."

And Orrick Johns goes on with the story:

Babe Connors imported the pick of the girls from Louisiana. She advertised them as "Creoles" and no doubt they had the old blood of the Creoles in their veins, but they were octaroons. They danced in little more than stockings, and Mammy Lou [thus Mr. Johns; she seems to be more generally known as Mama Lou], a gnarled, black

African of the purest type, sang, with her powerful voice, a great variety of indigenous songs.

She was among the first to sing "Frankie and Johnnie" for entertainment, and she excited hair-raising emotion when she sang the refrain of that song. . . . Mammy [sic] Lou was one of the first to sing the Negro spirituals and field songs to the white men. Paderewski wanted to go to Babe Connors'. They took an old hack and drove through the streets, which were lighted more by the bright doors and gaslit windows than by the feeble street lamps. After the very formal and polite introductions—Babe Connors insisted on the most polished manner in her parlor—a dozen beauties danced to the music of a blind pianist, and Mammy Lou sang her raucous songs. Among them was Ta-Ra-Ra-Boom-De-Ay. [On the published song cover the title is given as "Ta-Ra-Ra-Boom-Der-É".] It was still unknown to the wide world, and it caught Paderewski's fancy. He went to the piano and asked her to sing it again and again. He learned that, and a number of other songs from her; but Ta-Ra-Ra-Boom-De-Ay seemed the favorite. . . . In a season or two the song, like many others that originated with Mammy Lou, got into vaudeville by way of some manager who visited Babe's and became a sensation.

Jim Kiley, a well-known song writer of the '90s, author of "The Little Boy in Green," which Helene Mora, a female baritone star of the period, sang with much acclaim, assured the writer that Mama Lou originated the "Bully Song," which was associated with May Irwin to her retirement. The published copy says Charles E. Trevathan wrote the words and music. (But Delaney published an almost identical version in his No. 12 *Song Book* in 1896 as written by Will Carleton and composed by J. W. Cavanagh. The Essex Music Publishing Co. is cited as the copyright owners.) It is presumed that Trevathan gave the song to May Irwin, who, hearing him sing it in a Chicago-bound Pullman, asked him to set it down. Trevathan, a Chicago sports writer, was of Southern origin and may first have heard the song on the Mississippi levees— so, perhaps, had Mama Lou. Trevathan's version is printable:

> Have you heard about dat bully dat's just come to town?
> He's round among de niggers, a-layin' their bodies down.

I'm a-lookin' for dat bully and he must be found.
I'm a Tennessee nigger and I don't allow,
No red-eyed river roustabout with me to raise a row.
I'm lookin' for dat bully and I'll make him bow.

Chorus: When I walk dat levee round, round, round, round,
When I walk dat levee round, round, round, round,
When I walk dat levee round,
I'm lookin' for dat bully an' he must be found.

May found her bully and dispatched him with the proper degree of bloodletting associated with the razor-armed African.

For additional data on the incredible Babe and her redoubtable songstress, Mama Lou, we are indebted to Clem Hurd, of the St. Louis *Post-Dispatch*, who was kind enough to round up what old-timers still were left and forward a dossier of their assorted recollections.

Babe's original *maison de joie* was at 210 South Sixth Street. It was within "easy staggering distance," as Hurd says, from Faust's restaurant or the Southern Hotel bar. It was known as "The Castle," and, "Let's go storm the Castle" was a phrase among masculine adults in St. Louis as familiar as observations on the weather. The place still stands, or did at this writing, a three-story white-painted brick house with a narrow porch, mounting to a door bearing a neat brass plate— BABE CONNORS—a modest-enough identification, but which to the initiated meant a rendezvous that was virtually the hub of St. Louis' red-light wheel.

Near by were Priscilla Henry's Negro establishment and Molly Barnum's white emporium. Molly seems to have lacked the drive of the brassy Babe; yet she was expansive, albeit in a softer way. With tears welling, she would invariably relate, in repetitions that never lost their poignancy, of the folly of trusting scheming males constantly seeking the downfall of sweet innocence. The bitter experience was sound; had been hers. Molly, too, had had a boy friend whose love—alas, only apparently—equaled his ambition. This was to captain a river steamer, and Molly, who could not resist his charms, was an equal prey for his financial appeal. She advanced him $30,000 and he bought his boat. When the packet heaved off on her maiden voyage, Molly took her girls down to admire the craft and its handsome captain. "Then," said Molly, upon one of countless tellings, "he rang the bell, he tooted the whistle— and I never saw the son-of-a-bitch again."

Once inside of Babe's place, one was blinded by the brilliance, partly from the prisms of the $250 chandeliers, mainly from Babe's diamonds. Babe, in full panoply, resembled a Tiffany window. She enhanced the natural sparkle of her front teeth with diamond inlays. Diamond pendants dangled from her ears; strands of diamonds encircled her neck. She wore diamond bracelets, not only about both wrists, but both of her ankles were similarly decked. So far as any one knew, the jewels were real; Babe was a woman of substance; she detested fakes.

She was a handsome, bronze-complexioned Negress, a bit plumpish, but her height—five feet seven inches—easily molded her weight of 165 pounds. On fair days it was her custom to summon her open carriage, driven by a white coachman in fancy livery that included white doeskin breeches. Whereupon, Babe, with parasol and feather boa, would enter and be driven about the city, perhaps as far as Forest Park, her diamonds catching and sending back the brilliance of the sun. Occasionally, if the horses were running, she drove out to Fairgrounds Park, perhaps with her white lover, Willie Frank, whose average daily losses of $100 to the bookmakers Babe covered from the profits of her house. Babe leaned to horse players; Scottie the Tout enjoyed her favors when she found Willie a bore.

At night, presiding over her hostelry, she was always fashionably attired in evening dress. Her girls were beautiful. They were very young and very light, of the Negro mixture known to the trade as "pink skins." She usually kept eight or ten, and on less-occupied nights, Babe, for the diversion of her customers (many were national names; it is said that one of the Republican party's platforms was written in Babe's domicile) would have the girls dance in the nude, perhaps reluctantly, for Babe was never all-out, preferring finesse, subtlety. Her favorite variant was to attire her girls in long skirts but without underclothing. Thus costumed, they would dance on a huge mirror.

A number of Babe's customers came only to hear Mama Lou sing. She was short, fat, black, often belligerent, and always herself. She never made the slightest effort to imitate Babe in dress or manner. She wore a calico dress, gingham apron, and head bandanna, and nine tenths of her songs were obscene. The original lines of "Hot Time in the Old Town Tonight," for example, had nothing to do with a conflagration, marching men, Rough Riders, or Negro revivals. It told of a darky whose dusky sweetheart was enmeshed in another amour. Here is what is printable of Mama Lou's lines:

> Late last night about ten o'clock,
> I knocked at the door and the door was locked.
> I peeked through the blinds,
> Thought my baby was dead—
> There was another nigger in the folding bed. . . .

The chorus began with the line "When she heard that bell go ding-a-ling" and ended with the outraged buck's "God damn her," instead of the well-known, "My baby," which, presumably, she was no longer. In the song of Joe Hayden and Theodore A. Metz, now universally known, the verse celebrates a Negro revival.

The song had an amazing response. It was sung virtually everywhere. Its rhythm was irresistible, and even the words in the cleaned-up patter of Hayden convey unmistakable abandon. Our troops in the Spanish-American War adopted it at once as their marching song, and from this derives two stories—one amusing, one confounding. Clayton Hamilton, distinguished critic and litterateur, says that a newspaper in Paris, reporting the victory of Colonel Theodore Roosevelt at San Juan Hill in 1898, included this delicious paragraph:

> The American soldiers gathered round their campfires and sang the American national anthem, "Il Fera Chaud dans la Vieille Ville ce Soir. . . ."

Mama Lou would have been delighted with this given title which, roughly, is "There Will Be Warm Weather in the Old City This Evening." Ten years later President Theodore Roosevelt who, so is the legend, led his men in the famous charge to the strains of "Hot Time," directed that the song be omitted from a collection of war songs he had asked the Congressional Library to assemble. According to Joseph Flanner, an early publisher of "Hot Time," the President's objection was that the tune was ragtime and not music.

Mama Lou and Babe finally parted, probably still friends, although Mama Lou opened in direct opposition with a house in Lucas Avenue, establishing there what one might call the wellspring of the '90s' popular songs. She was extraordinarily kind to her girls financially, and with advice which she put into songs whose scarlet lines would set this page in flames. She was functional too. An old-timer recalls this instance: One night two stalwarts came into her place, found it full of slender fops. "Git out o' here, you skinny boys!" screamed Mama Lou. "Here comes a couple o' men wiv juice in 'em."

Babe, about 1898, removed to the new red-light district in Chestnut Street, where she occupied a double house. One, called "The Palace," she used strictly as a residence, which she furnished in admirable *décor* with the finest of rugs, tapestries, and objects of art. It had a connecting door, of course, with her business establishment, for Babe had the practical side of a Madam—her only definable expression. Before her death she was converted to Catholicism by Harry Bridgewater, Negro proprietor of a saloon at Eleventh Street and Lucas Avenue. She was buried from St. Theresa's Church.

BLOOMER GIRLS AND KISSES SLY

BABE CONNORS' influence, or rather that of Mama Lou, was pronounced, discernible in many of the pop tunes of the '90s. A song Neil Price wrote and sang all over in that decade achieved remarkable success because of a *double-entendre* attached to its meaning which Price never intended—presumably. This was "Pump Away Joseph." And as the women in the audience buried their blushes behind fans or handkerchiefs, their escorts rocked uproariously when Price went into the chorus:

> Pump away Joseph, do;
> Pump away Joseph, do.
> Be ready and willing, the kettle be filling,
> While I make tea for two.
> Get there, Joseph, do.
> Some day I'll pump for you.
> Don't stay there and dandle but collar the handle,
> And pump away, Joseph, do.

It's an interesting ditty. It doesn't parse for sense, and although some of its lines are silly, the sentiment is pretty. And its situation unique. Observe the verses:

> Now I love a lass whom none can surpass
> And she is devoted to me.
> She lives down by the square, oft times I go there
> Of an evening to take tea.
> One night when I called I was nearly appalled
> When she passed me the kettle and said,
> "The pump is close by so to it now fly
> While I the tea table do spread." (*Chorus*)

The second verse was the rouser; its tag line a fillip:

> Now I rushed to the pump feeling much like a chump,
> For pumping was not in my line.
> I would rather have been far, far from the scene,
> But of course 'twould not do to decline.

So provoking was she as we sat down to tea,
And I asked her if I'd loved in vain.
She hung down her head as she blushingly said,
"The kettle needs filling again."

Despite the depression of 1893, the songs of the '90s were rollicking. There were, certainly, numerous ballads and "motto" songs, mostly tear jerkers. These were immediately spoofed. One was "Just About to Fall." Its theme was the plight of a boy or girl sorely beset by temptation, and it preached the advisability of extending a helping hand when he or she was "just about to fall." This was red meat for Lew Dockstader, who promptly parodied the croaker in lines ribbing the bloomer-girl cyclist of the period.

Did you ever see a maiden when she's riding on her wheel?
How she wears her baggy bloomers that her limbs she may conceal?
As she rolls along the highway at a brisk and lively pace,
Suddenly a look of horror spreads itself across her face.
Let us pause a minute, stranger—kindly look the other way,
Sympathy give to that maiden, for I think I hear her say,
"My suspenders they have busted—If I only had a shawl—"
With both hands she grabs her bloomers for—
They're just about to fall.

In the autumn of 1890, Emma Pollock applied for a role in *The Fakir*, a farce comedy. She was younger than the age minimum required by the Gerry Society (now the Society for the Prevention of Cruelty to Children), and so Mrs. Fernandez, theatrical agent and mother of Bijou Fernandez, suggested that she wear a long dress belonging to Evelyn, Emma's sister. It was a white dotted Swiss. Hurrying to the theater, she passed a saloon as a man came through the swinging doors. He paused a moment, and, as though at a target, sprayed her entire dress with about a pint of tobacco juice. But she got the job, perhaps because of the sympathy of Harry Hamlin, who was casting the company. All went well until it was decided to put Emma in tights with a number of other girls who were to support a turn of Ann Sutherland, whose curves were superb. When Emma's mother heard of the number, she promptly ordered Emma and Evelyn out of the cast and home. They were playing Chicago at the time.

Emma came back to New York with a letter from Alice Harrison (later of the famous act, "Fun in a Photograph Gallery") to Martin Hanley, manager for Ned Harrigan, of Harrigan and Hart. Harrigan was opening his new theater (it became the Garrick, in Thirty-fifth Street east of Sixth Avenue) with *Reilly and the Four Hundred*, and he needed a soubrette. Hanley sent Emma to Harrigan, who lived in Perry Street in Greenwich Village. She dressed to kill for the interview, topping her costume with Evelyn's hat, which was trimmed with Prince of Wales feathers. As she sat in the parlor awaiting Harrigan, a wet towel splashed across the top of her head, crushing the feathers and ruining her hair. As Emma says: "Young Bill Harrigan was at the top of the staircase peering down at me. My first impulse was to cry, for if I didn't get the part I could never go home with Evelyn's hat spoiled. I took it off, and waited, and presently Ned Harrigan came in. The first thing he did was to grab my bunch of curls and say, 'Just the wig for the part.' " Emma was hired, the show opened December 29, 1890, and Emma sang "Maggie Murphy's Home."

It not only stopped the show—it is still a known song. For Emma, thereafter and wherever—in England, the Continent, South Africa, Australia, and on the battlefields of France—sang it continuously. It is a fresh and lively lyric with a homey graciousness, a gas-lamp, boys-in-the-street touch that was precisely the flavor of the period. Dave Braham wrote the music, and Ned Harrigan the lines.

Emma, who, happily, is still alive and still as sprightly, now confesses that Maggie Murphy's Home actually was in Brooklyn, and that when she removed to New York, her change was sadly noted in the Brooklyn *Eagle*.

In her role, Emma danced a "Challenge Jig," and she had to do it very well, because it was necessary to the plot of *Reilly and the Four Hundred*. The "Challenge Jig" had a peculiar connotation. It was an old form of program billing attached to any type of artist—jig, reel, clog, or sand-jig dancers, harmonica players, bone soloists, skaters—and it meant the equivalent of our modern "tops," or "supercolossal."

An actual challenge-jig contest, however, was quite a different thing. There were a number of these in the '90s, especially clogging contests, and for this dance the contenders were assembled and announced, and three judges were appointed— one for time, one for style, and one for execution. The time judge sat on the stage in the right first entrance, the style judge sat in or near the orchestra pit, and the judge of execution sat *under* the stage. There, with pad and pencil, the execution judge checked the missing taps, defective rolls and heel work, the lagging in the breaks. At the conclusion of the contest the judges compared notes and awarded the prize on points. Thereafter, the winner was billed as the champion of the state in which the contest was held.

In the '90s the popular song definitely improved. The tunes were better, and the lyrics reflected the wanton times. The English music-hall songs, many of which were imported, were an influence. Indeed, in the '90s, as American publishers visioned the golden days to come in the first decade of the twentieth century, and the industry awakened from its disorganized, hit-or-miss policy of previous years, exchanges were made with London houses, some of whom had New York affiliations.

To the humors and jibes of the American ditties, the English songs added a sophisticated note. A song of this type is "You Don't Have to Marry the Girl." It was written by Murdoch Lind to the music of George Rosey and was published in London by Sheard. Joseph W. Stern & Co. brought it to the United States, and it became a pronounced success through its use by Lottie Gilson, who was billed as "The Little Magnet" and who could wring sex from a dissertation on integral calculus. She gave the song a piquancy decidedly risqué. Here is a verse and chorus, with the interlude spoken by Lottie:

> When you go a-courting, boys, life is full of bliss,
> And you find a thousand joys in a hug and kiss.

With your sweetheart every night, walking you will go,
Where there's no electric light to spoil the fun, you know.
Seated in a cozy nook, in some quiet park,
Right into her eyes you look, squeeze her when it's dark.
Tell her that you worship her, call her "darling dove,"
All those sort of things occur, when you're making love—

Spoken: Yes, boys, that's just about the way it goes. Spooning?
Why it's great! First you hold hands. I don't mean poker hands, but
real, clean, warm, velvety hands, with plenty of eau de cologne on
them. Then you get your arm around her waist. She may object, at
first, and say, "Why Mr. Williams! I'm surprised at you! I always
thought you were a gentleman!" But that's only a bluff. In two
minutes she'll be calling you Algie again, the same as ever, with a
look in her eyes that says, "Kiss me just once, and save my life!" So
you kiss her. Then you kiss her again. And the more you do it the
better she likes it, and the better you like her. But whatever you
do, don't lose your head. Spooning may be all very well for a little
recreation—

Chorus: But you don't have to marry the girl,
       Though your brain she may set in a whirl.
       She will simper and sigh
       But it's all in my eye—
       For you don't have to marry the girl.[1]

The American tours of the English music-hall performers—
and splendid artists they were: Vesta Victoria, Vesta Tilly,
Marie Lloyd, Albert Chevalier, and a score more—were a tonic
too, bracing and effervescent in their effect on our own troupers
and tunesmiths.

       The music hall girl is the rage,
       The pet of both youth and old age.
       With plenty of chic and one dear little kick,
       She makes a success on the stage.

So wrote Ilda Orme in a song called "The Music Hall Girl,"
which Oliver Ditson published in 1896. It may have been of
English origin, but it caught the fling of the period—flirt, smirk,
and leer—deftly:

[1] Copyright, Edward B. Marks Music Corp., RCA Building, Radio City, N. Y.
Used by permission.

The hubby sits in the front row,
But wifie is not there—oh, no!
She thinks her dear hub, quite safe at the club,
For there pretty girls never go.
But where is the harm after all,
In the darlings of the music hall?
If they give you spice with your champagne on ice,
They want but a curtain call.

Here are the laces, flounce, and wine days; the violets-tossed-on-stage days, the top-hat-raised-and "May I?" days:

The mischievous music hall girl,
She will set all your brains in a whirl,
When she sings naughty songs which to Paree belongs;
When her laces they twinkle and twirl.
In his mind then each man forms a place,
For a supper, champagne and can-can;
She will throw you a kiss while you watch her in bliss,
But she'll go home with some other man.

In the '90s the girls were in on much of the fun; at first with a shy grace that was charming, latterly with an openness suggestive of the coming sex equality. The setting of Richard R. Hanch, to music by G. R. E. Kennedy, caught this spirit nicely in their song, "That Up-To-Date Girl of Mine":

You talk about your maidens with hearts of gold,
Your bleached blondes and dashing brunettes;
But I've got a sweetheart that knocks 'em all cold,
An up-to-date girl, you may bet.
She wears flashy bloomers and carries a cane,
She's a girl you don't meet every day.
She has plenty of dough and wherever we go
She will say, "Now, dear boy, let me pay."

Chorus: She bets on the horses
At all the race courses,
Her equal you never could find.
Each day all the papers
Give space to her capers,
She glories in poker,
At billiards she's a corker,
This Up-To-Date Girl of Mine.

Except for the *ouch* line, "At billiards she's a corker," Hanch's lyric is acceptable, with a neat, sophisticated twist. His use of the slang term "dough" is unusual. Nowhere has the writer seen this contemporary term for money in any of the '90s' songs. The slang of the period for money included "mazuma," "rhino," "filthy lucre," etc. It was such songs as Hanch's (they were numerous) that drove Comstock and Dr. Parkhurst nearly out of their minds.

YIELDING, SHE FELL

THE REV. DR. CHARLES H. PARKHURST was called to the Madison Square Presbyterian Church, New York, in 1880, and on February 29 of that year preached his first sermon. He remained in character and personality a scholarly pulpit pip-squeak until February 14, 1892. On that Sunday he tossed a bombshell at his fashionable congregation, and the subsequent detonation was as civically important to the city as Luther's inkpot was to Protestantism. The Tenderloin, then an area approximately bound on east and west by Sixth and Eighth avenues, respectively, and on south and north by Fourteenth and Thirty-second streets, was one vast brothel. Row upon row, the Madams holed up in sinful warrens; and at men who were without entree or inclination, streetwalkers clutched with Hogarthian frenzy. A number of songs reflected that looseness —most of them comparable to those set down in previous pages. There were some moralizations. Ed Marks and his partner, Joseph W. Stern, took cognizance of the expression, neatly turning it, however, upon the masculine tendency to regard the humble maid as fair game in a lush field.

Their song had a vast sale—over 1,000,000 copies. It was conceived in the birthplace of Theodore Roosevelt at 28 East Twentieth Street, now a dignified memorial to the "Big Stick" President, but then, in the mid-'90s, harboring a basement saloon. There, on an afternoon about 1894, Marks and Stern repaired for sandwiches and beer. Two men sat at a table near them, and when the comely waitress deposited their victuals, one made an off-color remark. The girl, poor but honest, to preserve the idiom, remonstrated. "If Jack were only here," she added defiantly.

Marks overheard the reply and, a professional of the pop tune, realized its worth at once in relation to the situation. He gulped his beer and motioned to Stern, and they hastened across the street to their office and wrote what seems to be the imperishable, "Mother Was a Lady."

Marks prettified the setting, as any poet might—but his feat, that of the all-time high in pop-tune history for quick courtship (one must assume the girl fell into the arms of the repentant drummer) still stands. So does the song. It is still sold. As were hundreds of thousands of records.

It is possible the record company was chagrined at its sales in one instance.

Some years ago a man took the song, gave it a hill-billy version, labeled it "If Jack Were Only Here," and the company paid off to Marks on some 300,000 records of the thefted version.

Charles Archer, less deft, possibly, certainly more precise, limned the lady Parkhurst's heart bled for in

ONLY A FALLEN ANGEL

Who is the woman in scarlet so gay,
Hidden in shadows just over the way?
Once she was pure as the snowflakes of white,
Now shunning brightness, she hides in the night.
Once loving arms rocked her gently to rest;
Once a fond mother clasped her to her breast.
Then came a tempter, and, yielding, she fell,
Loving not wisely, alas, but too well.

Chorus: She's only a fallen angel, doomed to a wretched life.
She's only a fallen angel, living midst want and strife.
Under the flick'ring gaslight, wasting her youth away,
She's only a fallen angel on earth today.

This was Parkhurst's Sylvia, and he set out to learn more about her. What he learned, after months of field work, going into the houses, visiting the saloons that nested the harlots, talking with pimps, cops, and prostitutes, he noted in chapter and verse. For years an indifferent public had sanctioned the hand-in-glove (and pocket) policy of organized politics with organized vice—indeed, enhanced it by patronage. The eminent reformer was well aware of it, seethed over the situation in his study, nursed his anger and hatred until, that fourteenth of February, he spewed out against "the polluted harpies that, under the pretense of governing this city, are feeding day and night on its quivering vitals. . . ." And he called the politicians "a lying, perjured, rum-soaked, libidinous lot."

The congregation fretted, and there was the usual buzz-buzz at their Sunday dinner tables. Beyond that, nothing, and Dr. Parkhurst's bomb possibly would have sputtered in his manuscript (he read his sermons), a dud. For some unexplainable reason, a newspaper reporter, one W. E. Carson, happened in on that Sunday. He plastered the sermon all over his paper. The exposé brought about the Lexow investigation and, in 1895, the overthrow of Tammany with the election of the reform candidate, Mayor William L. Strong. The reformation lasted two years, when Tammany was returned to power with Mayor Robert A. Van Wyck its puppet front.

Reform was unpopular in the '90s. Mayor Strong holding forth at City Hall particularly dismayed Arthur J. West, a popular singer and song writer of the period, who set his feeling in lines that were jingled until Van Wyck removed the Parkhurst governmental halo. "When They Get Through with Reform in New York" was West's song (1895), and here are three pertinent verses:

Have you thought of the fate of the city
When they get through with reform in New York?
And won't things look awfully pretty,
When they get through with reform in New York?
The trees will all stop blooming,
Perhaps, maybe, stripped of their bark.
And the police will never need booming
When they get through with reform in New York.

Saloons on Sunday will all be closed
When they get through with reform in New York.
And no more gambling or pawning your clothes,
When they get through with reform in New York.
Horseracing then will be stopped,
They'll then turn saloons into policy shops,
And next election Tammany Hall will give us a grand hop—
Then there'll be no reform in New York.

They'll put Dr. Parkhurst up for Mayor of this town,
When they get through with reform in New York.
And not one single vote in the ballot box will be found,
When they get through with reform in New York.
Tammany Hall then once more will have a say,
And all these good government people they'll then send away,
Lock them all up in Sing Sing without a word to say,
When there'll be no reform in New York.

What was more to the glow of the times was *Trilby*, the
novel of George L. P. B. Du Maurier, published by Harper's,
and the play made of it by Paul M. Potter (Walter A. Maclean),
produced in 1895 with Wilton Lackaye as Svengali, the musician with hypnotic power, and Virginia Harned in the title
role. This preposterous tale of the nude model with the tiny
feet who died with her lover for love raised the national eyebrows to hitherto unattained heights and modeled New York
for a straitjacket. The songs tell the story. Scan a verse and
chorus of "Since Trilby Came to Town." Its words and music
are by W. C. Parker, and it was published in 1895 (the year
before Du Maurier died) by Howley, Haviland & Co.

There was once a simple little maiden, so the story goes,
Who had such dainty little feet, and such lovely pinky
toes.
She was noted everywhere she went for what she didn't
wear,
And the only dress she had was—well, so small it couldn't
tear.
She was not the coming woman, for she came from gay
Paree,
She managed to get through the quarantine, and started
on a spree,

And now it's very hard to tell just what the end will be.
For everywhere you go, it's nothing but Trilby, Trilby,
Trilby.

Chorus: Trilby dinners, and Trilby plays, Trilby wagons and Trilby
sleighs,
Trilby corsets and Trilby thread, Trilby bakers and Trilby
bread;
Trilby hats and Trilby shoes, Trilby drinks and Trilby
booze,
Trilby living and Trilby dead, Trilby pains in the side of
your head.

Almost at the same time, M. Witmark & Sons published a
better lyric by J. W. Herbert to the music of Charles Puerner.
Herbert's was a saucy turn; his lines were too subtle for the
popular taste, but he got the champagne flavor of the daring
novel. His song:

THE NAUGHTY ALTOGETHER

I love a maid, I love her well,
Is she sincere? I cannot tell;
The soothing sob, the soughing sigh,
The heavy heart, the humid eye,
Proclaim aloud my weighty woe.
Ah! Thrilby mine, I love you so!

Chorus: You girls can never understand
How strongest men become unmanned.
Though I am free from jealousy
My heart's not made of leather;
Ah! Thrilby mine, pray draw the line
At naughty altogether.

It is not meet your dainty feet
Should be on view, I fondly sue
You won't expose your shrimp-pink toes.
Ah! Thrilby mine, you must decline,
Your perfect charms you will agree
Should be your sweetheart's property.

Well, Comstock gnashed and Parkhurst heaved and the Puri-
tans screamed. But everybody went on singing, literally lifting
their spirits in the myriad saloons where liquor was cheap and

food was free. In Cincinnati, in the early '90s, one could feast on an excellent meal for twenty-five cents. The same was asked in San Francisco, where the victuals were embellished with a large dish of shrimp—gratis. Large five-cent beers were available everywhere in the country, and in many saloons a free lunch was served all day and evening. Some of the high-class bars in New York, Chicago, and other cities served chicken salad, oysters fried in olive oil, Edam cheese, and small pickles at free buffets. Many of the Chicago saloons gave a hardboiled egg or a clam with a glass of beer, and some of them festooned the entrances to their emporiums with egg shells by the hundreds, which were strung on string and draped over the doors and windows. There was even sectional criticism:

NEW YORK ISN'T IN IT AT ALL

Now listen, gay New Yorkers, and lend to me your ear,
While I do quickly tell you the way that things appear.
Chicago got the World's Fair, and now she has the call,
When anything is given out, New York isn't in it at all.

Chorus: New York isn't in it at all,
Chicago gets there every time,
Politicians yell themselves hoarse,
Their actions are very sublime.
Conventions are all held out West,
Our club don't know how to play ball,
'Tis easily seen by one who's not green,
New York isn't in it at all.

Just look at all our barrooms and see the dizzy lunch,
The hardtack and bologna that drinkers have to munch;
Out West they get a sandwich, with every whisky ball,
For treating lushers good and white New York isn't in it at all.

Take in a show some evening and see the foreign fakes,
Who gather in our dollars, they'd give a man the snakes.
Out West they chase them quickly, home talent has the call,
To see good plays, we understand, New York isn't in it at all.

Johnny Morgan wrote the song, a parody on "Take A Day Off, Mary Ann."

Some of the Chicago saloons served free hot meals. The customer bought an immense glass of beer for a nickel, took a seat at a table, and a waiter brought him a plate of soup, a chunk of boiled beef or spare ribs, a boiled potato, and bread, butter, crackers, and pretzels. Of course, a number of customers would buy two or more beers with the meal. These places were meccas for bums. Some of the experts would watch for departing guests to leave a couple of half-filled beer glasses. They salvaged these promptly, filled one glass with the leavings of the other, stepped over to another table, and pounded loudly for the waiter. There was continual skirmishing between the bums and the waiters, but the bums were wizards and seldom lost.

H. T. Wilkins expressed the liquid sentiment of the times with his parody on "My Sweetheart's the Man in the Moon," "My Hobby's a Drink of Good Rye," warbled often by the bibbers as a hymn of excuse.

> Everybody has a hobby, underneath the rose,
> Everybody likes their "hopper," so the saying goes.
> I've a hobby, you all know it, quite as well as I,
> Every evening I do hit it, always on the sly.

> *Chorus:* My hobby's a drink of good rye.
> I'll take one on you by and bye.
> 'Twould fill me with fun
> Just now to hit one,
> And I don't think a dozen
> I ever would shun.
> I'm going away very soon,
> And will go into some great big saloon,
> And all very slyly where no one will spy me
> I'll drink down my hobby alone.

In 1893 the Chicago saloonkeepers and the ministers of the Gospel clasped hands in an unusual—and unholy?—alliance for

a common cause—Sunday closing of the World's Fair. Each
contended he would lose patronage. Both lost. The Midway
and the cooch dance romped merrily on; the penetrating, reedy
notes of the Armenian pipes droned night and day while the
coochers naughtily shook their rumps to the whine.

Nations stress their virtues, says Bolitho, and the people
respond with lip service. The mass cry, unfettered, is as funda-
mental as a privy. Ribaldry was often the note of the '90s, and
in high places a curious naïve sacrilege occurred in song. Perhaps intentionally—because there lay the heart of the herd—
perhaps victimized by parodists, the Salvation Army beat its
tom-toms in street-corner settings to such borrowings as

> There are no flies on Jesus;
> There are flies on you,
> And there are flies on me,
> But there are no flies on Jesus.

A variant:

> A friend we have in Jesus,
> For Jesus set me free.
> There are no flies on Jesus
> Though there may be flies on me.

The lines derived from, and were adapted to, a popular '90s'
song called "There Are No Flies on Dolan." There were others.
One, said to have been sung to a melody by Neil Moret, composer of "Hiawatha," a song of excessive popularity at the turn
of the century, and—the gamut in popular music—composer,
too, of one of the best of the jazz-era numbers, "Chloe," was
this:

> And the devil said to me
> Don't you see?
> Won't you come along with me?
> Says I, Oh, no, my friend,
> For Jesus is good enough for me.

Another, of which but a fragment exists:

> In the Salvation Army barracks,
> In a place away out West. . .

It may have been a hymn; it may have been a dirty rib. The recollection of the source goes no further, and the writer's effort to trace it has been fruitless.

A tune is a tune. "The Irish Dancing Master" is an old comic ballad:

> Two by two away we go,
> Not too fast, and not too slow.
> Mind your heel and point your toe,
> Says the Irish dancing master.

This tune is Number 72 in the *Christian Science Hymnal;* the lines:

> Glory be to God on High,
> God whose glory fills the sky.
> Peace on earth to man is given;
> Man, the well-beloved of heaven.

"Sweet Bye and Bye," and "Shall We Gather at the River" were frequently worked into sand jigs by dancers in the old variety halls and the free and easies as a medley.

> Hurrah! Hurrah! We bring the jubilee.
> Hurrah! Hurrah! From sin we all are free.
> Let us sing a song of praise for Jesus beckons me,
> While we are marching to Glory.

This the Salvation Army shouted to "Marching Through Georgia." None will take offense. But the Protestant Church was riled by the Salvation Army's adaptation of the pop tunes and said so at the Detroit convention of the Religious Educational Society in 1901. Among those who deplored the practice was the Rev. Dr. S. Parkes Cadman, nationally known divine and founder of the radio church of the air. The practice was stopped.

THAT IS LOVE—THAT IS TOUGH

BUT THE COMEDY CONTINUED. In no other decade were there so many comic songs. (The term is used generically; they weren't always funny.) The readiness for laughter by the audiences and the people generally, the prevalent spoofing of politicians, stuffed shirts, reformers, and poseurs by vaudeville's singing comedians were noted by the writers and composers. Two—E. C. Center and Jackson Gouraud—ribbed a famous hotel, its phony "patrons," and even the impeccable Oscar in a song they called "The Waldorf 'Hyphen' Astoria." Oscar was then (1897) headwaiter of the hotel at Fifth Avenue and Thirty-fourth Street, now the site of the Empire State Building.

> To be in the smartest set, or what is better yet
> I'm the Johnny that knows the proper tip.
> For if you only knew, the proper thing to do,
> Why—daily in the Waldorf you must sit.
> Have your clothes in the latest style,
> (Though your tailor waits awhile),
> But to you that doesn't matter, not a bit.
> Though little people know at night just where you go,
> But in the afternoon that's where you sit.

> *Chorus:* At the Waldorf "Hyphen" Astoria,
> No matter who or what you are,
> Be sure you nod to Oscar as you enter.
> Just speak to him by name,
> And for "ten" he'll do the same—
> That's the proper thing at the Waldorf "Hyphen" Astoria.

> We have all met those guys who affect to patronize
> The hotel with the hyphenated name.
> But if it should befall that on them we'd try to call,
> It would be hard to find them just the same.
> After hunting long and well through each separate hotel,
> Without result, a fellow must decide,
> They may be on the square, but if they are living there,
> It must be on the "hyphen" they reside.

Felix McGlennon, a prolific English writer (he'd bring fifty songs at a time into Witmark, the publisher, who swore he had a factory), wrote a number of comic songs, though his forte was the serious and the sobber. One, "And Her Golden Hair Was Hanging Down Her Back," had an amazing success.

> There was once a simple maiden came to New York on a
>   trip,
> And her golden hair was hanging down her back.
> Her cheeks were like the roses, she'd a pout upon her lip,
> And her golden hair was hanging down her back.
> When she landed at the station here she took a little stroll,
> At everything she wondered till she lost her self control.
> Said she, "New York is quite a village, ain't it! Bless my
>   soul!"
> And her golden hair was hanging down her back.

Chorus: But, oh, Jane doesn't look the same.
> When she left the village she was shy.
> But alas, and alack! she's gone back,
> With a naughty little twinkle in her eye.

This song was popularized largely by Dan W. Quinn, a favorite comic singer of the times, but it was first introduced by Eunice Vance, an English comedienne. In the stage presentation, a girl stooge with flowing blond hair was used who simpered and smirked and winked to the strains.

McGlennon's American idiom was perfect; he spent much time in New York. But it is possible the lines may have been pointed by Monroe H. Rosenfeld, who wrote the music to them. Rosenfeld was an interesting character. He drank nothing but water, not even soft drinks, and it is believed by his colleagues that he started the "stamping" craze at redheaded girls and white horses. This was a practice taken up by children who, upon seeing a redheaded girl or a white horse, would wet the tip of the right-hand index finger, place it upon the palm of the left hand, remove it, then "stamp" the spot with the right fist.

He wore an old-fashioned puff-fold tie, establishing it with a diamond bowknot pin, and a round hat with silk facing under the brim, which he had specially made for him by Yeoman. And when it wasn't in McAleenan's pawnshop, a handsome fob dangled from a gold watch in his vest. Horse racing kept him constantly insolvent, a status he once found more dangerous than embarrassing. As police closed in upon him in a bank against which he had drawn a fraudulent check he leaped into Broadway from the second-story window, painfully injuring himself and insuring his arrest.

Sam Lewis, who wrote an astonishing number of hit songs in the 1900s and who knew Rosenfeld intimately, insists that Rosenfeld was psychic and he swears that this incident is true:

Rosenfeld once asked Lewis to accompany him to his home. He lived in a rooming house in West Thirty-seventh Street near Seventh Avenue, New York. They had hardly been in his room five minutes when Rosenfeld motioned Lewis to come with him. Together they walked down the hall to a rear room. Without knocking, Rosenfeld opened the door. Two young girls were in the room, one of them weeping. Rosenfeld said, "You must stop crying. And get that idea of suicide out of your head." The frightened girl, eventually calmed, then confessed she and her companion had planned to die together that night because they were without work, penniless, and starving. Food was bought for them, and Rosenfeld later got them both jobs. Lewis says Rosenfeld had never before seen the girls, nor could he have known of their presence in the house, for they had rented the room only that afternoon.

One of McGlennon's ballads, "That Is Love," was extraordinarily popular, possibly because of Imogene Comer. She had a big, heavy baritone voice and an artistic aptitude for dramatizing her material. She displayed a wealth of it in "That Is Love." Here are two verses:

> See the mother gazing on her baby boy
> With ecstatic eyes and heart that fills with joy.
> He to her is purest gold without alloy,
> For him how she praised to heaven above.

How she guides his footsteps through this vale of strife,
Watching o'er his bedside when infection's rife.
Risking for her baby boy her health—her life!
That is love—that is love.

See the father standing by his cottage door,
Watching baby in the gutter, rolling o'er.
Laughing at his childish pranks, but hark! A roar!
Save, oh save him, God in heaven above!
Dashing down the street there comes a maddened horse,
Out the father rushes with resistless force,
Saves the child, but he lies there a mangled corpse—
That is love—that is love.

This was pretty sobby stuff. But although the '90s appreciated its sentiment, listening in tears to Miss Comer's rendition, it was too big a target to go unshot, and Billy Ryan, popular eccentric comedian, let fly with a parody—rowdy, but more expressive of the decade. Mr. Ryan:

See the weary boozer at the barroom door,
He dares not brace the barkeep,
He's been worked before.
Soon he spies a dime upon the barroom floor,
Snatches it and cries, "I've got the stuff!"
Throws the coin upon the bar with gleeful shout,
Fills a can and places it beneath his snout,
The can is old—it springs a leak—the beer runs out—
That is tough—that is tough.

See the night stand actor as he struts about the town,
Gazing on his litho' pasted upside down.
Looks at the advance sale with an awful frown,
To the local manager makes a bluff.
"I'm the great and only, and I first produced East Lynne."
Calls upon the editor and works his chin,
At night the hall is opened, only two small boys come in—
That is tough—that is tough.

See the old maid sitting in her easy chair,
Twisting curling papers in her thin gray hair.
Suddenly she starts and says, "I do declare,
"Someone's moving in the room above."

"Quiet," said her roommate, "there's a man beneath the bed,
I am not mistaken, I can see his head.
I saw him first, so you go out. I'll stay instead—"
That is love—that is love.

In the '90s, racial allusions waned. They were revived again
in the 1900s, as we shall see. But the omnipresent Irish were
neglected in no period, and the comic note we are discussing
was his especial concern. Most of the Irish songs of the period
are of fisticuffs ("Throw Him Down McCloskey") and barroom battles, and they are not much good. One, though, was
really quite good and was deservedly popular. It comes to
hand through Jack Murphy, who does not recall its writer
though he remembers that it was in the repertoire of many
vaudeville comic singers. The song is "She Got It Where
McDooley Got the Brick." A verse and chorus:

> McDooley used to carry the hod to pass the time away,
> 'Till recently he met a sudden death.
> A brick fell from the scaffold and it landed on his neck,
> And separated Dooley from his breath.
> McDooley's friends assembled and they called upon the
> gang
> That should be made to pay for Dooley's life.
> They said as long as nothing could be done for Dooley
> now,
> That something should be done for Dooley's wife.

Chorus: She got it where McDooley got the brick,
She got it where McDooley got the brick.
The gang is still debatin'
And McDooley's wife is waitin'
And she got it where McDooley got the brick.

The Dillon brothers, Harry and John, were a splendid team
of vaudeville comic singers. They played all the desirable
American time in a novel act, for which they wrote all the
material, including their songs, which they delivered in a
curious but effective crossfire manner. Their comic songs
usually told a story, sometimes a good one. "Put Me Off at

Buffalo," which Witmark published for them in 1895, was their
best song, occasionally heard today. Here it is in full:

PUT ME OFF AT BUFFALO

He caught the train at Albany and to the porter said,
Put me off at Buffalo.
He was tired and took a sleeper and says, Now I'll go to
    bed,
Just to rest an hour or so.
In an undertone he murmured, Now I lay me down to
    wink,
Put me off at Buffalo.
Then he tipped the porter, saying,
Port, old boy, come have a drink,
Put me off at Buffalo.

Chorus: Oh, oh, don't forget to put me off at Buffalo,
Oh, oh, my berth is lower five.
If you find me hard to wake,
Oh, don't be afraid to shake,
Throw me off there dead or alive.
Mister Porter, when you call me in the morn, he says,
I'll kick, but of course it doesn't go.
No matter what I say, just remember I'm the jay
That goes off the train when you get to Buffalo.

The porter started drinking, and you'd think he owned the
    road,
When he got to Buffalo.
The train was 'way behind, the engineer he had a load,
Take water—he said, No, no.
When the porter went to call his man
He got at the wrong berth.
Says, get off at Buffalo.
Oh, the man he says, You're wrong, old boy,
Look out, you'll tear my shirt.
I don't get off at Buffalo.

Chorus: Oh, oh, don't tell me you won't get off at Buffalo.
Oh, oh, be quick and grab your clothes.
Here's the hardest guy to wake,
Said the porter with a shake.
They exchanged some good hard blows.
Oh, the porter got a soaker but he fired the man.

With a crash through the window he did go.
Then the man he should awoke in his sleep says that's a
    joke
Put me off the train when we get to Buffalo.
When the brakeman shouted Cleveland, why the man
    jumped out of bed
And says, We've gone through Buffalo.
Then he saw the poor old porter with a bandage on his
    head,
And his eyes swelled out, oh, oh,
His whiskers they were sandy in the sand he did a jig—
Put me off at Buffalo.
He says, My wife was waiting at the depot with a rig,
Take me back to Buffalo.

Chorus: Oh, I thought I told you to put me off at Buffalo,
    Oh, oh, there's trouble in the air.
    Oh, the porter shook with fright, yes, he turned from
        black to white
    Oh, how that coon did stare.
    I'm a dead nigger now, he whispered to himself,
    It's my last trip on this road, I know.
    My goodness sakes alive, here's the gent in No. 5!
    I put the wrong man off the train at Buffalo.

One of the most popular of the comic songs of the '90s was
Joe Flynn's "Down Went McGinty." It was a fluke hit. Flynn,
an eccentric comedian, had written a few songs that Witmark
published, two of which were "Paddy Shea" and "Number
Four, Second Floor." Both were unsuccessful. Flynn got his
idea for the calamitous McGinty while touring. He wrote the
song, but when he tried it out on his fellow actors, they showed
small interest, and he was discouraged. Flynn's vaudeville act
was really eccentric. He wore a very broad-brimmed straw hat,
a woman's blouse, and misfit pants, and he embellished his
comic songs and parodies with epitaphs, which he read from
a large book. One:

Here lies the body of Jerry Greer,
His mouth could stretch from ear to ear.
Stranger, step lightly on the sod,
For if he gapes you're gone, by God.

His comic song, "McGinty," fitted nicely into his act. And when it was introduced, probably at Hyde and Behman's Brooklyn Theater (as some say), it was received with shouts. Still, according to one version of the story, the larger publishers would have none of it, including Witmark, who had lost on Flynn's earlier efforts. So Flynn carried it to Spaulding and Gray, and it became one of the great money-makers of the '90s. Jay Witmark denies this. He said that Flynn never came near them with the song; regrettably, too, for Witmark then needed the money that it brought in.

Its lines are of no moment. But it has plenty of bounce, a lively tune, and good rhythm—qualities esteemed by baritones, parlor or professional, in any age. And it makes sport of suicide —an incredible violation of pop-tune canon. Here are the first verse and part of the fourth, and the first and fourth choruses:

> Sunday morning just at nine
> Dan McGinty dressed so fine,
> Stood looking up at a very high stone wall.
> When his friend, young Pat McCann,
> Says I'll bet five dollars, Dan,
> I could carry you to the top without a fall.
> So on his shoulders he took Dan.
> To climb the ladder he began,
> And he soon commenced to reach up near the top.
> When McGinty, cute old rogue,
> To win the five he did let go,
> Never thinking just how far he'd have to drop.

Chorus: Down went McGinty to the bottom of the wall,
> And tho' he won the five,
> He was more dead than alive.
> Sure his ribs and nose and back
> Were broke from getting such a fall—
> Dressed in his best suit of clothes.

Well, while he was in the hospital, Mrs. McGinty bore him a boy, and when he came out he got drunk in celebration and was clapped into jail for brawling before he could see his wife or child. Released, still misfortune marked him. He returned home, "And with joy to see his boy was nearly wild"; but no, Bedelia Ann had skipped with the baby. Then:

> . . . he gave up in despair,
> And he madly pulled his hair
> As he stood one day upon the river shore.
> Knowing well he couldn't swim,
> He did foolishly jump in
> Although water he had never took before.

Fourth Down went McGinty to the bottom of the say.
Chorus: And he must be very wet
> For they haven't found him yet.
> But they say his ghost comes round the docks
> Before the break of day,
> Dressed in his best suit of clothes.

One of the great songs of the '90s, "I'm the Man Who Broke the Bank at Monte Carlo," has an interesting legend. It is one of the finest examples in popular song annals of international *inter-changeability*, proof that a good rhythmic tune with a buoyant lyric knows no barrier. The song completely reverses the history of "Ta-Ra-Ra-Boom-Der-É," which, as we have seen, was pelvic negroid Americana but rejected here until London's insane acceptance. "Monte Carlo," quite the other way, was of absolute British origin, a furore in the English halls as sung by Charles Coborn, and later Maggie Duggan, who stampeded their audiences with it.

The first time Coborn sang it (at the Oxford Hall) he milked it for ten chorus encores and was soundly rapped by a critic for disgusting the audience and making the critic ill. But Coborn continued to plug it, largely because he liked it. He vowed he would win over his audiences, and he did. Once a disgraceful house in the Eden (now the Kingsway) was quieted by Coborn, who kept repeating the chorus until the rowdies, exhausted by the monotony, behaved.

The story is that one Arthur DeCourcey Bower, a sort of sandwich man in tails, of whom little else is known, "fronted" London in 1891 in foppish attire, tossing his money away

fanatically as the man who broke the bank at Monte Carlo—
the resort's advertisement for more suckers. On a night during
all this, Fred Gilbert, an English song writer, observed the headline on a Strand poster: "The Man Who Broke the Bank at
Monte Carlo." Its unmistakable beat impressed him, and mum-
bling the sentence as a rune, he went to his lodgings and the
following day wrote the song to the headline. But no performer
would touch it, and when Albert Chevalier declined its use, the
discouraged Gilbert timorously submitted it to Coborn. Coborn
also rejected it. In his autobiography, titled after the song, he
wrote that he thought it was "too high-brow for the average
music-hall audience."

But after he'd returned the song, he regretted his action,
caught up with Gilbert, begged it back, and got it, Gilbert
selling his share for £10, then about $50. When the popular
Maggie Duggan took it over, Coborn's royalties, according to
M. Willson Disher in his savory *Music Hall Parade*, soon
reached £600.

Originally William (Old Hoss) Hoey had teamed with
John Fields in a blackface comedy act in which Hoey did an
eccentric line of comedy; not much talk, but a lot of interruptions. Then he was slim, active, and danced while Fields
played the dulcimer. Later Hoey teamed up with Evans for
their memorable seasons in *The Parlor Match*, the full-length
farce Charles H. Hoyt derived from delousing *The Book Agent*,
a purple afterpiece of the '70s. The combination was subsequently dissolved, and Hoey went out on his own as a tramp
comic. He needed a song, and on a trip to London induced
Coborn to let him have "The Man Who Broke the Bank at
Monte Carlo." Hoey brought it back to America, where it
was not only immediately successful, it made Hoey a "one
song" man. It became a trade-mark, and he was forced to sing
it throughout his career. He had a hoarse, rasping voice. But he
took himself seriously as a singer, which gave an added comic
touch to the song:

THE MAN WHO BROKE THE BANK AT MONTE CARLO

I've just got here through Paris from the sunny southern
    shore;
I to Monte Carlo went, just to raise my winter's rent.
Dame fortune smiled upon me as she'd never done before,
And I've now such lots of money I'm a gent.
Yes, I've now such lots of money I'm a gent.

Chorus: As I walk along the Bois de Boolong with an independent
    air,
You can hear the girls declare, "He must be a millionaire."
You can hear them sigh, and wish to die,
You can see them wink the other eye
At the man that broke the bank at Monte Carlo.

I stay indoors till after lunch, and then my daily walk
To the great Triumphal Arch is one grand triumphal
    march.
Observed by each observer with the keenness of a hawk,
I'm a mass of money, linen, silk and starch.
I'm a mass of money, linen, silk and starch.

I patronized the tables at the Monte Carlo hell,
Till they hadn't got a sou for a Christian or a Jew.
So I quickly went to Paris for the charms of mademoiselle
Who's the loadstone of my heart, what can I do,
When with twenty tongues she swears that she'll be true?

THE RAGTIME COON

THE GAIETY OF THE PERIOD was enhanced at this time (about
1895) by three important developments in our popular-song
culture. These were the introduction of ragtime, the "coon
shouter" and coon songs, and the cakewalk, which, albeit an
eccentric dance, often had "coon" lyrics set to its tunes.

The greatest exponent of ragtime (a form of syncopation;
the delayed beat in classical music), and possibly its inventor,
was Ben Harney. No one could approach Harney's ragtime
piano prowess. It was said of him that he could "rag" the

Protestant hymnal in a way to win applause from a congress
of divines. G. A. Severance, a band leader and prominent
musically throughout the '90s, at this writing financial secretary
of Local No. 13 of the Troy, N. Y., Musical Union, says that
not one of today's swing pianists could equal Harney's technique or rhythm.

Harney began as a "back-room entertainer," playing for
throw money or a meager straight salary in the back rooms of
saloons. These were furnished with chairs, tables, and a piano,
and in them ladies, with or without escorts, could order re-
freshments, enjoy the music, and make social contacts often to
their financial advantage. In Kansas City and St. Louis, Harney
was a civic favorite. When he went into vaudeville in the
mid-'90s, audiences in the best houses all but rioted at his art.
For he not only introduced this new form of rhythm—ragtime—
but a new type of song—coon shouting. His first published song
(M. Witmark & Sons, 1896) was "Mister Johnson, Turn Me
Loose," and one has but to scan its lines (Harney wrote his
lyrics too) to observe the new lilt he gave to the pop tune.

> T'other ev'nin' eb'ryting was still, Oh! babe.
> De moon was climbin' down behin' de hill, Oh! babe.
> T'ought eb'rybody was a-sound asleep,
> But a old man, a Johnson, was a-on his beat. Oh! babe.
> I went down into a nigger crap game,
> W'en de coons were a-gamblin' wid a might an' main.
> T'ought I'd be a sport an' be dead game;
> I gambled my money, an' I wasn't to blame.
> One nigger's point was a little, a Joe,
> Bettin' six bits t'a quarter he could make de fo'
> He made dat point, but he made no mo'—
> Jus' den Johnson jumped t'rough de do'.

> *Chorus:* Oh, Mister Johnson, turn me loose;
> Got no money, but a good excuse.
> Oh, Mister Johnson, I'll be good.
> Oh, Mister Johnson, turn me loose,
> Don' take me to the calaboose.
> Oh, Mister Johnson, I'll be good.

The second verse relates the errant Negro's mishap when he met with Mister Johnson at a chicken coop. Mister Johnson opened fire to prevent the theft, and:

Second   I got no chance for to be turned loose;
Chorus: Got no chance for a good excuse.
           Oh, Mister Johnson, I'll be good . . .
           An' now he's playin' seben-leben
           'Way up yonder in de nigger heaben.
           Oh, Mister Johnson made him good.

The ragtime rhythm will be apparent in the lyric to those who remember. The response, "Oh! babe," is pure ragtime punctuation. As are "a-sound asleep," "a-gamblin' wid," and (especially neat) "a little, a Joe"—all literal slurs necessary to the slurred accent of ragtime's peculiar beat. More, the song is climactic in its social presentation of the new type of Negro that developed in the '90s—the "coon dandy," the "sport" in exaggerated peg-top trousers, russet ties (as low shoes were called), straw hat atilt, and equally adept at craps or dusky amours. Now he was "Bon Bon Buddie, the Chocolate Drop," as George Walker (one of them) was to sing at the turn of the century. The lazy, shuffling, good-natured Negro passed into limbo with the simultaneous advent of Harney's ragtime tune and characterization, along with the ol' massa songs.

Harney's Negro accent and tone quality were perfect. It was part of his vaudeville act to prove it. He carried along with him a Negro singer who sang the verse of a song from the front row of the balcony, one of the first, by the way, of the singing stooges. Harney would then repeat the verse from the stage, his exact imitation winning him rounds of applause. The Negro singer then joined him on the stage, and both went into their coon shouting to Harney's incredibly tangled ragtime obbligatos.

His act at once set a craze, and many imitators soon plagued him. Best was Mike Bernard, pianist at Tony Pastor's, who played the music for the show. When Tony finished his own specialty, he would announce Bernard, who thereupon tore into a ragtime number. For a time the ragtime style was confined to instrumental music. But in the late '90s, James J. Morton, the "nut" monologist and a performer of rank, originated the art of actually singing in ragtime. Morton's selection for this annihilation was Barney Fagan's "My Gal's a Highborn Lady." It was one of the first of the coon songs, and here is its original chorus:

> My gal's a highborn lady,
> She's black, but not so shady.
> Feathers like a peacock, just as gay,
> She's not colored, she was born that way.
> I'm proud of my black Venus,
> No coon can come between us.
> 'Long the line they can't outshine
> This highborn gal of mine.

And this is how Morton "ragged" it:

> My gal shezeheza high gaborn galady dady,
> She's blacka hacka wacka not so gashady dady. . .

The original song was highly successful. Burton B. Fagan, Barney's son, says that Barney lost $20,000 in royalties on the tune to the sharks who lifted it for publication in Canada and Great Britain, where its copyright did not hold. Were he alive, Barney could lament with Representative Sol Bloom, current chairman of the House Foreign Relations Committee, but in those days a song publisher, and proprietor, briefly, of "Highborn Lady." Impecunious at the time, Sol debated whether he should sell that song or another he owned, "I'm Happy When My Baby's Come To Town." He decided to sell the former, for which he received $25. Nobody ever heard of the other tune, but the Fagan song became a remarkable hit. "I could have made $100,000 on it," Mr. Bloom recently, and ruefully, remarked.

Fagan also typed the Lenox Avenue slick coon with a song he wrote in 1895 for Pete Dailey, a popular comic with the

Weber and Fields company. He titled it "A Red Hot Member," and here is a verse:

> There's a dead swell stranger on the promenade,
> A coon who's as black as night.
> Causing a commotion among the yaller gals,
> And putting every darky to flight.
> They don't care to pester with the gentleman,
> He'd surely sting 'em like a bumblebee.
> Cooler than December, and a red hot member—
> And that great, swell coon am me. Am me!

One of the best of the coon shouters was Hughie Cannon, a versatile performer who mainly wrote his own songs. But one of his most popular, "I Got Mine," was written by John Queen and Charles Cartwell.

I GOT MINE

> I went down to a turkey feed,
> The eatables certainly was fine.
> Half hour after the table was set
> The coons all formed in line.
> And when they brought that buzzard in
> They couldn't wait and commenced to grab—but
> I got mine!

> *Chorus:* I got mine, boys, I got mine,
> A-gettin' of that piece of fowl
> I had an awful time.
> One coon grabbed that eagle by the neck,
> And I snatched on behind.
> The nigger in front thought he had it all—but
> I GOT MINE!

The coon shouters were mainly masculine, but a few of the women challenged the art, one of them Artie Hall. She had a powerful, husky voice and used an artistic brown face make-up, highlighted with lavender powder. Her wig and costume completed her characterization of a high-toned dusky belle, and at the finish of her act she would roll up her sleeves and expose a bare, white arm. It was always good for a hand.

About 1897 the New York *Herald* responded to the vast interest in popular songs by printing occasional criticisms and reviews of them as the songs were published or sung from the city's stages. Most of these reviews were written by Monroe H. Rosenfeld. In an unsigned article dated Sunday, June 20, 1897 (very likely it was Rosenfeld's piece; the clichés and style match his signed copy), it is stated that since May Irwin popularized the "Bully" song, some six hundred Negro songs had been published. Two selected as being outstanding were "I Want Dem Presents Back," by Paul West, and Ernest Hogan's "All Coons Look Alike To Me." West's song is typical of the plaints of ruined amours, which, with the coon dandy, were the subjects of most of the coon-song lyrics. A verse and chorus:

> My gal Tildy, she's gone shook me,
> Shook me good and smart.
> She done say she'd be mah wife,
> But she gimme de marble heart.
> She skipped out wid a low down nigger
> Ain't got half my stack.
> She can go where she's a mind to,
> For I don't care where she's gwine to—
> But I wants my presents back!

> *Chorus:* I want dat bran' new cook stove,
> I want dat chair.
> I want dat lookin' glass, de comb
> To comb mah hair.
> I want dat carpet, yes sir.
> Won't get it? Well, I guess sir,
> Carve and starve me,
> I want dem presents back.

Ernest Hogan's coon had similar difficulty, although the relationship was not quite so intimate. His "All Coons Look Alike To Me" was an enormously successful song, and its popularity continued well on into the 1900s, a period in which through the talents of Cole and Johnson, the Negro song improved greatly.

ALL COONS LOOK ALIKE TO ME

Talk about a coon havin' troubles,
I think I have enough of my own.
It's all about my Lucy Jane Stubbles,
And she has caused my heart to moan.
There's another coon barber from Virginny,
In society he's the leader of the day.
And now my honey gal's a-gwine to quit me,
She's gone, yes, and drove this coon away.
She's no excuse to turn me loose,
I've been abused, I'm all confused,
'Cause dese words she did say:

Chorus: All coons look alike to me,
I've got another beau, you see.
And he's just as good to me
As you, nig, ever tried to be.
He spends his money free;
I know we can't agree.
So I don't like you no how—
All coons look alike to me.

Most of the coon songs in the '90s were written by white composers (and mainly of Irish extraction), but they had an excellent colleague in one Negro song writer, Gussie L. Davis, who wrote "The Baggage Coach Ahead." Davis, however, was mainly a ballad writer, and we shall take up with him in our concluding words on that type of song.

The cakewalk, an eccentric strutting dance, was largely associated with the Negro or blackface comics in vaudeville. It is possible Dave Genaro and his wife, Ray Bailey, a white song-and-dance team, originated the dance before Frederick Allen Mills wrote "At a Georgia Camp Meeting," which he published himself in 1897. But it became the greatest cakewalk tune of the '90s. It is a remarkable song. It was one of the first public dance tunes, forerunner of the two-step and the fox trot. Mills, a disappointed violinist, wrote the song (under the nom de plume of Kerry Mills) as a protest against the myriad coon songs of the period, which he said were out of harmony

with the true Negro spirit in rhythm and subject. Accordingly
he set his story in a Georgia camp meeting, brought in a bras
band, and staged a dance contest to the chagrin—and later delight—of the exhorting preacher:

> A camp meeting took place, by the colored race,
> 'Way down in Georgia.
> There were coons large and small,
> Lanky, lean, fat and tall,
> At this great coon camp meeting.
> When church was out, how the sisters did shout!
> They were so happy, but the young folks were tired,
> And wished to be inspired, and hired a big brass band.

Chorus: When that band of darkies began to play,
> Pretty music so gay, hats were then thrown away.
> Thought them foolish coons their necks would break,
> When they quit laughing and talking,
> And went to walking for a big chocolate cake.

> The old sisters raised sand when they first heard the band.
> 'Way down in Georgia.
> The preacher did rare, and the deacons did stare,
> At the young darkies prancing.
> The band played so sweet that nobody could eat,
> 'Twas so entrancing.
> So the church folk agreed
> 'Twas not a sinful deed,
> And joined in with the rest.

The song and its accompanying cakewalk (Genaro and
Bailey made it their outstanding number) first became a furore
and then an institution. Cakewalk songs were written by the
hundreds in an attempt to satisfy the insatiable public demand.

Severance says that a man in Troy, N. Y., by the name of
James Skully became so infatuated with the cakewalk that he
ordered one of the songs, "Rastus on Parade," a favorite, played
as his funeral dirge. And it was—to the consternation of mourners and pedestrians who looked on spellbound as the band,
blaring the Rastus tune, followed the hearse.

SWEET ROSIE—AND MAMIE O'ROURKE

THERE WAS GRACIOUS LIVING in the '90s, and even more of kindness—expressions that found their way into the decade's songs as easily as folks said "please" and "thank you." Who knows not "The Sidewalks of New York," "Sweet Rosie O'Grady," "The Band Played On," "Daisy Bell"? Just three of that type of the songs of the '90s, the lighter love or nostalgic lyric within the writer's memory), have failed to survive. These are: "Only One Girl in the World for Me," "The Sunshine of Paradise Alley" and "Somebody Loves Me." This last, by Hattie Starr, is more of an achievement in dauntless energy than a worth-while song. Miss Starr, trained in music in her Southern home, came up from the South in the early '90s, a sheaf of manuscripts under her arm—all of which were rejected by the song publishers. Although a winsome lass, they would have no part of her music, and probably "Somebody Loves Me" would never have found its way if Josephine Sabel, a seriocomic of extraordinary popularity, had not agreed to use it on the tearful plea of Miss Starr, who stormed her way one night into Miss Sabel's dressing room at Koster and Bial's.

Miss Sabel quickly started all New York humming the melody, and eventually Willis Woodward was persuaded to publish it. These, mind you, were the days of raucous ribbing, coon shouting, ragtime, and eccentric or slapstick comedy, and, aside from Miss Sabel's plugging, it is likely that Miss Starr's sentimental fiddle-faddle was successful because it was, for the moment, a novelty. (George Gershwin, who used the title thirty-odd years later for one of his best songs, probably never heard either of Miss Starr or Miss Sabel.)

George M. Cohan used to say that "Only One Girl in the World for Me" was the best popular song ever written. This is Hubertian praise. To the lay listener it is a good tune, and the lyric is fairish. It was written by Dave Marion, a fantastic creature you will love. First his song:

> There's only one girl in the world that I would call my wife,
> And the girl I sing of I love dearer than my life.
> My sweetheart's age is just eighteen—she greets me with a smile,
> And when she says "Good evening, John," I'm thinking all the while
> That there is:

Chorus: Only one girl in the world for me,
> Only one girl has my sympathy.
> She's not so very pretty, or of a high degree—
> There's only one girl in the world for me.

> My sweetheart is an orphan and I'm a factory lad,
> But if work were steady, why, it would not be so bad.
> We've been engaged just one year, and last night at the gate
> She said, as tears rose in her eyes, "My own true love, I'll wait."
> So there is: (*Chorus*)

Marion wrote words and music, and he also sang it. But he was not responsible for its success, for it was an "actor proof" song, and anyone with the semblance of a voice could get it over. It is one of those simple, easy, sure-fire tunes that occur from time to time and survive any amount of repetition and abuse.

In vaudeville, Marion worked with his wife, who was one of the Bell Sisters (they were really mother and daughter), and the team was billed as Marion and Bell. Their act was odd: they appeared as abnormally short, stout persons, resembling the reflection from a trick mirror. To produce this effect, they used egg-shaped wicker forms about two and one-half feet in diameter. They stooped or squatted inside these forms, exposing only their heads, feet, and arms, and the result was startling. It was no easy matter to remain folded up so closely during an entire song-and-dance number, but they did it. Years after Marion and Bell abandoned this act, a European team, Streb and Treb, appeared in this country. They used the same routine and costume, and their act was booked as a novelty.

When Marion and Bell separated, Marion went into burlesque, creating the character "Snuffy," a cab driver with a head cold whom many will recall, for it typed him well and he played it for years. He acquired, during this period, another wife—one of the Vedder Sisters, a buxom burlesquer. When Marion retired from burlesque, he opened a hotel in Toms River, N. J., where he—and his neighbors—had the time of their lives. Directly he was established, Marion posted a map showing the location of Captain Kidd's buried treasure. He summoned a committee of natives and proposed an expedition to recover the loot and use the money thus gained to finance a glue factory on the main street of the town. The glue was to be made from fish, and his detailed plans even included good wages to the fishermen.

The slightly skeptical natives grinned. But they were really alarmed at his next announcement, which was that he had rented a house he owned in a good residential neighborhood to a Chinese laundryman. They could never be sure about Marion. So a committee of town officials called upon him and pleaded that he reconsider. Marion listened soberly, and then magnanimously agreed to cancel the deal—which he had never made. Guests always found a flip of his hotel register diverting. It revealed all sorts of startling names: Lord Stanskenck, Robinson Crusoe, Thomas Carlyle, William Jennings Bryan, Robert E. Lee, Senator Priff, and a string of other synthetic notables to puzzle the natives.

New York of the '90s was a vast picnic ground, its streets and sidewalks a romping rendezvous for children, its brownstone stoops in spring and summer a lolling place for evening gossips, its "Bedbug Rows"—as many of the dingy tenements were dubbed—unlovely hives of sociability. The song writers caught the setting in homely verse. Precisely is it indicated in

"The Sunshine of Paradise Alley." To the lyric of Walter H
Ford, John W. Bratton set down the tune, and a few month
after the seriocomics of vaudeville dinned it across America
it became a minor classic of the era.

> There's a little side street such as often you meet,
> Where the boys of a Sunday night rally.
> Though it's not very wide, and it's dismal beside,
> Yet they call the place Paradise Alley.
> But a maiden so sweet lives in that little street,
> She's the daughter of Widow McNally.
> She has bright golden hair and the boys all declare
> She's the sunshine of Paradise Alley.

Chorus: Every Sunday down to her home we go,
All the boys and all the girls, they love her so.
Always jolly, heart that is true, I know—
She is the sunshine of Paradise Alley.

In previous pages we have referred to the influence of th
English music-hall song on the tunes of the '90s. Bratton, ar
active composer, says decisively that the '90s' so-called "smart"
songs—the parodies, the satires, the slightly risqué lyrics—wer
definite trends America imported from England. Thus in
fluenced, he wrote one himself: "I Didn't Think He'd Do It—
But He Did," a song obviously intended to ride on its *double
entendre:*

> Won't you stay and have a bit
> Of breakfast in the morning? . . .
> Dad found him on the couch,
> And I said, "Dad, I can vouch,
> I didn't think he'd do it—
> But he did."

Marie Lloyd sang it.

Also of influence in our popular-song culture were the "descriptive" songs and singers of the English music halls. These
songs were called "scenery chewers" by the profession, because of their delivery, which was to act out the song. They

were in ballad form; that is, they told a story. But contrary
to the ballads of the '80s (and some of the '90s we shall review), many of them were funny—or were supposed to be—
or gracious, or interesting. Decidedly, they were not the lugubrious handkerchief dabbers we have taken leave of. (An excellent scenery chewer was Jim Thornton's "Upper Ten, and
Lower Five," which he "acted" with Charles B. Lawlor. But
Thornton's major period was the 1900s, and he is not ready to
be cued.)

On a visit to London in the early '90s, Bratton was taken
with the descriptive type of song, observed their success with
the London music-hall audiences (he remembers hearing
'Across the Bridge He Goes" and "The Gold Miner's Dream"),
and when he returned to New York, he wrote one himself—
"The Old Stage Door." It is a precise hark back. On the night
of his return he prowled his former Broadway haunts, his
heart warming as he neared the old Casino Theater at Broadway and Thirty-ninth Street, where Lillian Russell was appearing in *Princess Nicotine*, a musical. It was a quickening sight.
Hansom cabs lined the curb, discharging their fares, and at the
stage door Airy Fairy Lillian was just darting through, followed
by Marie Dressler and other principals. As swells in Inverness
capes and toppers, ermined ladies on their arms, mingled with
Broadway's flotsam, Bratton took a final look and set off to his
hotel to write:

THE OLD STAGE DOOR

One fine evening while out walking through this city's
    crowded streets,
I passed by a grand theater with a great crowd buying
    seats.
To the curb the cabs were driven, loaded with the city's
    fair—
What a scene of mirth and splendor met my eye while
    standing there.
Then I strolled around the corner, what a very different
    sight;

There beheld the old, old stage door, with a single lamp
    for light.
Here I paused for a few moments, and I noticed as before,
Faces that were passing in and out that old stage door.

Chorus: First came the star, with a smile so bland,
    The greatest actor in all the land.
    Next came the soubrette, so blithe and gay,
    Just left her sweetheart across the way.
    Here comes the villain, how meek he is!
    In half an hour what a fiend he'll be.
    Extra girls, ballet girls, and many more—
    All of them passed through the old stage door.

De Novellis, an excellent fellow, himself as popular as a
song, led the orchestra at the Casino then, and the stage manager was one Max Freeman, the nadir of personalities, one of the
most-disliked men in show business. De Novellis used to pass
around small slips of paper to his men and ask them to write
their own characterizations of Freeman. Then he would collect
them and read them aloud to the guffaws of his men. It was
a sort of game. Their enjoyment was enhanced in knowing that
Freeman knew he was the butt of their laughter. One night
De Novellis, scanning a written characterization of Freeman,
looked again and read slowly aloud: "The impression he makes
does not seem to be favorable." The orchestra leader exclaimed,
"Zis mus' be some woman, ha? What she mean, Freeman he is
sahn beetch, yes? Ho! Ho!" A year later Freeman leaped to
his death from the window of his room in the Hotel Grenoble.

A bit of musical lavender that blossoms perennially from
its Bowery roots is "Sweet Rosie O'Grady," and it is pleasant
to set down that at this writing, Maude Nugent, who wrote the
song, is as alive as its melody. "Rosie" became a part of our
great American lieder in 1896, after Maude had popularized it
at Tony Pastor's in a ten weeks' singing engagement. The
tune is a natural; its melodic sequence is unforced and its
sentiment affectionate and simple. It could scarcely derive from
any other period—an admirable contrast to the highfalutin

hyperbole of the did-you-ever-see-a-dream-walking-I-did school that was to come. Here are its simple lines:

> Just down around the corner of the street where I reside,
> There lives the cutest little girl that I have ever spied.
> Her name is Rose O'Grady, and I don't mind telling you,
> That's she's the sweetest little Rose the garden ever grew.

Chorus: Sweet Rosie O'Grady, my dear little Rose.
　　　　　She's my steady lady, 'most everyone knows.
　　　　　And when we get married, how happy we'll be,
　　　　　I love sweet Rosie O'Grady, and Rosie O'Grady loves me.[1]

Although the song was a success, Maude very foolishly signed away all rights to the song five years later (1901) to Ed Marks (who had published it after she had plugged it at Pastor's) for $200 or $300, she forgets which. When the first copyright period expired in 1924, Maude says Marks renewed it in her name and offered her $100 for the rights to the succeeding period. (Songs are copyrighted on a twenty-eight-year basis. When the copyright expires, it can be renewed for another twenty-eight years. The expiration of the renewal, fifty-six years after publication, is final, and thereafter the song is in the public domain.) Maude refused Marks's offer and turned it over to Jack Mills, a rival publisher. It still brings her in about $400 annual royalties.

The German band, once an institution on New York's streets, and now happily out of hearing, was responsible for "The Band Played On," which in recent times enjoyed a radio swing vogue. It was written by John F. Palmer, an actor, who occasionally dabbled in song writing, at the suggestion of his sister, Pauline. According to James J. Geller, in his pleasantly nostalgic *Famous Songs and Their Stories*, Palmer, summoned to breakfast one morning, paused to listen to the street "musicians."

"Let the band play on," said Palmer.

"That's a good title for a song," said Pauline. And Palmer wrote it forthwith. But he could never sell it. One day, when typing a play script in a friend's office, he hummed his tune. It

[1] By permission of Maude Nugent Jerome and Mills Music, Inc.

was heard in an adjoining office by Charles B. Ward, a "Bowery coster" singer, who touched it up a bit (his name appears on the copy as the composer) and bought it for publication.

THE BAND PLAYED ON

Matt Casey formed a social club that beat the town for
style,
And hired for a meeting place a hall.
When payday came around each week they greased the
floor with wax,
And danced with noise and vigor at the ball.
Each Saturday you'd see them dressed up in Sunday
clothes,
Each lad would have his sweetheart by his side.
When Casey led the first grand march they all would fall
in line
Behind the man who was their joy and pride.

Chorus: For Casey would waltz with a strawberry blonde,
And the band played on.
He'd glide 'cross the floor with the girl he adored,
And the band played on.
But his brain was so loaded, it nearly exploded,
The poor girl would shake with alarm.
He'd ne'er leave the girl with the strawberry curl,
And the band played on.

In a few years it sold more than a million copies, and Ward, whom we shall meet again, made a lot of money on it.

And how does *this* come back across the years to you? "Daisy, Daisy, give me your answer, do . . ." Faintly, as of the rustle of broadcloth bloomers (Tst, tst! These, *our* girls! These, these *Jezebels!*) against the frame of a Columbia tandem? And how mean is the cantrip that again makes this lilting bicycle song pertinent to us! As we write, Leon Henderson is "scorching" down Pennsylvania Avenue, a pretty secretary a-rump his handlebars, to publicize for workers the "wheel," as the '90s called the bicycle, for partial substitution of the motorcar, rationed for the necessary weapons of war. Harry Dacre (nee Henry Decker), an English song writer, wrote it, too, against an economic note. There was an influx of British song writers to America in the '90s. Dacre was one, and he brought along his bicycle. When he disembarked, he was astonished that the customs men exacted duty on it.

"Lucky for you it wasn't built for two," observed his friend, Billy Jerome, the prolific American song writer ("Bedelia," "Chinatown," "Mr. Dooley"). Jerome's banter meant, of course, that, "built for two," Dacre would have had to pay twice the duty on his bicycle. But Dacre was heedless of the jest, thought only of "bicycle built for two" as a catch line. He soon used it in "Daisy Bell," a song with the identical history of "Ta-Ra-Ra-Boom-Der-É." For Dacre couldn't interest a single American publisher. Dejected, he gave it to Kate Lawrence, an English seriocomic returning to London. A fortnight after she sang it there, it swept the British Isles. Geller reports that it was played at the Duke of York's wedding.

> There is a flower within my heart,
> Daisy, Daisy!
> Planted one day by a glancing dart,
> Planted by Daisy Bell!
> Whether she loves me or loves me not,
> Sometimes it's hard to tell;
> Yet I am longing to share the lot
> Of beautiful Daisy Bell!
>
> *Chorus:* Daisy, Daisy, give me your answer, do!
> I'm half crazy all for the love of you!
> It won't be a stylish marriage,
> I can't afford a carriage.
> But you'll look sweet, upon the seat
> Of a bicycle built for two!

The gay lyric—and a good one it is—and the captivating sway of its waltz rhythm, had—*have*—a universal appeal. There are the snows of yesteryear.

On January 14, 1933, James W. Blake, then seventy years old, checked out of the Penn View Hotel, a dollar-a-night hostelry near Pennsylvania Station in New York. With his blind brother, John D. Blake, and his sister, Mary F. Blake, they proceeded to the railway terminal. Then they checked their few belongings and went over to a sandwich counter. Jim Blake spent the last few pennies they had for coffee and rolls, and the three started up Seventh Avenue. At Fortieth Street, Jim looked west, noticed the building of the New York *Herald Tribune*, and recalled that some years previously that newspaper had printed an interview with him. Leaving his brother and sister to await, he went up to the city room and, as it happened, walked right into the *Herald Tribune*'s front page the next day. For Jim Blake, with his friend, Charles B. Lawlor, a vaudeville singer, wrote the song that since 1894 has characterized the city and later became Governor Alfred E. Smith's Presidential campaign chant, "The Sidewalks of New York."

Jobless, penniless, and without food, he and his brother and sister had been dispossessed from their little flat in the Bronx. Blake had been a velour salesman. But velour and velvet were expensive materials that people found easy to forego during the depression, and the concern for which he worked no longer had need of his services. He explained his plight to a staff man of the *Herald Tribune*, and the newspaper speedily interceded. The Emergency Unemployment Relief Committee was notified, and presently charitable machinery began turning that ultimately re-established (with the personal attention of Al Smith) Jim Blake, his brother, and sister as housed, clothed, and fed citizens.

As Blake concluded his story in the *Herald Tribune* offices, he fetched out a decrepit wallet and extracted a yellowed cutting. It was a story a small-town paper had printed about him when he was on the road selling velour. The story detailed his career and closed with this comment: "His song has made Jimmy Blake the idol of New Yorkers, whose city he immortalized. He has but to ask and he has."

Blake folded the cutting back into his wallet. "That is rather ironic," he said. East side, west side, all around the town he had been, and there was no dancing in the streets. Blake, in 1894, was a salesman in the shop of John Golding, a hatter. One day Charlie Lawlor came in, hummed a melody, and asked Blake to write a lyric for it. "I want it to be something about New York," said Lawlor. And Blake, between customers, scribbled down these lines:

> Down in front of Casey's old brown wooden stoop,
> On a summer's evening we formed a merry group.
> Boys and girls together, we would sing and waltz
> While the Ginnie played the organ on the sidewalks of
> New York.

Chorus: East side, west side, all around the town.
> The tots sang Ring-a-Rosie, London bridge is falling
> down.
> Boys and girls together, me and Mamie O'Rourke,
> Tripped the light fantastic on the sidewalks of New York.

> That's where Johnny Casey and little Jimmy Crowe,
> With Jakey Krause, the baker, who always had the dough,
> Pretty Nellie Shannon, with a dude as light as cork,
> First picked up the waltz step on the sidewalks of New
> York.

> Things have changed since those times, some are up in G.
> Others they are on the hog, but they all feel just like me.
> They would part with all they've got could they but once
> more walk
> With their best girl and have a twirl on the sidewalks of
> New York.[2]

They are all originals in the song, all neighbors centering about the 312 East Eighteenth Street address that had been the Blake family's home for seventy-five years. They bought their bread from Jakey Krause, and a real Mamie O'Rourke had taught Jim to waltz. Nellie Shannon's beau *was* a dude—checkered weskit, pearl-gray bowler, and incredible trousers. He was probably James C. Shannon, a gallery-stooge singer for Lottie

Gilson, for he married Nellie. The brown stoop actually fronted the house of a man named Higgins, but Jim thought Casey sounded better.

Lottie Gilson sang the "Sidewalks" song at the old London Theater in the Bowery, and it scored an immediate success. A little later, Blake and Lawlor sold their interest in the song outright for $5,000. Blake died in 1935. He left a tuneful characterization of the town and its times and its simple people that amounts to a historical footnote.

It is a kindlier song than "The Bowery," although *that* satirical fling at New York's quaint avenue of derelicts and mulcters was of equal social significance. It accompanies virtually every reference in motion pictures and on the radio to the city's lower East Side. Like Jim Blake's casual classic, it pins the town to a tune now internationally known. It scored immediately when it was first sung by Harry Conor in Charles H. Hoyt's musical satire, *A Trip to Chinatown*. Soon its recognition became so pronounced that the furious shopkeepers of the Bowery protested—futilely, of course—its public presentation.

Hoyt, a Boston newspaperman and a prolific writer of farces, was the author of the words, and Percy Gaunt, musical director of *A Trip to Chinatown* (he had similarly served for Harrigan and Hart), put his name to the music. Its theme is fast, and the descriptive lyric, if commonplace, is authoritative. For the Bowery, when Hoyt produced his play on November 9, 1891, at the Madison Square Theater, was no cloister—is not today, except that the dives and brothels have been supplanted by one-night flop houses and "smoke" joints ("smoke" is slightly non-poisonous alcohol and water sold at five or ten cents per glass). Here are the first, fourth, and sixth verses and the chorus of

THE BOWERY

Oh! the night that I struck New York,
I went out for a quiet walk.

Folks who are "on to" the city say
Better by far that I took Broadway.
But I was out to enjoy the sights,
There was the Bow'ry ablaze with lights—
I had one of the devil's own nights!
I'll never go there any more!

Chorus: The Bow'ry, the Bow'ry!
They say such things, and they do strange things
On the Bow'ry, the Bow'ry!
I'll never go there any more!

I went into a concert hall,
I didn't have a good time at all.
Just the minute that I sat down,
Girls began singing "New Coon in Town."
I got up mad and spoke out free,
"Somebody put that man out," said she.
A man called a bouncer attended to me—
I'll never go there any more!

I struck a place they called a dive,
I was in luck to get out alive.
When the policeman heard my woes,
Saw my black eyes and battered nose,
"You've been held up," said the copper, "fly!"
"No, sir, but I've been knocked down!" said I.
Then he laughed, though I couldn't see why!
I'll never go there any more!

Yes, the lines are clumsy. But Hoyt was writing for a specific characterization: that of a rustic on his first visit to New York. And Conor caught the spirit of the song and character admirably. Rube types were often portrayed in the vaudeville of the '90s. But Conor added a touch of the coster to his performance that not only made it outstanding, it virtually created a new style in pop-tune technique. Critical banter, as we have seen, was acceptable practice in the '90s. But the coster twist, seemingly foreign to Hoyt's song, actually assured its success. Many coster types followed: "My Pearl's a Bowery Girl,"

"My Pet Is a Chelsea Girl," "On the Proper Side of Broadway on a Saturday P.M." It was a curious, unintentional derivation.

THE BALLAD MONGERS

IN THE LAST FIVE YEARS of the '90s, the ballad type of popular song enjoyed a renaissance, probably because of the success of "After the Ball." This song was written by Charles K. Harris, a Milwaukee bellhop, later a pawnbroker who became a banjo teacher. Harris published it himself in 1892, a fortunate decision, for the song became a sensation and the New York *Herald*, a year after, put Harris' earnings at $48,000.

"It has absolutely nothing to recommend it," wrote an anonymous critic (probably Rosenfeld) in the Sunday *Herald*, September 17, 1893. But everybody kept singing the song, and buying it too. In the life of the tune, the composer-publisher must have realized more than a hundred thousand dollars from its sales. As with almost all sensational successes of whatever type—books, music, plays—detractors, some presumably jealous, darted at it with their accustomed zeal. One even asserted that the idea was appropriated from *The Queen's Necklace*, by Alexandre Dumas, a work, and perhaps an author, Harris may never have heard of. Nonetheless, the germ of Harris' lyric is in the Dumas piece, a part of which reads:

> After the tragedy's over,
> After the playing is done,
> We must go home with the ladies
> Coupled, and not one by one.

Harris maintained that his song came of an actual incident. He said he attended a ball with his fiancée. When they left for home, he observed a girl entering a hansom, departing alone and obviously distressed. He inquired and was informed that she had been accompanied by her sweetheart but had afterward

become estranged over some trivial happening. There was a
story value to it, Harris said, and he went home and wrote

AFTER THE BALL

A little maiden climbed an old man's knee,
Begged for a story, "Do, Uncle, please."
Why are you single, why live alone?
Have you no babies, have you no home?
I had a sweetheart, years, years ago.
Where she is now, pet, you will soon know.
List to the story, I'll tell it all;
I believed her faithless after the ball.

Chorus: After the ball is over, after the break of morn,
After the dancers' leaving, after the stars are gone.
Many a heart is aching, if you could read them all,
Many the hopes that have vanished after the ball.

Bright lights were flashing in the grand ballroom,
Softly the music, playing sweet tunes.
There came my sweetheart, my love, my own,
I wish some water,—leave me alone!
When I returned, dear, there stood a man,
Kissing my sweetheart as lovers can.
Down fell the glass, pet, broken that's all,
Just as my heart was, after the ball.

Long years have passed, child; I'll never wed,
True to my lost love, though she is dead.
She tried to tell me, tried to explain,
I would not listen, pleadings were vain.
One day a letter came, from that man,
He was her brother the letter ran.
That's why I'm lonely, no home at all,
I broke her heart, pet, after the ball.[1]

An inspection of the lyric, especially the line "Down fell
the glass, pet, broken that's all," offers some support to the
Herald's critical reaction. Probably its simple melody was a
factor in its success. But its sensational sweep of the nation
undoubtedly was due to the plugging of J. Aldrich Libbey, a

[1] Used by permission of the copyright owners, Charles K. Harris Publishing
Co.

baritone of great popularity, who sang it as a musical interpolation in *A Trip to Chinatown*, the musical satire in which Charles H. Hoyt also introduced his song, "The Bowery."

Although Harris is remembered mainly for his "After the Ball," he was by no means a one-song man. He wrote also, "Hello Central Give Me Heaven," and "Always in the Way," both incredibly maudlin ditties of dead mothers, and enormously successful. He wrote "Hearts," and "Creep, Baby, Creep"; "Fallen by the Wayside," and "Break the News to Mother," a ballad of a dying hero soldier, commended in death by his general, who turns out to be the lad's father. He wrote "Is Life Worth Living?" an amazing ballad which must surely hold the all-time mortuary record: A mother dies in the first verse, a son in the second. The third verse, which tells only of the broken heart of a jilted girl, is a bit anticlimactic, but the murderous touch is quickly recaptured in the fourth and final stanza, which kills off a brother on the field of battle.

Harris' work is interesting. It reflected little of the spirit of the '90s. But he made much money. Most of his songs are tearful trivia of blighted love or the dire plight of orphaned children. He explored more graveyards than the ballad mongers of the '80s. Yet he was an astute music publisher, a field requiring always wits and occasionally weapons. He left a comfortable estate for his wife and blind daughter, Mildred, who was born virtually sightless and to whom he was devoted. Expensive operations failed to correct her disability, and her vision ultimately was destroyed. But in her father's devotion and her love for baseball she found partial escape. They scarcely ever missed a sunny afternoon at the ball park, where Mildred took delight in hearing the shouting and the crack of the bat.

Harris was small in stature, with reddish, curly hair and mustache, and he was voluble and vain. In 1920 he was one of a group who proposed to take over the Edison Motion Picture Studios in New York. Among those in the deal were Jerome H. Remick, a rival music publisher; John J. Murdock, of the Keith-Albee vaudeville interests; B. S. Moss, operator of a metropolitan chain of movie theaters; and J. J. Keit, who represented the Columbia Amusement enterprises.

The plan was to make two-reel comedies, for which they had an ideal outlet through the Moss-Murdock vaudeville chains, and to rent space to other companies for shooting interiors. Remick was to make illustrated songs, and Harris proposed more elaborate dramatizations of his songs in picture form. "No directors," he told Jack Murphy, whom he hired to manage the studio, "are capable of developing my ideas, so I shall make my own productions." Murphy was to attend to the rentals and laboratory charges and make the comedies, in which he was given a substantial interest. While Harris was telling of the masterpieces he intended to create from his songs, Murphy appraised and tabulated the wardrobe, the properties and settings (of which there was a warehouseful), the lights, scenic equipment, etc. The principal promoters then fell out over a pinochle game; nobody spoke to anyone else, and the proposition was abandoned.

Harris was the leading sob balladist of the '90s. But he was closely challenged by Gussie L. Davis (the Negro previously referred to), who wrote better songs; Edward B. Marks, whose masterpiece was "The Little Lost Child"; Charles Graham; and H. W. Petrie, a lesser light, but who will always be recalled by his publishers (and 50,000 bassos) as the composer of "Asleep in the Deep." Petrie, a sensible chap with a leavening modesty, was born in Bloomington, Illinois, and he had written about twenty-five songs before he published, to the words of Philip Wingate, "I Don't Want To Play in Your Yard," his first successful song. Almost everyone knew it, and its sales were ballyhooed as "in the hundreds of thousands." Yet when Petrie was asked about this years later, he replied, "Hell, I doubt if it sold more than 50,000 copies." For a reason the writer was never able to learn, Petrie and Wingate dedicated the song, "To the Ladies of the Charity Circle of La Porte, Ind."

Arthur Lamb, a prolific lyricist and a high-pressure lad of the first water, wrote the words for Petrie's "Asleep in the

Deep," certainly the most popular bass song ever written. Lamb was at first a nuisance and then a phenomenon alike to publishers and composers. One of his colleagues told this writer that, "Lamb was the only man in the history of popular music that ever was able to take the publishers. He had a line like a con man, and used it. He'd take a publisher out to lunch with advance money from a rival, and then tap his guest for $100. A lot of us often tried that, but Lamb got the money." It may have been because he had a happy way with lines. He wrote the lyrics of many successful songs: "A Bird in a Gilded Cage," "Mansion of Aching Hearts," "Splash Me," "The Bird on Nellie's Hat," and "Wait Till the Sun Shines, Nellie."

The success of "I Don't Want to Play in Your Yard" is a pronounced illustration of the inexplainable shifting of public tastes. It is a very simple song of childhood that was published in 1894. Its predecessor—that is, the "hit" song of 1893—was "Sweet Marie," a love song composed by Raymon Moore, a headline ballad singer of the '90s, to a better-than-average lyric.

It should have been; the lines were written by Cy Warman, popular author of railroad stories with authentic backgrounds ("Snow on the Headlight") and rated by contemporaries as high-class romantic fiction. Warman, Illinois born, was a sickly youth who early was required to remove to Colorado for his health. There he took up railroading, but became ill again and was forced to quit his job as a locomotive engineer with the Denver & Rio Grande for journalism. The *Chronicle*, of Creede, Colorado, a silver-mining town, gave him his first opportunity, and never regretted it. Like Eugene Field in Denver, Warman wrote verse for the *Chronicle*, and in 1892 he published a collection called *Mountain Melodies*. Thousands of copies of the slender volume were sold (many of them on trains), and Warman became known as "the bard of the Rockies." His fame spread to the East, and Charles A. Dana hired him for the New York *Sun*, for which he wrote numerous lyrics, among them "Sweet Marie." However, this does not appear to have been its first publication.

According to Geller, Warman was in the audience at a Denver performance (1893) of the George Thatcher Minstrels, with whom Raymon Moore was the star soloist. After the performance, Warman went to Moore's dressing room and showed him the lines he had written to his second wife, Myrtle Marie Jones, and asked Moore if they were not a suitable lyric for a song. Moore read them over and agreed. Some months later, Moore joined a musical called *Africa*, which had a college scene in the second act wherein Moore thought of home and his sweetheart. It was the setting for a song given to Moore which the singer considered no good, and he substituted his own "Sweet Marie" at the opening performance in the Euclid Opera House, Cleveland. It failed, and Thatcher, who had an interest in the show, ruled it out. Moore said he would quit if the ruling stood. It did, and Moore left the show in Pittsburgh—with some dejection, for the apathy of the Cleveland audience was also a blow at his reputation, which was immense.

The producers substituted Charles Hopper, who, naturally, learned of the reason for Moore's defection. He asked to see the song, liked it, rehearsed it secretly, and on the night of his first performance, while Thatcher and his co-producers, Rich and Harris, listening in the wings, writhed helplessly, sang it. This audience acclaimed it madly, and Hopper sang himself hoarse with encores. The song was made, and soon after swept the nation. A verse and chorus of

SWEET MARIE

I've a secret in my heart, sweet Marie,
A tale I would impart, love, to thee.
Ev'ry daisy in the dell
Knows my secret, knows it well—
And yet I dare not tell, sweet Marie.
When I hold your hand in mine, sweet Marie,
A feeling most divine comes to me.
All the world is full of spring,
Full of warblers on the wing,
And I listen while they sing, sweet Marie.

Chorus: Come to me, sweet Marie,
          Sweet Marie, come to me.
          Not because your face is fair, love, to see.
          But your soul, so pure and sweet
          Makes my happiness complete,
          Makes me falter at your feet, sweet Marie.

Rosenfeld, in his *Herald* column, says that Moore earned
$12,000 royalties on the song, which seems a modest estimate,
for its sales were heavy. As with other love songs, a bit mawkish
in sentiment, the parodists of the '90s dealt with this one too;
oddly, only with the chorus. Many of the parodies were saloon
obscenities. A few are printable:

> Sweet Marie, sweet Marie,
> She had fishhooks where her fingers ought to be.
> Every stud horse passing by,
> Seemed to know the reason why,
> When he winked his other eye,
> At sweet Marie.

> Sweet Marie, sweet Marie,
> When I think of what a sucker I used to be,
> For whenever I would call,
> A lot of sailors, short and tall,
> Used to jump the backyard wall
> At sweet Marie's.

> Sweet Marie, sweet Marie,
> You can tell her walk as far as you can see.
> She's so dainty and so neat,
> All the coppers on her beat
> Say, "Go work some other street,
> Sweet Marie."

Call them naughty-minded, but be fair and complete your
appraisal. They, these parodists, were critical stabilizers too—
the realists denied by Thomas Beer as an expression in the '90s.
Indisputable statistics would be difficult to assemble, but it is
a safe bet that more tarts walked the streets of our cities or
warrened up in evil hutches in the '90s than in any other decade
in our history. The Dr. Parkhurst-inspired Lexow investigation

proved it in relation to New York. There is a paradoxical denial of sex in nearly every heartthrob pop song; the lovers are so damnably pure they are heavenly wraiths. The parodists bring them down to earth. We have seen that not all of the '90s' expression was mush and treacle. Even in the sob-ballad period of the mid-'90s, Harris' heyday of tears, Gussie L. Davis, the Negro composer, was competing with realistic songs of life as it was (and still is). One of them, "Beyond Pardon, Beyond Recall," celebrates a wife as a rational adulteress, the story of a mother living in sin and liking it.

> A fond loving grandma with snowy white hair,
> Sits thinking of a daughter far away.
> A sweet little baby so thoughtless of care,
> Is on the floor by grandpa's knee at play.
> Deserted home and husband, the truth they soon must learn,
> The baby's mother bears another's name.
> The husband would forgive her if she would but return;
> For baby's sake he'd love her just the same.

Chorus: Gone beyond pardon, beyond recall,
> Left those that loved her the best of all.
> Lost all respect for the home she has wrecked;
> Beyond pardon, beyond recall.

Davis gets his moral in, but Ma is still bedding with her man.

Davis was an odd character. He was a composer of considerable versatility, and his talent was superior to most of the run of the pop-tune writers. He never drew full recognition, but he seems to have been the victim of inordinate shyness and modesty rather than of his color. The fact that Cole and Johnson and Williams and Walker were Negroes never jeopardized their success.

Davis had much imagination, milled everything he heard. His best known song, "In The Baggage Coach Ahead," derived from a story told him by a Pullman porter about a brat whose bawls annoyed the passengers in a sleeper. (Some say Davis was the porter and the experience his.)

Davis peddled it all over vainly until Howley and Haviland, with misgivings, finally agreed to publish it. Geller says that Davis sold it outright to them for its equivalent—a song—but Rosenfeld, in the *Herald*, who was in a position to know, says that Davis received $1,300 royalties for his "Baggage Coach" up to 1897, three years after it was published.

With Charles B. Ward, Davis wrote the music for the song "Picture 84," and it is another admirable illustration of how he profited by events and situations.

Ward, a short, plump, round-faced, good-natured lad, was a "newsboy" singer on the vaudeville circuits. He specialized in Bowery songs (he was largely responsible for the success of "My Pearl's a Bowery Girl," by Andrew Mack and William Jerome), which he delivered in agreeable coster style. While he was on tour in Boston, perhaps in the summer of 1894, when "Picture 84" was published, police authorities took Ward and a girl companion on an inspection of their criminal laboratory and departments of crime. They visited the rogues' gallery, and at Picture 84 the girl collapsed, told Ward it was her father. Ward related the incident to Davis, who immediately saw its value as a dramatic ballad, and the pair wrote the song: Ward the words, Davis the melody. A verse and chorus:

> On a pleasant day in summer at the Central Station door,
> Stopped a carriage with a couple, out sight-seeing, nothing more,
> And the gray-haired Superintendent kindly showed them through the place,
> First of all the great Rogue's Gall'ry, where they gazed on many a face.
> Characters of all descriptions—some were famous men of crime,
> Some were dead and some at freedom, some of them were serving time.
> Some had stories interesting, as the man explained them o'er,
> But the woman fainted when she gazed on picture eighty-four.

Chorus: 'Twas the picture of her father, there among the men of
       crimes,
       Though now a man of honor, but this tells of other times.
       Now he lives in style and splendor, worth a million now
       or more,
       Still his picture's in the gall'ry, picture eighty-four.

       "Listen, I will tell you the story," said the Superintendent
       then,
       "Though that picture's of your father, we have pictures
       of worse men.
       Men whose conscience knows no limit, would do anything
       for gold,
       Men with lives they do not value, child, the half has not
       been told.
       Once your father was a forger, forged a check which
       brought him shame.
       Though this gall'ry holds his picture, 'tis known by an-
       other name.
       You were not born when this happened, it was many years
       ago.
       And the world is none the wiser, still it's picture eighty-
       four."

Davis also wrote the music for one of the sobbiest tear jerkers
in our entire portfolio of pop tunes—"The Fatal Wedding."
Despite its wretched lyric, it was a successful song, probably
because of Davis' agreeable and unforced waltz melody. W. H.
Windom, who wrote the words, dedicated the song to the
Utica, N. Y., *Tribune,* a dubious honor that amounts to defiance.

It even dismayed the parodists. George F. McCann wrote
one, and so did Charles H. McIntosh, and they are almost as
bad as the original. The boys just couldn't top it. Indeed, the
lyric is something of a "sport" in the '90s' garden of song. Most
ballads are grave in essence, deal with broken hearts and sudden
death, and the writers of the decade adhered to the pattern.
Some of them were pretty awful (recall some of Harris' violent
lines), but Windom's doggerel stands alone for ineptness and
implausibility. Davis could have done a better job—did, in his
"Baggage Coach" and "Beyond Pardon"—both of which are

superior even to Ward's lines for "Picture 84." And although the tunes he left that are remembered are settings for doleful ballads, he could turn out a comic song, sometimes neatly ironic, as in his "Get on Your Sneak Shoes, Children," a catchy melody for which Davis wrote good lines.

> A dark night, a nigger and a chicken,
> You can bet that they are mighty close friends;
> When times are hard and poultry's high,
> And a nigger can't meet his ends.
> When he feels like he's been hoodooed,
> And business with him is slack,
> Just give him a basket with a covered top,
> And a chicken he'll bring back.

> *Chorus:* Get on your sneak shoes, children,
> Now listen to what I say:
> Don't disgrace the colored race,
> Do not go astray.
> Get on your sneak shoes, children,
> Now's the time to make your mark.
> Don't come yellow but come the right color,
> But for goodness sake don't come dark.

Will H. Fox, a popular comic pianist with an immense amount of skepticism, oddly enough wrote a tear jerker that was one of the great successes of the mid-'90s—"The Broken Home." Like Davis' "Beyond Pardon," the theme of "Broken Home" was the errant wife, and Fox being worldly, she stayed errant. The lines are rather good.

THE BROKEN HOME

> The church bells they were ringing,
> The choir was sweetly singing,
> In a far New England village
> Just two short years ago.
> The flowers they were blooming,
> The birds in tree-tops tuning,
> Two hearts had been united—
> Fair Lillian and Joe.

The husband he toiled daily,
And happy was their lot.
He loved his wife and baby,
His vows he ne'er forgot.
One day a former sweetheart
Came and, finding him away,
Through flattery and promises
Joe's wife was led astray.

Chorus: There's her picture on the table,
There's a baby in the cradle,
There's a husband crying bitterly alone.
There's no wife's voice to cheer,
In his sorrow to be near,
What was paradise is now a broken home.

His eyes are dim with weeping,
Yet faithful watch he's keeping
O'er his precious little treasure
For whom his heart does moan.
Forgetting all dishonor
Which she had brought upon her;
For baby's sake he'd gladly
Forgive if she'd come home.
Oh, why do people falter,
And lose all self-respect
For vows made at the altar
And make their lives a wreck?
These questions Joe has asked himself
With heart as heavy as lead—
When baby's smile prevents him
Being numbered with the dead.

The success of this song must have amazed even Fox, a curious fellow, whose slant on life was truly Horatian. Fox began as a café piano player in Providence, Rhode Island. He ribbed the piano, the job, himself, the café, and the customers with satirical slings and arrows, a sort of Jack White patter that actually kidded him into vaudeville with a headline specialty he called "Paddy Whiski," a billing that jibed the famous Polish concert pianist, Paderewski, then approaching the zenith of his popularity.

Fox made up in an enormous yellow wig. It was a foot in height and stood out in all directions. He wore a woman's shirtwaist, baggy black pants, one rubber boot with the price tag dangling from it, and one low shoe with a white sock showing. While going through the mockery of tuning his piano he'd strike with a hammer a large iron horse pinned to his shirt front. He was an excellent pianist, performing his trick and burlesque playing with a deceptive skill experts recognized and admired. Throughout his act he kept up a running fire of whimsical chatter, tossing out an occasional barb at himself, the theater, the audience, his instrument, the management, or a late-comer. For a number of years he was a novelty nut comedy act unrivaled in the American theater.

About the time of the Spanish-American War, Fox went to London, and on his first appearance tossed Webster's definition of the word "sensation" (a vivid emotion or experience attended by excitement) completely out of the dictionary. To his successive London music-hall audiences he was virtually the end of the world. Fox was the first music-hall performer ever to be advertised on the busses, a distinction hitherto only accorded Guinness' Stout, Wood Vestas, and Bovril. Banners announcing Will H. Fox as "Paddy Whiski" extended the full length of the busses, and on both sides of each bus. The populace gasped but vowed him the honor. We Americans, who are constantly prodded and nagged and drugged and scared by advertising, will attach little importance to Fox's exploitation and its acceptance. But its comparable use in New York would be the display of a burlesque poster of a well-organized blonde complete with G-string in the Cathedral of St. John the Divine.

Fox returned to America for a round of the vaudevilles, finished his tour, and went back to London to stay. When he was well along in years he married a very young non-professional English girl of the draper's apprentice type. Although the disparity of ages was marked, she seemed well satisfied with her bargain. Fox always said, "She was grateful and easily pleased." The couple lived in what the lodging house keepers optimistically called a "combined apartment," meaning the bedroom, living room, and dining room were all one room of ordinary size and that a toilet in another part of the house was available—sometimes. No one ever got Fox's explanation for this mode of life. He had made a lot of money and was no spendthrift. His friends considered him wealthy.

Before Fox went to England, he wrote a number of songs with Edward B. Marks, and one of them, "Break the News to Mother Gently," Fox sang with success. It was published by Frank Harding, whose Bowery shop, inherited from his uncle, E. H. Harding, adjoined the London Theater.

Fox and Marks also wrote "When McManus Went Down to the Track," a comic song they adjusted to the special talent of Polly Holmes. But Marks's best known song was "The Little Lost Child, or the Passing Policeman," which he wrote to the music of Joseph W. Stern, his partner. It was a sobber, probably would have blubbered out except for an idea of Marks that was to light up the times for ten years. "Little Lost Child" was the first of the illustrated slide songs.

Marks and Stern, in a handshaking partnership, formed the house of Jos. W. Stern & Co. and published the song in 1894. Then Marks asked George Primrose, of the Primrose and West Minstrels, to permit Allan May, a minstrel tenor, to sing it to illustrations. Primrose was indifferent, but West was emphatically opposed; said such monkey business didn't belong in a minstrel show.

Marks persisted and eventually gained grudging consent to put it on at a Wednesday matinee in the Grand Opera House, Eighth Avenue and Twenty-third Street, New York. The slides had been made from photographs by George H. Thomas, a competent photographer when working with a Niagara Falls backdrop, but who in this new medium felt like an explorer in paleozoic Hollywood. The original shots were authentic enough. The brazen Marks brought Thomas out to the Lee Avenue, Brooklyn, police station, and with the cajolery characteristic of all publishers induced a real cop to pose with as actual an urchin in the setting of a bona fide precinct house.

Thomas also did a pretty good job of transferring his negatives to slides. So Marks, elated at the chance and feeling sure it would go over, waited for that Wednesday afternoon, which came soon enough. At the olio, Allan May stepped out on stage as Thomas took his post in the balcony at the sputtering stereopticon machine. Now Jim Fisk, you may recall, bought the Grand Opera House, and the Admiral of the Fall River and Bristol Lines always did everything in spades, doubled, with technicolor. His Grand Opera House had two of everything and was twice as big.

Thomas, whose projection technique naturally was faulty through inexperience, flashed his first slide. It pictured a policeman fifteen feet tall standing on his head, and West, incensed, chased Thomas and Marks out of the theater. Surreptitiously, Marks rehearsed Thomas, who finally got the knack, and with Primrose's aid he got West to consent to one more performance at the Saturday matinee. It not only stopped the show—it started exploitation that sold more than a million copies of "Little Lost Child" and influenced others to make slide songs, among them Joe Howard, who illustrated Marks's song, "My Mother Was a Lady."

The Marks-Stern Company was an influential house, published many old-time hits, including Cole and Johnson's, "Under the Bamboo Tree." Marks, by the way, although recognizing its worth as a song, held up its publication until Cole and Johnson agreed to change its original title, "If You Laka Me." Marks argued the title didn't mean anything. The Jos. W. Stern Co. also published Paul Linke's "Glow-Worm" which was introduced in Lew Fields's *The Girl Behind the Counter*. The musical was a hit, but Marks told Fields the day after the opening that there was a bald spot in it. "You've got a nice summer scene in it with May Naudain doing nothing. Why don't you give her the 'Glow-Worm'?" "How much will you give me to put it in?" countered Fields. "Not a nickel," said Marks, "but if the song flops, I'll pay you $1,000." "Take him up," said Fields's company manager. It was the song hit of the show.

Years earlier, Jim Thornton, whom we shall have business with in the following chapter, sold Marks "When You Were Sweet Sixteen," forgot about it, and months later sold it to Witmark, who brought it out. It was a hit directly it was published, but Marks was heedless until one evening he heard someone sing the refrain,

> I love you as I never loved before,
> Since first I met you on the village green . . .[2]

Then he telephoned Witmark.

"I got the song in my safe and my common-law right is even greater than the copyright," said Marks. Witmark said go ahead and sue, but it never came to trial. Witmark settled for $5,000, and Marks sent him a photograph of the check.

For "Two Little Girls in Blue," which is still juke boxed in the bars and grills across America, Charles Graham, who wrote the words and music, received $10. The song may well have been inspired by Charles K. Harris' "After the Ball": the theme is the same; indeed, the first four bars of the chorus are a thin variant of the Harris song. Nobody paid any attention to that, the public just bought and bought and the money rolled in to Spaulding and Gray and the rival house of Witmark writhed.

The two little girls were sisters whose husbands were brothers, "But we have drifted apart," sings the narrator in the unhappy song. Because, as it is oddly explained in the verse, he "thought her unfaithful." Perhaps it was wish fulfillment, but whatever the reason, it is an unusual twist in the '90s' ballads, which, for all their crepe, were pretty specific about the immoralities and misfortunes of their characters. The uncle in Harris' "After the Ball" relates his sad story to a niece. Graham also used an uncle narrator, but his listener is a nephew.

[2]Copyright, 1898, by M. Witmark & Sons. Copyright renewed by James Thornton. Used by permission of Shapiro, Bernstein & Co., Inc.

The song also confused Witmark for another reason. Graham had been their writer, they thanked God, for one of his earlier songs virtually established them financially in the music-publishing business. It was "The Picture That Is Turned Toward the Wall," which cost them exactly $15. That Graham offered his "Two Little Girls in Blue" to Spaulding and Gray for $5.00 less only heightened his apparent "ingratitude" to his first publishers.

"The Picture That Is Turned Toward the Wall" derived from Joe Arthur's play, *Blue Jeans*, a well-known never-darken-my-door-again meller of the '90s about a farmer who, when his daughter ran away from home, turned her picture toward the wall. After Graham saw the play, he wrote his song.

> Far beyond the glamour of the city and its strife,
> There's a quiet little homestead by the sea,
> Where a tender, loving lassie used to live a happy life,
> Contented in her home as she could be.
> Not a shadow ever seemed to cloud the sunshine of her
>   youth,
> And they thought no sorrow could her life befall.
> But she left them all one evening and their sad hearts knew
>   the truth,
> When her father turned her picture toward the wall.

Chorus: There's a name that's never spoken,
> And a mother's heart is broken,
> There is just another missing from the old home, that is
>   all.
> There is still a memory living,
> There's a father unforgiving,
> And a picture that is turned toward the wall.

The song sold almost countless copies. Graham died in Bellevue Hospital, New York, in 1899, a pauper. Two years later police arrested a ten-year-old boy in front of the New York Produce Exchange. He was singing "Two Little Girls in Blue," "My Dad's the Engineer," and "The Picture That Is Turned Toward the Wall" for throw money. He said his name was Howard Graham, that the songs were written by his dead father, and that his mother, Mrs. Alice Graham, had sent him out to beg.

When the lad was arraigned before Magistrate Brann in Centre Street police court, Mrs. Graham, an office-building scrub woman, told the Court she had not sent her son out to beg. But she said she had three other children, that she was virtually penniless and could support the child only with the greatest difficulty. She asked that he be placed in an institution, and Magistrate Brann agreed to send him to the Catholic Protectory.

Thus Graham's life, and the fortunes of his family, closed on as tragic a note as ever he had gotten into his songs. It is a doleful, cello tone upon which to end the happy decade whose discussion is now concluded. We have traced its frivolity, found its other melodies gay as its girls' lace drawers. Nor were its sob ballads anachronistic. We are a three-handkerchief nation.

THE SOUND AND THE FURY—JUKE BOX, JAZZ, SWING, AND BOOGIE-WOOGIE

THE GIRLS DIDN'T GIVE IT AWAY!

THE TWENTIETH CENTURY! It was a miraculous phrase to char-
acterize that New Year midnight in 1900, and the nation hailed
it with wild acclaim. The phrase became first a slogan, signify-
ing awakening and advance, then a motto. Here was the beginning of man's inventive triumph over nature. It was, said the
pundits, the new era of modern things, of modern thought, for
modern men whose scales, as if by some calendrical magic,
had dropped from their eyes. Joyously they mated man with
what they called his true handmaiden—Science—then a shy lass
whose maiden blush and gentle mien concealed the snake in
her brain. We would go forward from this laboratory marriage
to new goals, easing our labor the while, comforting our lives,
making more glorious our achievements. We know now what
a tragic *mésalliance* it was. The issue of that union was Franken-
stein. At Kitty Hawk, North Carolina, on December 17, 1903,
Orville and Victor Wright conquered the laws of gravity, and
the world soared with them to new heights. Other men of
genius labored with them through the years to perfect the airplane—and an ape has got hold of it. Science, says Professor
Joad, has shown us the way to a better life, but it has not taught
us how to live.

In 1900 his words would have drawn scornful laughter.
Those seeking escape from this miserable world can do no better
than look backward to those times. They were happy, but the
gaiety, unlike the '90s, was not feminine. We were conquerors.
It was the joy of possession, of wealth, of industrial advance, of
empire building. The period from 1900 to the first World War

was a great sprawling era, geyserish in effort, fulsome in tone, hilarious and jerky. The growing pains of our people were fostered by an imperialism inspired by our victory over Spain, the acquisition of the Philippines, and our avuncular interest in Cuba.

The decade was a paradise for con men, quacks, and gold-brick peddlers. Many a sucker let go a dollar for that "steel engraving of George Washington," receiving by return mail a United States postage stamp. It was precisely the era of the "city slicker." Oh, it got into the songs all right, sometimes in unusual manifestations, curious variants, displaying a sophistication and morality often metallic, and largely engendered by the metropolitan press. Paul West put it neatly to a song by John W. Bratton that was published by Witmark in 1902.

SHE READS THE NEW YORK PAPERS EV'RY DAY

> Once there lived a farmer's daughter down in old Con-
> necticut,
> Where they get the New York papers ev'ry day.
> She was shy, and oh, so tender, unsophisticated, but
> She read the New York papers ev'ry day.
> She had never dined on lobsters or had tasted of cham-
> pagne,
> She'd never smoked a cigarette nor ridden on a train,
> But those who tried to fool her found their labors all in
> vain,
> For she read the New York papers ev'ry day.

> *Chorus:* Down in the meadows fair where the lambkins play,
> There's many a maid with a golden braid,
> Who rakes the new mown hay.
> But you'd best beware what you do or say,
> She may look quite green, but she's not, I ween,
> She reads the New York papers ev'ry day.

> Her papa took summer boarders and she entertained them
> well,
> Reading from the New York papers ev'ry day.
> All the latest city scandal she could always, always tell,
> She read the New York papers ev'ry day.

But a rich young chap one summer came, she led him on
  to woo,
And when he popped the question she'd a phonograph
  there, too,
Her daddy made him wed her, so she didn't have to sue,
For she read the New York papers ev'ry day.

Their wedding was a marvel and they lived in style, of
  course,
For she read the New York papers ev'ry day.
But her hubby was a rounder so she sued him for divorce,
She read the New York papers ev'ry day.
Then she took her alimony and she off to Europe flew,
She captivated dukes and earls and even princes, too,
But she didn't let them marry her, too much for that she
  knew,
For she read the New York papers ev'ry day.

Ev'ry paper printed stories of the way she carried on,
And the people read the papers ev'ry day.
She soon came back very famous, tho' unknown where she
  had gone;
Her name was in the papers ev'ry day.
She is now a prima-donna on the comic opera stage.
Her jewels look like headlights, and her gowns are all
  the rage.
And if you want to know her name, just look on any page
Of most any New York paper any day.[1]

Satire was the dominating note of the songs of the early
1900s. The demise of the dismal ballads had not yet come, but
they were getting delightfully fewer. In the Sunday issue of the
New York *Herald*, January 20, 1907, under the heading "Popular Songs Less Pathetic This Year . . ." an anonymous writer
observed that there is "not a single 'mother' or 'father' song"
being published and "a more cynical or humorous tone now
prevails."

It prevailed earlier than 1907. In 1900, Charles Klein and

[1]Copyright, 1902, by M. Witmark & Sons. Copyright renewed. Used by permission.

Grant Stewart to the music of W. T. Francis were caroling
of the fall and ruin of

THE DAUGHTERS OF A MINISTER

A clergyman who lives in a little country spot,
And has brought his daughters up in retirement;
Is not supposed to teach his children what is what,
And a child unburnt could never know what fire meant.
Therefore, when those daughters come up to the city
Too innocent to know what they're about;
If a man should write them, surely he would pity
Two girls whose mother doesn't know they're out.

Chorus: It shouldn't take so very much to urge a man
To be kind to the daughters of a clergyman.
No scoundrel ought to fasten
On the daughters of a parson,
And a man should never have a motive sinister
When he's talking to the daughters of a minister.

Then the Messrs. Klein and Stewart have the girls (with
tongue in cheek) relate their case histories:

Our father was a minister, as you can see,
And brought us up so innocently,
That when you first encountered us in gay Paree,
You should have known enough to treat us gently.
You should not have let us think champagne was cider,
And cautioned us 'gainst smoking cigarettes.
We were not fly, and yet you played the spider,
To two confiding, trusting little pets.

So innocent were we that we really did not know
At all how many beans made five.
Or the difference 'twixt a circus and a poultry show;
We almost were too good to be alive.
It was you who have destroyed each fond illusion,
Who taught us that our goodness was a frost.
And we've mutually arrived at the conclusion,
You must pay for the innocence we've lost.

The girls collected, too, as the tag refrain indicates:

Second   It shouldn't take so very much to urge a man,
Chorus: To make good to the daughters of a clergyman.
      If through you scandals fasten
      On the daughters of a parson,
      Why financial consolation you'll administer,
      P.D.Q. to the daughters of a minister.[2]

Some of the early 1900 pop songs were actually sacrilegious. John W. West wrote a lyric for a coon song in 1900 whose theme was a crap game in church:

MR. JOHNSON, YOU'RE KNOCKING YOUR OWN GAME

    Mister Johnson went to church last Sunday morning,
    And right beside him sat a gambling man.
    And not to give the congregation warning,
    Began to shoot craps while they pealed a psalm.
    But that cute old parson heard them bones a-rolling,
    So he just stopped that singing right away.
    He was awful mad, yelled right out loud,
    Said, "There's gambling going on in this crowd.
    I will mention no one's name!" Then he did say:

Chorus: "Mister Johnson, you are knocking your own game,
    "To gamble here you ought to be ashamed.
    "Now you might think it's fun, perhaps,
    "But church is no place to shoot craps,
    "Wait till after service, I'll join in the game."

The 1900s offer an interesting setting—socially, politically, industrially. Many of America's great fortunes were on the make or already made, and soon we were to hear the cry of the Oyster Bay Roosevelt—"Malefactors of great wealth"—which, in our time, the Hyde Park Roosevelt translated more tersely and colloquially as, "Soak the rich."

At the turn of the century, dudes became the counterpart of the dandies of the '90s—loud-vest sports in paddock overcoats, peg-top trousers, wide-flanged buttoned shoes of horrendous yellows, and "iron" collars of the type worn by the

[2]Copyright, 1900, by M. Witmark & Sons. Copyright renewed. Used by permission.

late Dan Frohman. Seasonal hats were a weighty derby or an enormous straw called a "Katy," which was battened against the wind by a silken cord affixed to the lapel of the coat—a fastening called a "trolley."

The pompadour of the Gibson girl was a synthetic creation fashioned over a wad of hair or roll of wire called a "rat." The ladies unleashed, too, their bustles of the '90s, and rumps appeared as is. In New York, Siegel-Cooper's ("Meet Me at the Fountain") was advertising corsets "reinforced to prevent bone and steel from cutting." Full bosoms were *de rigueur* . . . "The Bust Beautiful," reads a New York *Herald* personal of the times: "Our method of treatment is rational and healthful. Endorsed by the medical profession." Mechanical aids—bust forms—were available for unresponding patients. Fortunes were made in nostrums and panaceas. Widely in many prints, "Old Dr. Grindle" and "Old Dr. Gray" exploited their fakery in the treatment of the now-mentionable (and happily lessening) diseases of syphilis and gonorrhea—"advice free."

A great national consciousness was developing, influencing considerably the social expression, probably because political confidence was so great. With Teddy in the White House and Bill Taft, the trouble shooter, always with luggage packed to straighten out a tangle in Panama, the Philippines, or Rome, "people," as Mark Sullivan says in the third volume of *Our Times*, "felt all was well." Given two men and a potbellied stove, and politics is an inevitable discussion. Still, people of the 1900s found another topic—themselves. So, around the cracker barrels of America, in town bars and hotel lobbies, the talk was of labor (the Government in 1901 decreed an eight-hour day for Federal workers), of the Equitable Life Assurance Society's policyholders, of the National and American League ball teams and the new "World Series" launched in Pittsburgh between that city's National League team and the Boston Americans in 1903. (Boston won.)

They talked about the open-work stockings and the peekaboo shirtwaists the girls were wearing, about that feeble-minded man in Los Angeles, one Thomas J. Tally, who had opened, in 1902, a theater for motion pictures only. Five years later there were 400 nickelodeons in America. They talked about the Cherry Sisters, the freak act in vaudeville, so dreadful they were a box-office draw because people came to hoot. They talked about the Pan American Exposition in Buffalo in 1901 and stormed and raged at a Polish dupe named Leon Czolgosz, who, on September 6, 1901, proffering a handkerchief-covered hand to William McKinley, blazed a bullet into the President's abdomen of which he died eight days later.

They talked about the sheath gowns favored by women with sleek flanks in 1908, about the Henry C. Frick Co., a United States Steel subsidiary, which the same year forbade drinking by its employees on or off the premises. They talked about Harry K. Thaw, who in 1906 shot and killed Stanford White, America's best-known architect, on the roof of Madison Square Garden during a performance of *Mlle. Champagne,* to "avenge" the soiled affections of a girl named Evelyn Nesbit. They talked about "parlor socialism," which Woodrow Wilson, then president of Princeton University (1906) attributed to the use of the automobile, of which 25,000 had been manufactured the previous year. In truth, class lines were slowly vanishing as wealth obliterated birthright, and Berry Wall, the tailor-made fop, stalked the boulevards and kept his society rendezvous, a scented symbol even then of a moribund aristocracy that was to die in the democratic speakeasy gas chambers of the 1920s.

These were fecund days, the 1900s, for the popular-music publishers. New houses sprang up, older companies consolidated for expansion, and most of them holed up in the brownstone-front warrens of Twenty-eighth Street between Broadway and Sixth Avenue, where the pounding of myriad pianos led to the sobriquet—Tin Pan Alley—bestowed by some unknown dubber.

A curious phase of the early 1900s' songs is that they were social rather than topical. It sounds like a paradox, but the distinction is clear when the songs are examined. Their sentiment was intimate and personal, and the touch was not too maudlin. "Absence Makes the Heart Grow Fonder," for example, "Any Old Place I Can Hang My Hat Is Home Sweet Home To Me," "Go Way Back and Sit Down," "In the Good Old Summer Time," "Under the Bamboo Tree," "Ida! Sweet as Apple Cider," "Sweet Adeline," "Good-bye My Lady Love," "All In Down and Out," "Cheyenne," "Chinatown, My Chinatown," "I Just Can't Make My Eyes Behave," "I'd Rather Be a Lobster than a Wise Guy," "School Days," "Take Me Back to New York Town," "Down in Jungle Town," "Daisies Won't Tell," "Shine on Harvest Moon," "Take Me Out to the Ball Game," "Sunbonnet Sue," "Has Anybody Here Seen Kelly?" "I Wonder Who's Kissing Her Now," "Meet Me Tonight in Dreamland," "Let Me Call You Sweetheart" . . . That is a random, yet representative, selection of the songs most widely circulated in the period we are discussing. Some of the songs are critical in essence, but there are few specific references to scandals of the times, to politics (except for Tammany, of course), to the panic of 1907, the "Psyche-knot" hair-do of the girls in 1908, the principal crackpots, like John Alexander Dowie, or the insurance exposé by Charles Evans Hughes.

The writer has been unable to find a single song characterizing or relating to the Francophile, James Hazen Hyde, who sold his controlling interest in the Equitable Life Assurance Society (502 shares) to Thomas Fortune Ryan for $2,500,000 and then stole off to Paris, where he remained *ex patria* until the war returned him to America. The boys of the '70s and '90s, who had so much fun with Henry Ward Beecher, Jim Fisk, and the Reverend Dr. Parkhurst, would have had a wonderful time with Hyde. With Charles Evans Hughes too. Charles the Baptist Hughes, as he was called after his investigation of the insurance frauds. How they would have leaped upon his sobriquet for a song title! The scandals and corruption in high places unearthed by Hughes and championed by the crusading New York *World* of Joseph Pulitzer which would have provoked ballad upon ballad in tavern times went unsung in the 1900s.

The probable reason was the cleanup of vaudeville. Tony Pastor would permit no indecent or indelicate expressions, no ill-natured jibes at public figures in his Fourteenth Street house. Subsequently, B. F. Keith similarly censored performers' material and songs on the huge Keith and Orpheum circuits. A troubadour of the 1900s, daring enough to present a song of the comparable vigor of "Sons of Beecher-o," would have been banned from the theater.

Chicago was so sensitive its censorship was silly. For *The Burgomaster*, a musical by Gustave Luders (who composed the splendid score of the *Prince of Pilsen*), George Rollit, to the music of Howard Talbot, wrote a smart lyric called "Everybody Wondered How He Knew":

> There are often little trifles that were better left unsaid,
> But are uttered in an unaffected way.
> Which reminds me of a funny little matter which occurred,
> At a fashionable ball the other day.
> The host espied a silk-embroidered garter on the floor,
> And gaily dared the owner to declare;
> When a jolly-looking fellow said without the least concern—
> "Oh, I know it, it belongs to Mrs. Dare!"

> *Chorus:* Now wasn't that a silly thing to say?
> Wasn't it a silly thing to do?
> It came as quite a starter
> When he recognized the garter
> For everybody wondered how he knew.
> Now wasn't that a silly thing to say?
> Wasn't it a silly thing to do?
> But they didn't hear till later
> That she got it from his mater,
> So everybody wondered how he knew.

> Folks were gazing at the very latest painting at a sale,
> Labeled "Beauty Unadorned" upon the list.
> When a gentleman remarked to several others standing by,
> "It's not true, such perfect beauty can't exist."

"Excuse me, sir," a gentleman remarked,
"But you are wrong, and if you like I'll bet a case of fizz,
That this painting here before you is exactly true to life
And represents the girl just as she is!"

Chorus: Now wasn't that a silly thing to say?
Wasn't it a silly thing to do?
The ladies blushed and wriggled
And the men turned round and giggled,
For everybody wondered how he knew.
Yet nothing could be quainter,
You see, he was the painter,
Yet everybody wondered how he knew.

Chicago authorities suppressed the song. And in a date-line story amusingly captioned "Wasn't It a Silly Thing to Do?" the New York *Herald*, July 7, 1900, thus recorded the incident:

Chicago, Ill., Tues.—Everyone in town liked the song hit of the Burgomaster. Everybody Wondered How He Knew. Everybody is wondering what happened to it, for it is no more to be heard at the Dearborn theater. City officials must have suddenly gotten shocked. Since its suppression everybody sings the song everywhere, wondering why it shocked.

Thus the effect of censorship and prohibition was again exemplified.

About 1905, the publication of popular songs became a vast expression, and many houses made much money. Although the industry remained unorganized until 1916, with the formation of the Music Publishers Protective Association, there were stabilizing influences. The public response virtually guaranteed the financial success of a good song. In 1905, for example, there were forty-three successful songs, including "In the Shade of the Old Apple Tree," "My Gal Sal," Bert Williams' outstanding comedy song, "Nobody," "Wait Till the Sun Shines Nellie," James J. Walker's "Will You Love Me in December as You Do in May?" (to Ernest R. Ball's music), Clare Kummer's "Dearie," and Vincent Bryan's "Tammany" (to the music of

Gus Edwards). In 1906 there were thirty-six successful or "hit" tunes; the year after, forty-two. In the first decade of the twentieth century two songs were published whose sales can actually be called phenomenal. They were "Meet Me Tonight in Dreamland" (1909) and "Let Me Call You Sweetheart" (1910). Both sold nearly 5,000,000 copies each.

The competition of those two songs was interesting. Will Rossiter, the Chicago publisher who never paid royalties but bought his songs outright, brought out "Meet Me Tonight in Dreamland." The music was composed by Leo Friedman (who is understood to have been well paid) to a lyric by Beth Slater Whitson. Sales were moving along rapidly the first year when Harold Rossiter, an associate of his brother, quit the firm in 1910 to establish a rival house of his own. The first song he published was "Let Me Call You Sweetheart," written by the creators of "Meet Me Tonight in Dreamland."

Will Rossiter published Jim Thornton's song, "She Never Saw the Streets of Cairo," a rib of Little Egypt, the Midway dancer at the Chicago World's Fair in 1893 who wriggled herself into a sensation as the nation's naughtiest girl. Years later someone casually remarked that Rossiter reproduced her photograph on the first copies, which he supposedly recalled for destruction, fearing legal action by the dancer. There is not one word of truth in the story. But it persists, and there is still, today, a standing offer of $500 for the pictured Little Egypt on the copy of the "Streets of Cairo."

The sales of the brothers Rossiter's two hit songs were a barometer of the boom in the industry. The public's singing appetite was seemingly insatiable, and the total sales of all houses achieved astronomical figures. Indeed, the pop-tune counters were those most patronized. Shrewd publishers of operetta scores with individual numbers accepted as only so-so by audiences immediately reissued these songs in pop-tune format and exploited them in that medium.

Victor Herbert's "Gypsy Love Song," which was not in the

original score of *The Fortune Teller*, was marketed in this manner. Herbert had written it on the demand of Eugene Cowles that he be given a solo in the last act. But the talent of the great melodious composer thwarted the aim of the talented basso. Herbert added so charming an obbligato, and Alice Nielson sang it with such beauty, the audience thought Cowles was a piece of scenery.

But it was high-class for mass reception, and, realizing the value of the solo tune, Witmark republished it as a pop song and plugged it in vaudeville, cafés, honky-tonks, and singing-waiter joints, with the result, Jay Witmark says, that it sold 2,000,000 copies. The firm similarly exploited "Ah, Sweet Mystery of Life," ultimately making more money with that tune than with the hit song of *Naughty Marietta*, which was "I'm Falling in Love with Some One."

The industry was growing up. Its practitioners became self-critical, and it learned to take a generous amount of jibes from the press and pulpit (the ministers were continually scotching the pop songs as sinful in the early 1900s; families that gathered round the piano to sing "Just Because She Made Dem Goo-Goo Eyes" or "Bedelia" on Sundays were hell-bent), and from that same public that supported it so handsomely.

"The materialistic or dollar-getting spirit of the hour demands so much time and attention," lamented the New York *Herald*, January 26, 1902, "that no opportunity is afforded for the cultivation of serious thoughts in musical expression." This was the prelude to an article excoriating coon songs and ragtime "for getting more attention than they deserve." But the nation kept buying and singing, and the publishers just laughed.

They all sang, as Ed Marks so aptly titled his reminiscences. And the *Herald*, with petulant whimsy, editorially admitted it, August 1, 1907. It seems Isidor Witmark had told a European correspondent of the *Herald* of a new combination which would cut popular-song prices from fifty cents to one cent. Music publishers just do not think that way, and it is probable Witmark had something else on his mind. Nothing happened, of course. But the cabled interview gave the *Herald's* editorial writer pause, and he emerged with:

THAT DRAWING ROOM TERROR, THE AMATEUR VOCALIST

Among the many chats with Americans in Europe, published in the Herald's special cables this morning, is one with Mr. Isidor Witmark, a New York music publisher, which will fill this heretofore happy country with dismay and cause numerous urban residents to take to the woods.

Remembering all that that drawing room terror, the amateur vocalist, can at a present outlay of fifty cents inflict upon a company unable to escape, does Mr. Witmark realize what he is doing in providing him or her with fifty songs for fifty cents?

If Mr. Witmark desires that future generations shall see his figure in bronze in Central Park, placed there by a grateful country, he will think again and form a combination by which no singing amateur can possibly purchase any song whatsoever for less than $117.50; no more than one copy sold on any street, and no discount "to the trade." Then possibly we shall have something like peace in the land.

A year earlier, Vincent Bryan, a most successful Tin Pan Alley minnesinger, the lyricist of "Tammany," "Down Where the Würzburger Flows," "It Was the Dutch," etc., blistered his own profession in a *Herald* interview, January 7, 1906. In a statement astonishing for its frankness, Bryan told the *Herald*, "Filching tunes is the only thing that counts in the song writing business."

"There are no new popular melodies, ever," said Bryan. "If they are new they will not be popular. Songs we whistle today are variations of the ones we whistled yesterday. Musicianly songs are overlooked while inferior melodies are heard all over the place. Why? Because we are a quick lunch nation. We discourage originality in music because we are too busy to learn songs which have an unfamiliar air. Old songs are like old shoes —comfortable.

"All you need to compose a song that will sell is a good

memory. I'm a Yankee Doodle Dandy, sung by George M. Cohan in Little Johnny Jones, is a variation of the same tune used in Violets. Blue Bell comes from Nearer My God to Thee [which Rosenfeld in turn asserted was stolen from Thomas Moore's, "Oft in the Stilly Night"]. My own song, G.O.P., was adapted from John Brown's Body, and Right in This Old Town is a derivation of In the Good Old Summertime.

"Nor are our best poets our lyric writers. They can't reduce themselves to the commonplace level and phrases and the limited imagery which are necessary for a song to be popular with commonplace people. Edgar Allan Poe's Annabelle Lee was changed by a writer to fit a pop tune, a writer, incidentally, who became a bartender in Harlem."

This is plain talk. But the Jeremiad against the pop tune was delivered by Herbert H. Taylor, a topical verse writer and compiler of *Taylor's Popular Recitations*, which bears the 1903 copyright of Will Rossiter. Taylor put his invective in rhyme—lines incredibly bold for their insulting racial allusions. Here is Taylor's

THE POPULAR SONG

If you want a receipt for that popular mystery
Known to the world as a popular song,
Take a fake story from newspaper history,
Get a soubrette to help push it along.

Never write sense, if you do you will rue it,
For no one will learn it or sing it for long.
Every bum actor will always go through it,
For he is the one who is making the song.

Never write words one could call clever,
For audiences never expect such a thing.
Then let 'em screech 'em for ever and ever,
For who the —— hears what the chorus girls sing?

Let 'em have goblets, pretend to pour wine in 'em,
Then let 'em sing anything they durn please.
Dress 'em in tights, if they only look fine in 'em,
People will then think of nothing but these.

As for the music, you'll manage that easily;
Get a few songs that were written before.
Swipe 'em and change 'em and have 'em sung breezily;
Get an arranger, you'll want nothing more.

A Sheeny to publish your song is superior,
He'll force himself where a white man will duck.
No thin cuticle mars a Hebrew's exterior,
He's got the nerve and the devil's own luck.

So take my advice, throw your paper and ink away
If a big hit for next season you'd write.
Don't be afraid or endeavor to slink away,
Bow in response to your call the first night.

Though musicians may sneer at your work and pooh-pooh it all,
You needn't mind—not a line did you write.
You can laugh in your sleeves at their knocks, while you through
    it all
Fight for your royalties—and you bet you fight.

Writing song lyrics in the 1900s became an obsession with
folk in all walks of life. Mike Scot, for example, was well aware
of Taylor's line (not wholly unjustified), "Never write sense,
if you do you will rue it," and was incensed at the apathy
toward a "lyric" he had written. Mike was an eccentric performer, not exactly a nut, but an odd character. His act wasn't
much—a meaningless song and dance followed by a Lancashire
clog on a pedestal which was about a foot high and resembled
a milking stool. The slab on top was the size of a brick, which
forced Mike to do all his dancing on his toes. He made a serious
announcement in reference to this and also told his audiences
that he was "the best singer of any dancer, bar none." He
worked the dumps, slabs, and honky-tonks, never made the big
time, but he was well known to performers, all of whom feigned
great interest in his lyric. He spent all his spare time trying
vainly to get it published. He would give anyone a copy and
was hurt if not asked for it. He must have given away a thou-

sand handwritten copies. Still the publishers would have nothing whatever to do with it. Possibly this is why:

IN THE GARDEN I SAW STARLIGHT AT THE PARTY

By Mike Scot

> One day when I was rambling all alone,
> Taking pleasure of the many beauties fair,
> I was invited to a party on the green,
> And politely I said I didn't care.

Chorus: Oh, my heart is overpowered with its joy,
> For many pretty faces there I seen.
> At the garden there was starlight in the sky,
> As I stepped into the evening.

Anyway, Mike meant well. And if we accept the critiques of Bryan and Taylor, the publishers were amiss, for Mike's technique is faultlessly within the genre: his sentiment is tender, his action—a pleasant stroll to a garden party—is simple, and his assonances unique in their juxtapositions. No Alley genius has ever approached "I seen" and "evening," and Tin Pan Alley has bred some Titans. It is probably Mike's pinnacle of effort. Ring Lardner would have published it at his own expense; Gertrude Stein would have awarded it the Toklas Rose Is an Alice. Of such is the understanding of great minds.

THE MIGHT—THE POWER—THE U.S.A.

ALTHOUGH THE TURN-OF-THE-CENTURY songs were less critical and less specific in their reference to customs, events, and people than those of the periods we have examined, they did mirror the times in a general reflection that, while abstract, was spontaneous—proof that the influence was genuine. For example, songs directly relating to the Spanish-American War were meager. But throughout the decade, hundreds of songs hymned the spirit of our newly won imperialism. Indeed—and quite apart from his merit—it was on this very nationwide consciousness of America's world importance, the pride and exultation of Americans generally, that George M. Cohan, the theater's Yankee Doodle Dandy and author of many of the flag wavers, red, white, and blued his way to a fortune.

When, in 1902, Witmark bought out "My Own United States," which Julian Edwards composed to the lyric of Stanislaus Stange, the press ecstatically exclaimed, "Has the American Marseillaise been found at last?" And the *Herald*, January 18, 1903, extolling the song in a full-page patriotic spread picturing a soldier, sailor, and eagle and reprinting the music, set forth its delight that we had done with the "makeshifts and plagiarisms" that heretofore had been our national hymns.

MY OWN UNITED STATES

The poet sings of sunny France,
Fair olive-laden Spain.
The Grecian isles, Italia's smiles
And India's torrid plain.
Of Egypt, countless ages old,
Dark Afric's palms and dates—
Let me acclaim the land I name,
My own United States.

Chorus: I love every inch of her prairie land,
Each stone of her mountain side.
I love every drop of the waters clean
That flow from her rivers wide.
I love every tree, every blade of grass
Within Columbia's gates,
The queen of the earth is the land of my birth,
My own United States.[1]

Currently apposite is "In Germany You've Got To Do the Goose Step," by R. L. Johnson, to a tune of Ellis R. Ephraim, that Witmark published in 1901. Here is the chorus:

Oh, the goose-step is the walk where you neither glide nor stalk,
'Tis a leggy, laggy, limber, lamber loose-step.
The Yankee boy is bred to a firm and martial tread,
But in Germany they always do the goose-step.

[1] Copyright, 1902, by M. Witmark & Sons. Copyright renewed. Used by permission.

Oh, the goose-step is the walk and the goose-step is the talk,
That leggy, laggy, limber, lamber goose-step.
I'd rather march, you see, in my dear own country,
For in Germany you've got to do the goose-step.[2]

The unwitting foresight of Johnson, alas, has been tragically confirmed.

The fervor of the patriotic song writers expressed itself in a surprising number of diversions, and in one instance, Frank Abbott's "The Military Maid," a precise reference is made to the soldierly style of girls in dress and bearing that for a time in the early 1900s was à la mode. It was influenced by the Latin battlefields—Cuba and the Philippines—and the prevailing martial spirit. Abbott's verse is good in character, shows a nice observance, and Ben M. Jerome gave it a properly vigorous musical setting.

THE MILITARY MAID

The cycle girl has had her day, the golf girl, too, has
    passed.
The Dewey girl, the Sousa girl have lately been out-
    classed.
The martial maiden has appeared and she has come to stay.
She's ev'rywhere and ev'ry one can see her ev'ry day.
Straight as a dart with head up in the air,
Uniform smart and dimpled shoulders square.
She's not afraid of a brigade,
What antagonist could long resist this military maid?

Chorus: She is a military maid,
    Look out, your heart she will invade.
    And with her eyes of blue will run you through,
    Her smile's an ambuscade.
    Red cheeks a very pretty shade,
    Her colors never, never fade.
    A thoroughbred from her heels to her head
    Is the military maid.

[2]Copyright, 1901, by M. Witmark & Sons. Copyright renewed. Used by permission.

There were even military coon songs; Ed Rogers wrote one:

Chorus: When this darky is parading ev'rybody steps aside,
    All the ladies promenading watch his manly stride.
    Head erect with eyes a-rolling made him leader soon.
    To see him on parade
    Places others in the shade,
    For Jackson he's the military coon.

One of the most successful of the military songs was Paul Barnes' "Good-By Dolly Gray," which he wrote to the lyric of Will D. Cobb. Many today will recall its chorus—all will recognize its poignant pertinence:

    Good-by Dolly I must leave you,
    Though it breaks my heart to go.
    Something tells me I am needed
    At the front to fight the foe.
    See the boys in blue are marching
    And I can no longer stay;
    Hark! I hear the bugle calling—
    Good-by Dolly Gray[3]

All these songs were written subsequent to the Spanish-American War, some of them even after the Philippine insurrection had been halted.

But the truth is that the patriotic song, the battle chant written specifically for the boys in service, is received almost with apathy by the armed forces. Soldiers and sailors lean to sentiment and comedy; songs extolling character and bravery and that are full of chauvinistic pride, they find embarrassing. The rallying tune of 1898 was "Hot Time in the Old Town Tonight." George M. Cohan's "Over There" was a successful song of 1917—over here. On the Western Front the boys sang the stutter song, "K-K-Katy," "The Trail of the Lonesome Pine," "There's a Long, Long Trail a-Winding," "Pack Up Your Troubles in Your Old Kit Bag," the British marching song, "Tipperary," and various versions, mainly unprintable, of "Mademoiselle of Armentieres." In our time, the pre-December

[3]Copyright, 1900, by Morse Music Co. Copyright renewed by Will D. Cobb. Used by permission of Shapiro, Bernstein & Co., Inc.

7 training-camp favorite was the "Beer Barrel Polka," which the boys called "Roll Out the Barrel." And as we write, it is "Deep in the Heart of Texas." The lads paid little attention to "You're a Sap, Mr. Jap," "Goodby Mama, I'm Off to Yokohama," or the rest of the topical martial tunes.

Originally, the "Beer Barrel Polka" was a Czech melody called "Skoda Lasky"; in English, "Unrequited Love." The composer is Jaromir Vejvoda. W. A. Timm, an executive of the Standard Phonograph Co., heard it on a foreign record and suggested it to Shapiro, Bernstein for American adaptation. The publishers accepted, and Timm, after titling it, wrote the American lyric with Lew Brown. Elliott Shapiro then called the broadcasting chains to learn if they objected to the word "beer" in the title. Columbia Broadcasting System officials said they would admit the title, but banned "beer" in the lyric. They also insisted that the lyric contain no emphasis on drinking. When the National Broadcasting Co. officials saw the copies, they immediately notified Shapiro that the word "beer" would have to be eliminated from the title also. The publishers refused. Although it was played often over NBC's chain, it was always announced as "The Barrel Polka," to the amusement of the entire industry.

There is a gentle apology for the fussy broadcasters. An enormous number of crackpot listeners daily pester the chains with complaints of outrageous stupidity, and since they are also potential purchasers of tooth paste, soap, and breakfast foods, they must be mollified. Moreover, some states do not sell beer (Kansas for one) and object to all references to liquor. The chains must be constantly on the alert for innocent words that have taken on evil or vulgar connotations. "Pansy" and "Fanny" are obvious, but others are so recondite they are known only to special groups. Not long ago, one of the chains broadcast for several months the song "Seafood Mama," with the gloating line, "I get my favorite dish—fish," until, to the horror of executives, it was learned that in Negro colonies from Harlem to the Coast, "fish" is an obscene homosexual term. During its popularity, the National Broadcasting Co. debated for some time whether it would admit to its air George Gershwin's song "Nice Work if You Can Get It" because of its oblique allusion to prostitution. It was finally allowed.

DIAMOND RINGS FOR SWEET SIXTEEN

MOST TOPICAL of the song writers of the 1900s was the irrepressible James Thornton. Likable, genial, bibulous, and undependable, yet he was still respected by the vaudeville managers and by the music publishers, probably because of his tremendous assurance which, drunk or sober, was greatly enhanced by his unusual dignified appearance. If not too unsteady, he could double for an usher at a society wedding. Thornton's first wife was Bonnie, a singer who later teamed with him and whose real name was Lizzie Cox. It was for her he wrote "When You Were Sweet Sixteen," and he wrote it precisely as he wrote nearly every one of his songs—to a chance remark that he considered a title.

"Don't you love me any more?" she once asked him, after he'd broken his promise not to drink. "Why, Bonnie," he said, "I love you like I did when you were sweet sixteen." And there, as Jim knew, was his title, and the song followed. For a title was all Jim needed. "When You Were Sweet Sixteen" sold by the thousands. Ed Marks, as we have seen, claimed $5,000 forfeit from Witmark because of Marks's prior ownership. But the only revenue Thornton derived from it was $15 throughout its long years of popularity. Witmark, who was lucky enough to get "Two Little Girls in Blue" from Charles Graham for $10, purchased "Sweet Sixteen" from Thornton outright for but $5.00 more. Kathleen Barry, Thornton's second wife, who still lives, was so incensed at the publisher's failure to reward Jim for his hit tune that she took it from Witmark upon the expiration of its first copyright and renewed it through the house of Shapiro, Bernstein.

In those days, and in the '90s, it was the custom of some newspapers (in New York, the *World*) to offer prizes for song-writing contests. Indeed, many newspapers throughout the country issued reprints of popular songs, words and music, as Sunday feature supplements. The New York *World* was pro-moting such a contest at a time when Thornton was paying one of his periodic visits to Bellevue Hospital. He was recognized by an attendant, who said, "Jim, you've got only twenty-four hours to get your entry in to the *World*." Jim said, "If you'll give me a drink, I think I can write the song." The attendant forthwith poured him out a drink. It was third-rate stuff and Jim, wry of face, said, "It don't seem like the same old smile. Say! Wait a minute! That's a title!" And he wrote to it the song which won the contest. ("Smile" was slang for a drink; one had a "smile" at a bar.)

"When I took the Keeley Cure," and "Curious Cures," both well-known topical songs of Thornton, originated from his ex-periences at the nationally known alcoholic clinic, a branch of which was at White Plains, N. Y. As Thornton was leaving, discharged after completing the treatment, a drunk drove up for admittance. Thornton, in Prince Albert coat, scholarly in ap-pearance, was mistaken by the drunk for the doctor.

"I'm here to take the cure," he said to Thornton.

"Yes, I know," said Thornton. "But before I can prescribe treatment, I shall have to test your cardiac reactions. I want you to run up and down that hill over there three times." The drunk complied, and as he finished his last trip, Thornton's cab arrived to take him to the station. He got in as the actual phy-sician arrived. "Who are you?" asked the drunk. "I am the doctor in charge." "I suppose you've got a hill too," said the drunk, and as Thornton drove off, the drunk swung a right to the doctor's jaw.

In the late '90s, Thornton, in his vaudeville act of satirical im-personations and songs, could pillory the Rev. Dr. Parkhurst, and did, characterizing the divine crusader as "Dr. Piecrust."

The humorless minister protested, but Jim kept on in this style blithely—until the puritanical vaudeville managers—Keith, Albee, and Pastor—obtained control and censored all such personal references, an exaction that was to bleed the pop-song expression of its puissance. Thornton was, however, permitted to burlesque, in the 1900s, Dr. Munyon, purveyor of a nostrum called Palmetto Berry Wine, who was widely known through his advertised product, which pictured the "doctor" as a professorial figure with an arm raised and a finger pointing heavenward.

> My name is Dr. Munyon,
> I can cure a corn or bunion,
> As a skin doctor I am immense.

So sang Thornton. And Munyon, like all great fakers a grand showman, loved it. Munyon's offices were in the St. James Building, at Broadway and Twenty-sixth Street, in which also were quartered, in the early 1900s, the vaudeville managers. One day, after calling upon the managers in relation to booking, Thornton entered the elevator in which Munyon was a passenger.

"I am very much obliged to you for your act, Mr. Thornton," said Munyon. "It has done me a world of good. Really, it has been much better than my advertising. You are getting me more publicity than any other medium, and I should like to reward you. I am going to give you some lots in Florida, where you and Bonnie can build a nice home when you retire." A few days later he sent them the deed, but Bonnie, skeptical, had the lots appraised. When she was advised, "You had better hire a diver to make the survey," she threw the document away and forgot it. It was expensive advice. The lots were located in what is now West Palm Beach.

Bonnie was a bright lass, not much of a performer, yet an able foil for Thornton. She had two quirks, one of which Jim never knew about—her critical interest in art. She prowled the gallery exhibitions constantly and was known to virtually every professional connoisseur. A few years after her death, Jim, who continued in vaudeville as a monologist, was playing Chicago. His hotel adjoined Knoedler's branch, and after a matinee one afternoon, the manager accosted Jim. "Would Bonnie like to come in and see the paintings?" he asked. "Bonnie has been dead since 1920," said Thornton, "and what the hell would she be wanting to see the paintings for?" "She was a constant visitor at our galleries in New York," the manager replied. "We always took heed of her opinions."

Bonnie was also, along with many in the theatrical and song-writing professions, a victim of the diamond craze, which, beginning in the '90s, continued well on into the 1900s. It was the belief of everyone that purchase of the stones was an investment. The stones of the 1900s ran to size. Large diamonds, eight carats or more, were worn by capitalists, Colonial Dames, debutantes, burlesque queens, faro dealers, bartenders, and banjo players. These are facts, not a jest.

All the money Bonnie could salvage from their vaudeville salary she used to purchase diamonds. At the height of their theatrical popularity, when Jim was behaving rather well, her collection was fabulous. Her inordinate love of the stones approached the idiosyncrasy of Henry Ward Beecher, who carried a handful of jewels in his pocket, which he drew forth for frequent public admiration and personal gloat. Bonnie, and this Jim never knew either, was an expert in diamond values. A well-known New York jeweler once asked Jim to send Bonnie to his store. "She's not buying any diamonds now," said Thornton. "It isn't that," said the jeweler, "we would like to have her appraise some new stones we just bought."

Diamonds were classified by dealers as commercial white, water-white, blue-white, charcoal, canary, feather, and smoke. Most expensive was blue-white. Commercial white and water-white diamonds were more moderately priced. "Charcoal" characterized a stone with tiny black flecks, really specks of carbon, which, while not diminishing the brilliance, lessened the value greatly. "Canary" referred to stones whose color ranged from pale amber to light brown. They had much fire but were low in price. "Feather" meant a flaw in the stone that resembled a wisp of thistledown. Sometimes it was discernible only through a magnifying glass. Diamonds that were murky or opaque and lacking luster were termed "smoke." Pear-shaped, square, triangular, oval, or flat stones were generally undesirable, regardless of color or quality.

A well-known banjo player of the 1900s owned a three-carat derelict that had all the imperfections nature and uncraftsmanlike cutting could crowd into a stone of its size. It was pear-shaped, flawed, and murky. But by holding it at a certain angle in very strong light, it would sparkle occasionally. It was set in a ring and cost twenty dollars. Worn on the little finger of the left hand of the banjoist, it compensated in a way for an occasional mangled chord.

Song writers and the theatrical profession went all out for diamonds, and stage-door stone peddlers were numerous in all the cities. Any fairly well-known performer could buy diamonds on credit without red tape, endorsers, or security. The sellers took small risk; a performer's whereabouts was always known or the information could be obtained from agents or bookers. A player could not hide and still remain in show business, and it would scarcely pay him to quit for the sake of a few hundred dollars in diamonds. Clusters in the shape of stars or crosses, interrogation marks, birds, crescents, and many other designs were fashionable. Wilkes Andress, a circus advance man, wore a nine-stone cluster of two-carat diamonds, which made a pin about the size of a half-dollar. Large pins of this type were attached to a light, but strong, gold chain, the other end of which was fixed to a safety pin or catch fastened to the shirt under the vest.

Louise Llewellyn, a ballad and character singer of the 1900s, wore a pair of eight-carat earrings while portraying poverty-stricken flower girls or news vendors. Fancy a comely, well-fed outcast, wearing a battered hat over beautifully coiffured blond hair, and a ragged skirt through the holes of which one could peak at her pink silk tights! Her earrings glittered as she plaintively offered newspapers ("Just a penny, mister"). Of course, it was ridiculously incongruous, but so accepted was the diamond as a personal adjunct that audiences never commented. Louise's earrings were white and clear and cost $900. Had they been blue-white and clear, they would have been priceless.

Frank McNish, the minstrel man, wore a valuable seven-carat stud, which he frequently left with some bartender for security when short of cash. At the close of a hilarious adventure, McNish could never remember where he had left it and had to begin his saloon tour all over to recover his stud. He once sold it to Ned Monroe, of Monroe and Mack, for fifty cents. After letting McNish spend a week of sorrow and remorse, Ned gave it back to him, which, naturally, called for another celebration. Billy Lowande, who presented a trick-mule act in vaudeville, wore a seven-carat solitaire ring. Because of the rough nature of his act with the mule, he was constantly losing it or knocking the stone from its setting, and in a fit of peevishness one night he gave it to a Salvation Army lassie who was canvassing the saloons.

Few performers, however, acquired diamonds that excelled the collection of Bonnie Thornton. One was Lillian Russell, and there is an amusing story recalled by oldsters that points her adornment with personal authenticity. Jerry Mahoney, a stone mason and contractor who had done considerable work for Proctor's theaters, called upon J. Austin Fynes, Proctor's general manager, during a matinee at Proctor's Fifth Avenue Theater, where Lillian was headlining for the week. Mahoney was a well-liked character, and Fynes took him backstage to meet Lillian. The brilliance of her diamonds matched her beauty, and Mahoney for a moment was speechless. When he recovered, he asked, in his characteristic forthright manner, "They're some fine-lookin' bits o' jewelry you have on you, are they any of them real?"

"Oh, yes," said Lillian. "They are all real—I hope."

"About what did the lot o' them cost ye?"

"Oh, about $15,000."

"Fifteen thousand!" gasped Mahoney. "And what wages do they pay you here?"

"They pay me $600 a week."

Mahoney pondered this a moment: "Six hundred, is it? And the jewelry cost $15,000? Tell me this—how do you do it?"

"Well," laughed Lillian, equally frank, "I have to give it up."

"Begorry," said Mahoney, winking slyly, "I thought so."

It is easy to rationalize the diamond craze of the period. What better symbol for dollar-getting days? What better badge to mark the "malefactors of great wealth"? What better insignia for the rise of trusts, the development of monopolies, the advance of big business, the octopus clutch of corporations, nationally garnering the small man's enterprise to build up their gigantic concerns? Ah, yes; this, too, was singable—oddly enough in a coon song that is a melodic epitome of the decade's economics. Leon Berg, who wrote "The Coontown Billionaire," had no notion that his extravagant lines were a mirror. They were, and here they are:

THE COONTOWN BILLIONAIRE

When I get up at half-past nine,
I take a bath in sparkling wine,
For milk baths only are the rage
For certain beauties of the stage.
Use almond paste to clean my face
For I'm the swellest of my race,
In place of towels use shawls of silk,
For gargling I take lily milk.

Chorus: For I'm the coontown billionaire,
I own in every trust a share,
Have palace cars on every road,
A gold keel on my pleasure boat.
I own the largest hunting ground,
Where bears with golden teeth are found,
My bank account is ten miles square,
For I'm the coontown billionaire.

My parrots have a boudoir and all my dogs a private car,
My horses have a billiard room, and every cat a swell-
dressed groom,
The rats get meat three times a day, the mice a Steinway
for their play,
And all the flies that light on me, get Force for breakfast
with their tea.

Dick Mansfield with his latest play reads me to sleep
'most every day,
And Melba warbles lullabies when I do close my tired eyes.
Before at morn I leave my bed, Paderewski plays the
minuet,
Henry Irving reads the news, while dusky princes lace
my shoes.

The gardeners of my floral park have blue-blood vaccina-
tion marks,
And milkmaids on my dairy farm wear diamond bracelets
on their arm.
My coachmen graduated all from Yale and Harvard late
last fall.
And all my servants have to speak high German, Latin,
French, and Greek.

The song was published in 1903 by Shapiro, Bernstein and
was sung widely in the music halls of Keith, Albee, Proctor, and
Pastor. The milk-bath reference is to Anna Held's press-agent
stunt. Such subtlety one could get away with. But most of the
song writers, reasonably imaginative factualists, studiously
avoided the precise critical tone. Instead of flaying out at gross
social and economic abuses or notching their guns at murdered
(in song) public fakers, they stuck to sure themes like love,
home and mother, the fire that burns fiercely in the hearts of
the brave, and in the process thereof discovered the geographical illimitation of America. With all stops open, they sang of
Dixie's glorious terrain and the honor and virginity of Southern
girlhood.

They thought it was true what they said about Dixie.

THE MINSTRELS WANDER

THE CENTENNIAL STATE (and John D. Rockefeller, Jr.), as though returning the compliment to the New York song writers for their discovery of the West, sent "Where the Silvery Colorado Wends Its Way" back to Tin Pan Alley.

Thus, with their song, C. H. Scoggins, the lyricist, and Charles Avril, the composer, two Denver letter carriers, sang their way into the heart of John D. Rockefeller, Jr. The song was popular throughout the state about the time of the butchery between the Colorado mine operators and their employees, a bloody war that filled press and public with horror in 1903 and 1904. Its doleful note wails the death of a wife by a widower who, in the second verse, succumbs himself. It has no specific relation to the terrorism at the mines. Yet all sorrow is akin, and the beleaguered miners took it to their hearts. According to the story, Rockefeller, emerging from a stockholders' meeting of the Colorado Fuel & Iron Co., heard the song, liked it, asked for Scoggins and Avril, and gave them $500 to publish it. A dispatch to the *Herald* from Denver, October 11, 1903, partially supports this story, adding that possibly it would counteract unfavorable publicity regarding Rockefeller's personal frugality in the matter of a twenty-five-cent cab for himself and luggage. It *has* the stamp of the late Ivy Lee, Rockefeller's public relations representative until Lee's death in 1934.

"The Silvery Colorado" is still popular, its copyright held by Jerry Vogel, a unique publisher, the only house in America whose catalogue is devoted exclusively to old songs. Vogel, incidentally, acquired all George M. Cohan's songs in 1932, a coup in salesmanship, with an assist from Ed Raftery, of O'Brien, Driscoll, and Raftery, theatrical lawyers who were attorneys both for Vogel and Cohan.

Well, south, west, along the Mississippi, down the beautiful Ohio, into New England the song writers roamed, forsaking

Broadway and the offside satirical lyrics, to pal with Indian
maids, Hiawatha, and "Come Be My Rainbow, My pretty Rain-
bow, I love you so"; to ride the range in cowboy chaps, "Pony
Boy, Pony Boy, won't you be my Tony Boy"; or, "Cheyenne,
Cheyenne, hop on my pony." It was an exhaustive itinerary,
and it is still being kept—sectional songs are currently popular
("California Here I Come," "Deep in the Heart of Texas").
But it was broken for a time when the boys, homesick for
Broadway, returned in mid-decade to consort for a time with the
Italians:

> My Mariuccia take a steamboat
> (*Toot, Toot—from the gallery*)
> She's gone away . . .[1]

or the pretty East Side Jewish girls:

> Don't do that dance I tell you Sadie,
> It's not a business for a lady.
> 'Most everybody knows
> That I'm your loving Mose,
> Oy, Oy, Oy, Oy, put on some clothes![2]

And the Irish:

> Bedelia, I'd like to steal ye,
> Bedelia, I love you so.[3]

Which Blanche Ring turned down, and thought better of her
decision when, playing London, she realized what a success it
was.

But the London managers were strict about songs. A singer
identified with a successful song was permitted to use it exclusively. Finally, Blanche admitted to Bernstein that she had
been wrong about the song, and Bernstein induced Francis, Day
and Hunter, British owners of the copyright, to let her have it.
With what success, those over fifty-five will recall wistfully.

[1]Copyright, 1906, by Barron and Thompson. Copyright renewed by Al Pian-
tadosi. Used by permission of Shapiro, Bernstein & Co., Inc.

[2]Copyright, 1909, Irving Berlin Standard Music Corp. Copyright renewed
1937, Irving Berlin. Used by permission.

[3]Copyright, 1903, Remick Music Corp. Copyright renewed. Used by permission.

Most earnest of the geographical song writers ("On the Banks of the Wabash") was Paul Dresser, a decent man who dripped his weight—300 pounds—in sentimentality. Yet often there was a facts-facing ring to his stuff. Thus he treats of the girl gone wrong in

JUST TELL THEM THAT YOU SAW ME

While strolling down the street one eve upon mere pleasure bent,
'Twas after business worries of the day;
I saw a girl who shrank from me, in her I recognized
My schoolmate in a village far away.
"Is that you, Madge?" I said to her—she quickly turned away.
"Don't turn away, Madge, I am still your friend,
"Next week I'm going back to see the old folks, and I thought,
"Perhaps, some message you would like to send."

Chorus: "Just tell them that you saw me,"
    She said, "They'll know the rest.
    "Just tell them I was looking well, you know.
    "Just whisper, if you get a chance,
    "To mother dear, and say—
    "I love her as I did long, long ago."

"Your cheeks are pale, your face is thin, come, tell me, were you ill?
"When last we met your eyes shown clear and bright.
"Come home with me when I go, Madge, the change will do you
    good;
"Your mother wonders where you are tonight."
"I long to see them all again, but not just yet," she said.
" 'Tis pride alone that's keeping me away.
"Just tell them not to worry, for I'm all right, don't you know.
"Tell mother I am coming home some day."

Dresser's tears were endless. Still, he never shed them upon the silly implausibles that made up the paper-flower characters and incredible shams of his sobbing, poetasting brethren. "The Pardon Came Too Late" is borderline gush. But the soldier boy deserter is not unreal, and his mission is understandable:

A fair-haired boy in a foreign land
At sunrise was to die.
In a prison cell he sat alone,
From his heart there came a sigh.

Deserted from the ranks, they said,
The reason none could say.
They only knew the orders were
That he should die next day.
And so the hours glided by . . .
A messenger on wings did fly
To save this boy from such a fate—
A pardon—but it came too late.

Chorus: The volley was fired at sunrise,
Just after break of day.
And while the echoes lingered,
A soul had passed away
Into the arms of his Maker;
And there to hear his fate.
A tear, a sigh, a sad goodby—
The pardon came too late.

And 'round the campfire burning bright,
The story then was told,
How his mother on a dying bed
Called for her son so bold.
He hastened to obey her wish,
Was captured on the way—
She never saw her boy so fair;
He died at break of day.
And when the truth at last was known,
His innocence at once was shown.
To save from such an unjust fate
A pardon sent—but 'twas too late.

"On the Banks of the Wabash" became a Tin Pan Alley legend. At the peak of its favor, Dresser one evening attended a honky-tonk show and to his horror heard a girl sing,

Through the syse-a-moors the candle lights are gleaming.

After her act Dresser went backstage. "My little girl," he said, "that word in the song is 'sycamore'—pronounced 'sick-a-more'—not 'syse-a-moor.' The sycamore is a tree. Try to remember it, won't you?"

"Well, who the hell do you think you are?" snapped the girl.

"I—I—well, I wrote the song," stammered Dresser.

"That's a good one," said the girl. "Lemme tell yuh sumpin'. The publisher learnt me that song 'n' I guess he knows his business, so beat it."

Howley, Haviland & Co. published the song, and it might have been Pat Howley's gag.

There is an unlovely but dramatic story about Dresser and his wife, May Howard, in no fashion a Calpurnia. Embittered by her indiscretions, it is said that on his vaudeville appearances he always awaited her attendance, had a standing order at each theater that, should she appear, she was to be given a box. She did appear. When Dresser came out for his act, knowing she was in the audience, and her location, he addressed himself solely to her in a song he had expressly written for the instance, called "The Curse." Its indictment was so severe that women screamed and fainted, and Howard, a handsome, shapely brunette featured in burlesque for years, was so mentally deranged it closed her career. Thereafter, the plates of "The Curse" (it had been set up) were destroyed, and Dresser wrote a milder version, which was peddled as "The Curse of the Dreamer."

Dresser was a prolific composer of heart throbs but his emotion was at least real. He wrote a number of hit tunes—"Just Tell Them That You Saw Me," "The Blue and the Gray," "The Pardon Came Too Late," and "My Gal Sal," which, save for the "Wabash" song (now the state anthem of Indiana), is his best known. It is often broadcast, and about the time of this writing, a motion picture, *My Gal Sal*, a sentimentalized verisimilitude of Dresser's life, was widely distributed and quite popular. He was well paid in vaudeville and drew considerable royalties from his songs, but his heart was bigger than his purse, and he died in 1906 virtually penniless.

Although there were a number of comedy songs published in the 1900s, the leaning was toward the serious side. Love, as we know, was gay, and sometimes light, in the preceding period. But the boom of industry, the advance of science, the spread of education in the early years of the twentieth century were sobering influences, and the most successful songs of the period were ballads of love and courtship with the little church just around the corner. Mostly they were reasonable in style and presentation—the lugubrious note seldom heard. And of all the song writers of the period, Ernest R. Ball had the golden key to this reaction. He wrote an incredible number of hit ballads; it is estimated that Ball's total sales were 25,000,000 copies. He wrote "Love Me and The World Is Mine," "Mother Machree," "Till the Sands of the Desert Grow Cold," "In the Garden of My Heart," "Let the Rest of the World Go By," "A Little Bit of Heaven," "When Irish Eyes Are Smiling," "Goodby, Good Luck, God Bless You," and, with James J. Walker, "Will You Love Me in December as You Do in May?" He wrote hundreds more, but those cited were amazing successes.

Ball, generally regarded as the outstanding ballad writer in the music industry, was an astonishing fellow himself. His personal humor was keen, and so was his fortitude and balance. He came to New York from Cleveland at the turn of the century, a thoroughly grounded pianist. But the publishers would have none of him, and he was forced to accept the part-time piano playing job at the Union Square Theater. Ball relieved the orchestra, thumping the piano from 5 P.M. to 8 P.M. Geller says that he first played "Love Me and the World is Mine" at this theater; played it so often, in fact, that the weary manager threatened dismissal if he didn't drop it from his repertoire.

But Ball thought well of the tune and took it to Witmark, who asked Dave Reed, Jr., a successful vaudevillian and song writer, to fashion a lyric to it. Reed at first refused, but when Ball played it over for him, he admitted its possibilities and set to work. He turned out an undistinguished lyric; in fact, dismisses the sweetheart in the line, "Yet, lo, dear heart, 'tis only thee," when he was certain she was the angel of his paradise. But it is a good illustration of the change from the gooey ballads of the '80s and '90s.

> I wander on as in a dream,
> My goal a paradise must be.

For there an angel waits 'twould seem—
Yet, lo, dear heart, 'tis only thee.
Suns may shine to light my way dear,
Wealth be mine for aye dear,
Queens may pledge their riches too.
Yet the world would still be lonely,
With such virtues only,
Life to me, dear, means just you.

Chorus: I care not for the stars that shine,
I dare not hope to e'er be thine,
I only know I love you,
Love me and the world is mine.[4]

Ball's original title was "I Love You and the World Is Mine," which was speedily changed to the more direct and better caption.

The song was an immediate success, and after Ball wrote several more hits, Witmark's, realizing they had a find, signed Ball to an exclusive contract, the terms of which were said to have been $10,000 annual guarantee for a song a month, plus royalties. Ball added to this revenue with vaudeville appearances, teaming up with Maude Lambert, a singer whom he later married. (His first wife was Jessie M. White, of Cleveland, who bore him three children—Roland, Ruth Mary, and Ernest A. Ball.) Yet he always said song writers never made any money, including himself.

During the 1900s, two actor colonies flourished in the East; one in Fairhaven, N. J., the other in Freeport, L. I. Ball and Lambert were residents of the latter and, with their actor neighbors, were frequent visitors to Tony Farrell's roadhouse in St. James, a town not far from Freeport. About 1915 there was a deluge of war songs, and comment on this at one of the sessions in Farrell's provoked the challenge that Ball and his friend, J. Keirn Brennan, write a war song *with no war* in it. Ball and Brennan accepted, and wrote, "Good Bye Barney Boy."

Brennan, the lyricist, was a striking character. In his youth he

---

[4]Copyright, 1906, by M. Witmark & Sons. Copyright renewed. Used by permission.

had been a middleweight pugilist. The Klondike boom drew him to Alaska, where he engaged in freighting, cooking, wood chopping, song writing—apparently everything except gold mining. When Alaska got too tame, he worked his way back to Chicago, where he tried hard to sell the lyric, "A Little Bit of Heaven" ("Sure They Call It Ireland") for $5.00, but no one would take the frightful risk. Ball later put music to it and, on publication by Witmark, the song became a sensational seller.

Ball died, May 3, 1927, of a heart attack while playing a fill-in date at the Yost Theater, Santa Ana, California. He left half his estate to his mother, Nannie Ball, the other half to his first wife, Jessie, in trust for the three children. He made no provision for Maude Lambert, "for reasons which she understands."

Ball was not a "sectionalist" composer, held close to love and mother, and his songs seldom wandered from the hearth. But he did carry on the "serious" tradition of Dresser. So did another able writer, Harry Von Tilzer, but he got more humor into his songs. Von Tilzer, brother of Albert Von Tilzer, also one of the Alley's noblemen, composed as many hits as Ball. His is an impressive list; most readers can probably hum the choruses to each of these: "Wait Till the Sun Shines, Nellie," "On a Sunday Afternoon," "Down Where the Würzburger Flows," "A Bird in a Gilded Cage," "All Alone," "I'd Leave Ma Happy Home for You," "The Cubanola Glide," "What You Goin' to Do When the Rent Comes Round?" "I Want a Girl," "Take Me Back to New York Town," "Down on the Farm," "My Old New Hampshire Home," and "On the Old Fall River Line." Here is a sheaf of which few of the Alley's most prolific writers could boast.

Harry Von Tilzer, a vaudeville singer and pianist playing his own accompaniments, wrote hundreds of tunes before he brought out his first successful song. This was "My Old New Hampshire Home," and according to Von Tilzer, it grew out of stark want. In 1898 he shared a furnished room with Andrew B. Sterling, a lyric writer, in East Fifteenth Street near Irving Place, New York. They owed three weeks' rent. Sneaking in one night, they had scarcely closed the door before someone knocked. They ignored the summons, and presently a note was slipped under the door, informing them to pay up at once or vacate. On the reverse of this sheet of paper they wrote "My Old New Hampshire Home," the chorus first, which was their invariable technical routine.

Next day they peddled it all over in vain, so they started disconsolately up Broadway, when at about Twenty-ninth Street they met a song-writing friend, Bartley Costello ("Where the River Shannon Flows"), who told them to take their song to the Orphean Music Co., then owned by William C. Dunn. He was closing for the day when they arrived but consented to listen to the song, said that he liked it, but wouldn't accept it until he had taken it home for his daughter's approval. However, Dunn advanced them $5.00, and that night they ate a regular meal instead of free lunch. The next day Dunn said his daughter had liked the song and offered to buy it outright for $15. The writers sold and collected the balance of $10. The song eventually sold 1,000,000 copies, but the conclusion is nicer than were the experiences of Graham and Thornton.

Von Tilzer later went out on the road as a pianist and singer with the Irwin Brothers Burlesquers, and, while playing Philadelphia, he was astonished at the close of a matinee when Maurice Shapiro, father of Elliott Shapiro and founder with Louis Bernstein of the house of Shapiro, Bernstein & Co., came backstage to propose that he quit the road and come back to New York and write songs.

Shapiro told Von Tilzer that he had acquired the catalogue of Dunn's Orphean Music Co., which included "My Old New Hampshire Home," and offered him $4,000 in royalties on the song if he'd join with them. Von Tilzer accepted with delight, and it was a decent gesture; Shapiro was under no legal obligation to make the payment. Later, Von Tilzer joined the firm. "It was cheaper to make him a partner than to pay him royalties," Bernstein subsequently explained.

On some of his songs Von Tilzer teamed with Arthur J.

Lamb. One, previously mentioned, was "A Bird in a Gilded Cage." Its origin is interesting. Lamb brought the lyric to Von Tilzer in Chicago. The title appealed to the composer, and he wrote the melody the same afternoon. That night, Von Tilzer visited a tawdry pub and played and sang it to get the reaction. One of the girls wept, "And I knew I had a hit," said Von Tilzer. It was published in 1900, and it was one of the last of the "mistress" weepers. Here again morality drew a sharp line between the acceptance of the '90s and that of the new century. Ballads of fallen girls and "kept" women, admissible in the previous decade, were now *de trop*. Lamb's "caged bird" was unmarried in the original lyric. "Why, you've written a song about a whore," said Bernstein. But Lamb refused to marry his girl—until Bernstein told him he wouldn't publish the song unless he did. The "corrected" line is the penultimate in the first stanza:

A BIRD IN A GILDED CAGE

The ballroom was filled with fashion's throng,
It shone with a thousand lights,
And there was a woman who passed along,
The fairest of all the sights.
A girl to her lover then softly sighed
"There's riches at her command."
"But she married for wealth, not for love," he cried
"Though she lives in a mansion grand."

Chorus: She's only a bird in a gilded cage,
A beautiful sight to see,
You may think she's happy and free from care,
She's not, though she seems to be.
'Tis sad when you think of her wasted life,
For youth cannot mate with age,
And her beauty was sold for an old man's gold,
She's a bird in a gilded cage.

I stood in a churchyard just at eve,
When sunset adorned the West,
And looked at the people who'd come to grieve,
For loved ones now laid at rest.

A tall marble monument marked the grave
Of one who'd been fashion's queen,
And I thought, "She is happier here at rest,
Than to have people say when seen:" (*Chorus*)[5]

The Lamb-Von Tilzer gilded bird was still in the '90s genre. The vaudeville restrictions and sobering influences already referred to were not apparent in the popular song until some three or four years later. When these influences were felt, the song writers shifted to melody, and the composers took over.

THAT STRAIN AGAIN

It was a change of necessity, and withal a happy one. Although composers still wrote for the vaudeville singers' technique of the day—the sixteen-bar verse and eight-bar chorus, the accent then being on the verse—they brightened up their music, got cleanly away from the dum-dum-diddle style, leaned less on repeat phrases, and touched up their pieces with a lilting rhythm, turning out such singable ditties as Eddie Leonard's "Ida, Sweet as Apple Cider" (1903), Harry Von Tilzer's "Alexander, Don't You Love Your Baby No More" (1904), Harry O. Sutton's "I Don't Care" (1905), which Eva Tanguay bosomed as her own for her entire vaudeville career, Egbert Van Alstyne's "In the Shade of the Old Apple Tree" (the same year) and "Chinatown My Chinatown" (1910).

Jean Schwartz wrote "Chinatown" to the lyric of Billy Jerome. It was an interpolated number in a revue by Edgar Smith called *Up and Down Broadway*. Speedily forgotten, it was revived some years later on the Coast and sold fairly well. "Then, about twenty years later," Jean told the writer, "Louis Armstrong played it hot, and it was a hit all over. I still wouldn't give you a nickel for the tune."

In 1907, Williams and Van Alstyne wrote "I'm Afraid to Go Home in the Dark," a lilting comic song that held up for at least three years.

[5]Permission to author by courtesy of copyright owners, Harry Von Tilzer Music Publishing Co.

"Pull up the shade, nurse. I'm afraid to go home in the dark," said O. Henry the last time he spoke, in Polyclinic Hospital where he died in 1910.

Jack Norworth and Nora Bayes wrote "Shine On Harvest Moon" in 1908, the hit of the year; and the hit, too, of the 1930s, when Ruth Etting revived it on her radio broadcasts.

A wonderfully melodic year, 1908! A great warbling burst, a threnody before the offbeat of rhythm conquered the Alley's melody in 1914 and sent it tumbling away from the nation's pianos toward the Calvary of the juke box, Hollywood's sound track, and the ersatz tone of the radio engineer.

Thrust at random at the publishers' lists of 1908, and this could be your garner: "Down Among the Sugar Cane," "Down in Jungle Town," "Good Evening, Caroline" (and having seen who could ever forget the Bayes-Norworth rendition, say at the old Colonial in Columbus Circle!), "Cuddle Up a Little Closer, Lovey Mine" (written by Otto Harbach and Karl Hoschna for *The Three Twins* and not strictly a pop tune but so pretty every singer in vaudeville begged for it), "In the Garden of My Heart," Herbert Ingraham's, "Roses Bring Dreams of You," Albert Von Tilzer's, "Smarty," Gus Edwards' melody to the lyric of Will D. Cobb, "Sunbonnet Sue" (almost as popular as this same team's "School Days," published the year before), Albert Von Tilzer's "Take Me Out to the Ball Game," "You're in the Right Church but the Wrong Pew," by Cecil Mack and Chris Smith, Negro writers who will bow in again for these pages, and "Yip-I-Addy-I-Ay," which Will D. Cobb wrote with John H. Flynn.

In this first decade of the twentieth century, the punch was in the melody. Everyone had a song on his lips, if not of social significance, at least a pleasing air, and the Alley swarmed with one-fingered artists who, not too sure on the piano, nonetheless could give a tune to the publishers' music demonstrators that needed little retouching.

They were a colorful lot: Bob King (nee Keiser, and heaven knows how many aliases); Fred Fisher, who once threw a typewriter into Broadway because his visitor said he was bored; George Meyer, who wrote 500 songs, fifty of which were hits; Benjamin Hapgood Burt, who, despite the acute hearing of Keith and Albee, wrote such sophisticated songs as "Robinson Crusoe's Isle" (sophisticated for 1905):

> *Chorus:* Robinson Crusoe lived alone,
>   No bills to pay, no friends to loan.
>   No wife to say when he came home:
>   "Robinson Crusoe, why do you do so?"
>   He wore the same clothes all the while—
>   A string of beads and a heavenly smile.
>   They very seldom changed the style
>   On Robinson Crusoe's,
>   (Robinson Crusoe's)
>   Robinson Crusoe's Isle.[1]

Marie Cahill ("a singer who can act, an actress who can sing," as she was billed) liked it so much—and it is a graceful tune—that she appropriated it for her musical, *Marrying Mary*. "A great mistake," Ben told us. Interpolated songs in musicals, "stage hits," as the Alley termed them, were unprofitable. "They died with the show, and you never made a nickel on them," said Ben. Unreasonably, for another he wrote, "The Best I Get Is Much Obliged to You," which was introduced in *It Happened in Nordland*, made a lot of money.

More than the money he made was the accolade to Burt that his song was introduced in a Victor Herbert musical. "As though Herbert couldn't write his own music!"

There was A. Baldwin (Baldy) Sloane, who, with Edgar Smith, a superb lyricist, wrote that delicious razz to end all pop tunes—the unforgettable,

HEAVEN WILL PROTECT THE WORKING GIRL

> A village maid was leaving home, with tears her eyes were
>   wet,
> Her mother dear was standing near the spot.

[1]Copyright, Edward B. Marks Music Corp., RCA Building, Radio City, N. Y. Used by permission.

She says to her: Neuralgia, dear, I hope you won't forget
That I'm the only mother you have got.
The city is a wicked place, as any one can see,
And cruel dangers round your path may hurl.
So every week you'd better send your wages back to me,
For Heaven will protect a working girl.

Chorus: You are going far away, but remember what I say,
When you are in the city's giddy whirl.
From temptations, crimes and follies,
Villains, taxicabs and trolleys—
Oh! Heaven will protect the working girl.

Her dear old mother's words proved true,
For soon the poor girl met a man who on her ruin was
    intent.
He treated her respectful as those villains always do,
And she supposed he was a perfect gent.
But she found different when one night she went with him
    to dine,
Into a table d'hôte so blithe and gay.
And he says to her: After this we'll have a demi-tasse!
Then to him these brave words the girl did say:

Second Stand back, villain! go your way!
Chorus: Here I will no longer stay,
Although you were a marquis or an earl,
You may tempt the upper classes
With your villainous demi-tasses,
But Heaven will protect the working girl.[2]

This was written for Marie Dressler, who sang it in *Tillie's Nightmare*. A woman of wide acknowledgments, remembrance of the ribbing tang of it eased, somewhat, the tragedy of her approaching death.

These men were more than cards. They were spades—redoubled, some of them. Bob King, he who was born Keiser, was one surely of the melodic tribe of Ben, a true master of the revels. "Mary Earl" wrote "Beautiful Ohio"; the music, that is. So it is printed on the sheet copy. Why King signed it "Mary Earl" he told only to the rushes along the river. It was pub-

[2]Jerry Vogel Music Co., Inc. Used by permission.

lished as a song in 1918, but King's "Ohio" music existed before that as an incidental theme for allez-oop acts in vaudeville. It was a soothing antidote to the acrobats, and so the pantomimists borrowed it. The melody both pleased and plagued audiences, who were eager for words to sing to it, and Ballard Macdonald was summoned to supply a lyric. Then it was issued as a song. You will remember that Louis Bernstein said it sold in excess of 5,000,000 copies, the largest sale of any song of our times.

King's career as a composer covers several decades in popular music. He was a facile writer who never lost his touch because of his ability to adapt himself to the contemporary scene. His versatility was astonishing. He wrote the frumpery, "I Scream, You Scream, We All Scream for Ice Cream," and "Beyond the Gates of Paradise." He wrote, too, "America's Fair Women," which Victor Herbert, a co-editor, included in the anthology, *The World's Most Famous Music*.

His affiliations with publishers and performers were vast, and he is constantly bobbing up on the covers of hit tunes under pseudonyms (most of them women's names, strangely) confusing to the researcher. He signed the "Gates of Paradise" with his right name. But a successful lugubrious number—"Apple Blossoms"—which chased "Hearts and Flowers" off violin strings as a tear jerker for the handkerchief sequences in plays and silent movies, he composed under the pseudonym of Kathleen A. Roberts. The first issues of his song "Anona" bear the name of Vivian Grey. It was popularized by the greatest of our Indian pop-tune exploiters, Mabel McKinley, a niece of the assassinated President. When it went into the hit class, "Vivian Grey" was removed from the cover and the song attributed to Miss McKinley, who legally defended her "ownership."

On the night of September 18, 1903, Doris Wilson, a vaudeville singer, was just beginning the chorus of "Anona" when a process server stomped down the aisle waving his summons, shouting to Miss Wilson to stop. She did, and so did the orchestra, for a near riot followed in which four women fainted. The audience believed he was brandishing a pistol. The action was said to have been initiated by Miss McKinley to prevent Miss Wilson and others from singing "her" song that King wrote.

King had a fine sense of irony, and of illusions regarding the song-writing business, none whatever. His technical training consisted of four music lessons on the piano in early youth at fifty cents each, and he contended, seriously, that a fifth would have ruined him for his work.

When Feist brought out the Century Edition of ten-cent titles, King composed more than three hundred numbers for it, taxing his inspiration no whit. He went to the countryside, putting up at a place on a lake. Daily he hired a rowboat and bought a case of beer. Then, flat on his back as the boat drifted aimlessly, and fortified with a sheaf of best-selling teaching pieces, he filled in a right-hand melody to their left-hand accompaniments. At any rate, it was an exercise, not Chopin, Tschaikowsky, or Grieg note for note. And if he erred, so did Gounod, whose obbligato to Bach's first prelude in the *Well-Tempered Clavichord* is a well-liked "Ave Maria."

At the time King wrote "Beautiful Ohio" in 1918, he was a salaried man on the staff of Shapiro, Bernstein, for whom he was to furnish four songs a month. "Beautiful Ohio" was one. The profits from its amazing sales the firm could well have pocketed, yet Bernstein says he paid King $60,000 in royalties on the sales, a stroke of justice virtually incomparable in the industry.

King, with Theodore Morse (who wrote "Dear Old Girl"), F. B. Haviland, later a prominent publisher, and Herman Snyder, who afterwards managed the Crown Music Co., had all begun as music clerks with the Charles H. Ditson Co. when that firm was at Broadway and Eighteenth Street. The four were in poor circumstances and sought to increase their earnings by writing songs for publication. This ambition was occasionally achieved in an unusual way. Whenever orders for titles came in that could not be located, King or Morse or Haviland or Snyder would oblige by writing a song for the title that was ordered. One was "Wait Till the Clouds Roll By," another, "While Strolling Through the Park One Day," which was published under the title, "The Fountain in the Park." Which one of the four wrote which song no one knows and no one ever will, but the Park song was dedicated to Robert (King) Keiser.

Some of the "frauds" were surprising. "Bring Back My Bonnie to Me," and "Goodbye, My Lover, Goodbye" were faked for two years before the originals came to hand. Then they were reissued correctly. In the industry, such incidents were casual. Any writer who couldn't crib a grand-opera aria or lift entirely a foreign song wasn't seasoned. The Neapolitan song made famous by Caruso, "Sul e Mar," is note for note the chorus of William J. Scanlon's "My Nellie's Blue Eyes." King died in 1932, when he was seventy-two, and Thomas (Fats) Waller at the organ played "Beyond the Gates of Paradise" at his services.

John Flynn, who wrote the successful song, "Sweet Annie Moore," Will D. Cobb, and Gus Edwards virtually formed a corporate stock interest in Safford Waters, a fancy fellow who Flynn, Cobb, and Edwards were certain was a stockbroker because of his attire—frock coat, worsted trousers, spats, and a top hat. The rendezvous of the trio of song writers was the office of Howley, Haviland & Co. in Twentieth Street, and on Saturday afternoons steadily for years Waters would arrive with a song lyric for submission to one of the trio for polishing. For this service they charged Waters $25, which he paid gladly. His visits were so regular that the trio took turns in their assistance and kept news of their gold mine carefully guarded from the rest of the fraternity. And all on his own, Waters wrote one song that has lived as long as any of those of his three advisers—"The Belle of Avenoo A." Nor was it disclosed until years later that he was never a stockbroker but a fashionable interior decorator.

S·W·E·E·T AD—DUH—L·I·N·E

A COLORFUL FIGURE of the early 1900 period (and still is; he is sales manager for Shapiro, Bernstein), was Tommy Hughes, who actually was responsible for the formation of the firm of Waterson, Berlin and Snyder, an important publishing house until its dissolution in 1929. Henry Waterson, a wealthy diamond merchant, in 1906 was the financial backer of the Crown Music Co. and also of the firm Helf and Hager, another publishing house that ultimately was forced out of business through the success of the song Bert Williams made popular, "Play That Barber Shop Chord," about which more a few pages later. A contemporary firm was Rose and Snyder, whose financial support came from George Krey, a Boston music dealer.

Waterson admired the business ability of Ted Snyder greatly and once observed to Tommy Hughes that he would gladly back Snyder if he desired to quit Rose and form a new house. Tommy, of course, immediately informed Snyder. "But how shall I get in touch with him?" said Snyder. "I'd like to do it in a way that would introduce me to him in an unusual manner." Tommy then suggested that he write a couple of songs and submit them to Waterson. He did, and after the examination Waterson said, "These seem to be all right, but who are you?" "I'm Ted Snyder." Thereafter the men got together and organized the firm in which Irving Berlin was subsequently made a member, because, as in the instance of Harry Von Tilzer with Shapiro, Bernstein, it was cheaper than paying Berlin royalties.

Tommy was once approached by Dick Gerard, who offered him a lyric. Tommy was just closing the shutters of Howley, Haviland and Dresser, at 4 East Twentieth Street, and was annoyed. "I'll give you $5.00 for it," said Tommy. But Gerard held out for $10—vainly, for he subsequently accepted the first offer. Tommy put his name on it as the author of the lyric, and it was published as "She's Sleeping by the Silvery Rio Grande." It proved a profitable investment, for Tommy drew $450 royalties on the song during its life.

Afterward, Gerard explained that he had a date and needed a new hat. He did considerably better with a song called "Sweet Adeline," the bacchanalian chant of the nation's bibulous for years, the lyric of which he wrote to the music of Harry Armstrong. The tune was originally called "Down Home in Old New England" but nobody would buy it, because the lyric was considered inferior. Armstrong, who knew Gerard, asked him if he had another lyric, and Gerard produced one he'd called "Sweet Rosalie." This lyric was fitted to Armstrong's tune, but again the publishers were apathetic, because there was another Rosalie song currently popular. Gerard mended that fast. At the time (1903), Adelina Patti was making one of her farewell tours, and so he borrowed the English equivalent of her name.

The song has been a consistent seller, and in 1933 Gerard said he had realized about $4,000 as his share of the royalties. Gerard, whose full name is Richard Gerard Husch, wrote a number of other songs, one of which drew the concern of Anthony Comstock. It was called "The Guessing Coon," and when somebody told the smut ferret that Gerard's lyric was about the Negro father of twins—one white, the other black—Comstock had the song suppressed.

They were days of color, the 1900s. True, the poets of the Alley were curbed in their expression, but the composers piped merrily some of the best songs in pop-tune history during the first decade of the new century, several of which may endure. The more imaginative of the poets who also possessed a dash of subtlety, occasionally, too, crossed the line so vigorously drawn by the vaudeville managers and to which the publishers were forced to hew. Sam Lewis, or Edgar Leslie, say, both inglorious Miltons, for who among our readers will recall that Lewis wrote, with Joe Young, Al Jolson's "Mammy," "Dinah," "King for a Day," "Sittin' on Top of the World," "In a Little

Spanish Town," "Beautiful Lady in Blue," and with George Meyer, "Tuck Me to Sleep in My Old 'Tucky Home"?

Some of Leslie's best known lyrics are "Oh, What a Pal Was Mary," "For Me and My Gal," "America, I Love You," "Romance," "Get Out and Get Under," and, in later years, "I Left Her by the River St. Marie," "Rose of the Rio Grande," "In a Little Gypsy Tea Room," and "Moon Over Miami." One of Leslie's most successful songs was "Among My Souvenirs," which he wrote to the music of Horatio Nicholls, nom de plume of Lawrence Wright. Leslie wrote the lyric on the Isle of Man on a holiday during which he read Anatole France's *The Crime of Sylvester Bonnard*, Lafcadio Hearn's translation. The chapter, "The Daughter of Clementine," citing the memories of an old man, interested him greatly and inspired the "Souvenir" lyric. Leslie is the only song writer of any substance who never hired out to the publishers; he remained a free lance for the thirty-six years of his career.

Before "'Tucky Home" was published, somebody on the staff wanted Lewis to add more "tucks" to "'Tucky Home," which Sam, as an artist, refused to do. "Even after the song reached 500,000 copies, they still wanted me to add more 'tucks,'" Sam once told the writer. If lyricists are quite mad, they have reason to be. During the height of Lewis' acclaim, he walked one day into an Alley office with his latest lyric, which included these lines:

> I'll build a palace
> To the aurora borealis
> In your eyes.

It was an unusual poetic conception, and Lewis was justifiably proud. The music editor read it over, and Lewis saw the gleam. It was sold, all right. But not without the literary mayhem lyricists perpetually suffer.

"Sam," said the editor, "it's wonderful. But them French words gotta come out."

Lewis was an adept at "catch" lines. These are the final

couplet or tag lines of a chorus which were supposed to snap the song to an arresting finish, a technique that was demanded in the 1900s. Here is one of Lewis' from his song, "Oh, How I Wish I Could Sleep Until My Daddy Comes Home":

> Oh, mama, that's when I thought
> God made the nighttime too short.[1]

Song writers are born in the light of a gibbous moon when the little people walk. Surely this was the setting at the nativity of Fred Fisher. Tossing typewriters into Broadway to relieve the ennui of a friend was but a mild aberration of the eccentric Fisher. A five-dollar bill slowly and casually shredded during a street-corner conversation was another of his interesting diversions. His passionate disregard for new neckties was a boon to the haberdashers, for Fisher only purchased them for destruction.

When *The Jazz Singer*, first of the talking pictures, loosed its thunderbolt in the entertainment industry in 1927, song writers fled to Hollywood in droves, Fisher among the first. Before packing, he sold his catalogue to Jack Mills for $15,000. Among Fisher's songs were "Dardanella," "I'm Always Chasing Rainbows," "Ma, He's Making Eyes at Me," "Daddy, You've Been a Mother to Me," "Wee, Wee, Marie," and "Chicago." When the picture companies subsequently bought up other catalogues for their own use (Warner Brothers today control 30 per cent of the popular-song catalogues) for hundreds of thousands of dollars, Fisher was made painfully aware of his mistake.

It was partially recovered in a typical Hollywood experience. Fisher went to the Coast for Metro-Goldwyn-Mayer. The first day he entered the studio, the late Irving Thalberg passed him in the corridor. "Who is that guy?" he asked. "That's Fred Fisher, the symphonic writer," his companion replied.

Thalberg turned, halted Fisher, and led him back to his office.

[1]By permission of the copyright proprietor, Mills Music, Inc.

"Can you write a symphony?" he asked.

"Get me a pencil, boy," said Fisher, adding, "When you get me you get Beethoven, Mozart, and Chopin."

And Thalberg hired him to write a symphony. For four months thereafter Fisher ambled stealthily about Hollywood, adopted a slouch hat and gait, carrying a large portfolio under his arm, presumably music scores. When anyone addressed him, he responded in Weber and Fieldsian dialect. The act was so perfect that Fisher received $500 a week for sixteen weeks without question.

Fisher's biggest hit was "Dardanella"—and his biggest nuisance. The piece was first brought to him by Johnny Black, a vaudeville actor, who called it "Turkish Tom-Tom." It was an instrumental number. Fisher was struck by the peculiar beat of the bass, but it had no chorus, and Fisher asked Black to write one. He did. Fisher then labeled it "Dardanella," and a few weeks after the song was published, Felix Bernard, another vaudeville actor back from a tour, told Fisher the piece was written by him. Fisher brought the two together, and a satisfactory adjustment was made. Bernard's name, incidentally, always appeared on the sheet copy.

The song didn't go at first, because the bass was too strong for the melody. Fisher corrected that with a new arrangement by Arthur Lange that gave the melody to a solo B-flat saxophone, with all the other instruments, subdued, carrying the bass. This was a novelty, and the song started to sell. During the rise in sales, Bernard wrote Fisher that he would like to sell out. He asked $100 for his interest, Fisher bought it, and Bernard went out on the circuit again. When he returned, "Dardanella" was a smash hit, and Bernard sued Fisher, contending that he had been deceived. Bernard lost the suit on the basis of testimony that the song was not a hit when Fisher bought the plaintiff's rights. Less than a year later the song sold 2,500,000 sheet copies and 6,750,000 records. Fisher told the writer that he cleared more than $1,000,000 on "Dardanella" and that he paid bonuses to his staff, comprising Ben Edwards,

Jack Mills, George Friedman, Jack McCoy, and Harry Mittenthal.

Just before his death in 1942, Fisher capped the history: "And Mittenthal, McCoy, and Friedman went into competition against me, opening up a rival publishing house with the bonus I paid them." He said it without rancor; everything was a laugh to him. He thought they were smart. And he rewarded Johnny Black; gave him a year's contract.

But "Dardanella" as a legal *cause célèbre* was by no means exhausted. In 1922, Jerome Kern introduced a song in the musical *Good Morning, Dearie,* called "Kalua." Fisher called it a steal from the bass of "Dardanella" and sued Kern, Charles B. Dillingham, the producer, and T. B. Harms, Max Dreyfus, president, publishers of the score of the musical.

Fisher speedily turned the trial into a judicial floor show. It began before Federal Judge John C. Knox, who, because of the illness of his mother, relinquished the case to Judge Learned Hand. Harms subpoenaed Artur Bodanzky, Leopold Stokowski, and Victor Herbert. ("And what did you write?" the learned court asked of Victor Herbert.) Each of these musical pundits denied that the bass of "Dardanella" was original, and Fisher countered with an eight-piece band, introducing May Singhi Breen and her ukelele as an added soloist. Fisher also obliged, playing "Dardanella" on the piano.

"Your Honor," asked Fisher, when he had finished his rendition, "may I now play another melody?" The court nodded, and Fisher played "Nearer My God to Thee" against the harem thump and wriggling rhythm of "Dardanella's" bass.

After the trial there was a meeting in chambers, and Fisher offered to settle with Kern for a suit of clothes. "But Kern was an egotist," said Fisher, "and said he wouldn't settle for a thousand suits of clothes."

Judge Hand ruled for Fisher, awarding him $250 damages, with the comment that the suit was "trivial pother of scarcely more than irritation and a waste of time for everyone involved."

"Knox would have given me $50,000," lamented Fisher. But

what hurt worse was the court's angular implication that the industry was juvenile and its practitioners doodlers who might better improve their time with paper dolls. Songs, may the court please, come from the heart and rate only second to a publisher's till.

To his death, Fisher never forgave Joe Goodwin for ribbing him about the song, "Daddy, You've Been a Mother to Me," for which Fisher wrote the words and the music. The blight of prohibition had just descended, and the optimistic Sam Dolliver, believing the nation would stop its nonsense and effect an immediate repeal, continued his lease of the Globe Café, a rendezvous of song writers on Broadway near Forty-seventh Street. He hacked out the bar, sold his stock, and set up, temporarily he hoped, an exhibition of freaks, stationing them on platforms and permitting them the usual concession of selling their photographs. Joe wandered into the exhibit one afternoon, and aware that Fisher was about to publish "Daddy, You've Been a Mother to Me," bought a picture from the bearded lady and sent it to Fisher as an illustration for his song cover.

A hit song is a valuable piece of property, and the writers and publishers will fly to the law at the slightest infringement. Lawyers, in fact, derive almost as much revenue from songs as they do from divorces. "My Melancholy Baby" was a famous litigant. Originally titled, "Melancholy," it was written in Denver, Colorado, by Ernie Burnett to a lyric by his wife, Maybelle E. Watson, in 1911. The following year Burnett placed it with Theron C. Bennett, a Denver publisher and owner of the nationally known Dutch Mill Café in that city.

Bennett thought the lyric needed polishing and asked George A. Norton to rewrite it. When it was published in 1912, Norton was named as the author, with no credit anywhere to Miss Watson. The song was an outstanding success, and in 1914 the rights were purchased by the Joe Morris Music Co., of Philadelphia. In 1940, Miss Watson, whom everyone thought dead and who had been divorced from Burnett for years, brought suit to establish her interest in the copyright renewal. She proved her authorship by the manuscript copy filed with the Library of Congress, and the defendants were forced to settle. She obtained a sum for back royalties and won an agreement compelling the publisher to print her name on the copy as co-author with Norton.

The legal ramifications in relation to one of Bert Williams' best songs, "Play That Barber Shop Chord," were graver, funnier, and more dramatic. In 1910 Ballard Macdonald who, the reader may recall, wrote the lyric for Bob King's "Beautiful Ohio," was under contract to Jos. W. Stern & Co. He was constantly at odds with Ed Marks because he contended that Marks would never advance him any money. In the same year, Lewis F. Muir wrote the music of "The Barber Shop Chord." Macdonald wrote the lyric to it, and a good one it is:

Chorus: Mister Jefferson Lord, play that barber shop chord,
        That soothin' harmony, has made an awful, awful,
        Awful hit with me.
        Play that strain, just to please me again.
        For Mister when you start that minor part
        I feel my fingers slippin' and a grippin' at my heart!
        Oh, Lord! Play that barber shop chord.[2]

He gave it to Muir and asked him not to mention his part in it. The song was unfinished, and Muir went to William Tracey, then a singing waiter in the Third Avenue Rathskeller, told him he had only a "dummy" lyric and asked him to finish it. It was Tracey's first song.

Muir was satisfied and placed it with J. Fred Help, who published it, as was previously observed, to his ruination, perhaps the only instance in the industry wherein a publisher was ruined by a hit song. Tracey said he was told that Help had interested Bert Williams in the song and that Williams would introduce it for the first time at the opening matinee at Hammerstein's Victoria Theater, Broadway and Forty-second Street. Tracey herded all his friends together, and they went up to hear Williams, a great artist, sing the song. After he had sung seven or eight songs, Williams bowed off, and Tracey's friends made ungentlemanly remarks about song writers with delusions.

The applause continued, and after about six more bows, Williams nodded to the orchestra leader, who began the introduction of "The Barber Shop Chord." Actually, the reception was riotous. The *Morning Telegraph*, a theatrical paper, headed a lengthy review of the vaudeville bill thus:

BERT WILLIAMS DISCOVERS
TWO NEW WRITERS; SCORES
A TREMENDOUS SUCCESS

When "The Barber Shop Chord" went into the hit class, Macdonald became interested. He went to Helf with a claim for money on the grounds that he had written the lyric. Helf said no. Besides, he added, there was some trouble about the song. As a prophet Helf was wonderful. From the Helf office, Macdonald went over to Ed Marks, head of the Jos. W. Stern Co., and told Marks he had written the lyric of the song, and Ed said goodness gracious or some unreasonable facsimile. Macdonald being under contract, Marks owned whatever he produced, and he promptly hailed Helf to the New York Supreme Court. Despite Tracey's testimony of his part in writing the lyric, and that Muir had told him he had adapted the song from a previously published number called "Play That Fandango Rag," Justice Joseph E. Newberger ruled that the lyric was Macdonald's and the victory Marks's.

Damages were assessed at $37,000. Helf paid and went out of business. And Tracey says he never made a nickel on the song. Because of instances like the foregoing, men in the industry to the time of his death called Carl Laemmle the wisest publisher in the business. He quit to make motion pictures.

The zany expression of the industry is beautifully characterized in "Yes, We Have No Bananas," a most apposite theme song. It was submitted to Shapiro, Bernstein by Irving Conn (nee Cohen) and Frank Silver. The lads came over after

Waterson, Berlin and Snyder had rejected it. They had asked for $1,ooo advance. Bernstein agreed to give it to them but insisted the song should be entirely rewritten. Originally it began, "Everywhere you go you hear a song," which Bernstein said was no good; it just talked about a song. So they went to work, and it emerged, finally, a perfect job of collaboration by virtually the entire Shapiro, Bernstein office. The late Jimmy Hanley contributed the line, "There's a fruit store on our street," and Elliott Shapiro offered, "It's run by a Greek," and Lew Brown, later of De Sylva, Brown and Henderson, finished the verse. The lyric of the second verse was touched up by Ballard Macdonald—everybody had a fist in it.

And the music is as lovely a bit of bastardy as was ever seminated in the Alley: the opening phrase is note for note the "Hallelujah" chorus of Händel's *Messiah*, there are distinct acknowledgments to Balfe's *Bohemian Girl*, and, worse, since it was still in copyright, a few bars from Max Dreyfus' "Old Fashioned Garden"—one, Bernstein recalls, of at least four infringements.

So they took it over to Dreyfus and asked permission to use the "Old Fashioned Garden" theme. Dreyfus said no. Then, scanning the sheet, "But if you use it this way," and he made a slight change, "it is o.k." Bernstein says Dreyfus actually improved it. They went back to the Shapiro office, and after Bob King smoothed the melody, it was ready to go. Then somebody remembered that the title was used as a catch line by the late cartoonist Tad Dorgan.

This was pretty disheartening, but they began a check that eventually disclosed the title was not even original with Tad. They learned that, in San Francisco, returning veterans from the Philippines were full of yarns about a fabulous fruit vendor in Manila whose pidgin English included the sentence Bernstein had accepted for the song title.

The labor and headaches were profitable. As the first of the goof ditties, criminally responsible for the "Music Goes 'Round and Around," "Three Little Fishies" (theme of the goldfish-swallowing college lads), "The Hut Sut Song," "Boogly Woogly Piggly," etc., it sold several million copies.

Later Bernstein placed "Bananas" with a Viennese music house, which had as hellish a time with it. It was virtually impossible to translate the title into German and retain the ridiculous contrast. They tried it first with, "*Ja, Wir Haben Keinen Bananen,*" which was perfect German but didn't mean anything. In final desperation the poor lyricist, before flinging himself from the window, exclaimed, "*Ausgerechnet Bananen!*" "Of All Things! Bananas!" There was his title.

At least it was an exciting way to make a song. And that is the way songs are made—impromptu, spontaneously. To this day, Bernstein insists that publicity was never a factor in selling a song. It can only be exploited by a singer or a band so that the public may hear and eventually learn the melody: Melodies learned mean melodies liked, then bought. He can prove his belief.

In 1915, William Randolph Hearst told Bernstein that he, Hearst, could make any song through publicity. Bernstein stuck to his theory, but agreed to a year's contract with Hearst that was really a gambling proposition: Hearst said he could make a song through his press; Bernstein said he couldn't. Immediately after, the Hearst newspapers and publications devoted column upon column to Shapiro, Bernstein songs and to performers who sang them in every city in which Hearst had newspapers. At the end of the year the largest sale of any one of the six songs (one was "Never Forget to Write Home," by Joe Goodwin and Jimmy Hanley) exploited by Hearst was 50,000 copies, and in a year—1915—when it was no trouble at all to sell 250,000 copies of a good tune.

MUSIC FOR PROFIT

THIS IS THE CURRENT APPRAISAL of a popular song: It means nothing intrinsically. It is several pieces of paper that is a product upon which it is hoped to make money. Most of the publishers (we speak of conditions today) and all of the professional song writers are members of the American Society of Composers, Authors and Publishers, a protective organization that guards the music of its members from piracy, infringement, and unauthorized performance, and licenses its members' music for performing rights for profit. Fees are collected from radio commercial and sustaining programs, motion pictures, restaurants, hotels, and dance halls. And up to 1941 they averaged $80,000 a week. Foreign-affiliation payments and operating expenses amount to about 28 per cent of ASCAP revenues. The balance is distributed 50-50 to the member song writers and publishers, not equally, but on a rating based on reputation, length of membership, and number of songs. Some win their double "A"s as board members. A number of states have challenged the organization in suits charging that its license system is illegal, and in March, 1941, Federal Judge F. Ryan Duffy fined ASCAP and its officials $35,250 for violation of the antitrust laws.

In the same year, 1941, the National Association of Broadcasters notified ASCAP officials it would no longer pay the licensing fees demanded, on the grounds that they were exorbitant. ASCAP officials refused to prune its prices, and the broadcasters barred ASCAP music from the air. Thus, for eleven months the music of Victor Herbert, Gershwin, Berlin, and other popular writers was not available to the listening public, which seemed not to care. Indeed, sturdy support of ASCAP in its fight against the broadcasters by many of the nation's most influential newspapers failed to arouse the apathetic public, and for interesting sociological reasons we shall subsequently examine.

Further to bolster its move, the broadcasters set up their own musical clearinghouse, calling it Broadcast Music, Inc., which was speedily shortened to the alphabetical BMI. It hired a number of renegade and non-ASCAP composers, set them to work on the assembly line, and produced typical pop tunes of average interest acceptable to the average listener.

The action of the broadcasters took a terrifying toll of ASCAP's revenue, reducing it to a tithe, and the organization asked for peace. New contracts were executed at lower fees, and the broadcasters capped their victory by refusing to dissolve their own BMI. This brought an internal revolt within ASCAP to the fore, and in the open internecine battle Gene Buck, ASCAP's president for eighteen years, was removed from office and supplanted by Deems Taylor, who now serves as a front without salary. This was hemlock for Gene. But the society made his drink non-poisonous. He was retained in an advisory capacity, and his annual salary of $35,000 was continued—an honorable and justifiable recognition of his long and militant service.

That, at this writing, is the status of the society that grew out of a casual observation by Victor Herbert to Nathan Burkan on an evening in 1914 at dinner in Shanley's, then a nationally known Broadway restaurant. The string orchestra was playing "Sweethearts."

"Listen to them," said Herbert to Burkan, a prominent theatrical attorney. "It must be the fifteenth time this week I have heard my score played in public places. And I don't get a nickel for it."

Burkan replied that something should be done. He held that a man's talent and work, giving pleasure to thousands, should be consistently rewarded financially. Soon after, Herbert, John Philip Sousa, George Maxwell, then head of the powerful music house of Ricordi, and Burkan organized the American Society of Composers, Authors and Publishers, and that same year Burkan brought a test suit against Shanley's restaurant for permitting its orchestra to play the score of Herbert's "Sweethearts" without license. Three years later (1917), the suit was carried to the United States Supreme Court, which unanimously concurred in the opinion of Justice Oliver Wendell Holmes, supporting the legal right of ASCAP to license its members' music for a fee. Shanley's maintained that the music was only incidental to the restaurant. "If the music did not pay," wrote

Justice Holmes, "it would be given up. If it pays, it pays out of the public pocketbook. Whether it pays or not, the purpose of employing it is profit, and that is enough."

The formation and subsequent vigorous administration of ASCAP was the first great stabilizing factor in the pop-tune industry. Its force policed dance halls, cafés, restaurants, hotels, taverns, and theaters, and, about 1921, approximated its goal of a general increase in financial yield for its members. But the serenity was short-lived. Out of the brains of Marconi, De Forest, and other inventive scientists, radio was born, and ASCAP faced a new dilemma. To the first stations ASCAP gave free licenses for its music or charged a nominal sum, a charity that was stopped with the development of radio advertising and the resultant enormous revenues that inhered to the chains through its sales of commercial time.

The next great stabilizing step of the industry was the organization, in 1916, of the Music Publishers Protective Association. Its instigation was to curb and eventually to eliminate the racket of song plugging. We have said that the current appraisal of a popular song is that it has no intrinsic value. That statement was made to the writer by Fred Fisher, an eccentric, but a confirmed realist. Fisher meant it in relation to the interest of the orchestra leader or prominent singer. If it is not played or sung, your song is a piece of paper. So a song becomes a hit only if it is exploited. The exploitation is devious in method, sometimes nefarious, and there are many in the industry who, up to 1942, would call "nefarious" a prize understatement.

Song plugging began in the '90s, and a great offender—but no apologist—was J. Aldrich Libbey, the great baritone of the period. In as frank an interview the writer has ever seen, Libbey admitted to the New York *Herald*, which published his statement on November 26, 1893, that he was responsible "for inflicting such songs on the public as 'After the Ball,' 'Kiss and Let's Make Up,' 'Two Little Girls in Blue,' and 'Sweet Rosabel.'" The rather impertinent reporter then asked Libbey if he did not find such trash repellent.

"Not altogether," said Libbey. "Of course, to the trained ear of a professional these songs are somewhat disappointing. But the recompense comes in the wider audience that a singer has for his simple themes. All of these songs, no matter how weak or tawdry from a classical standpoint, still contain a homely sentiment which is beneficial in its moral influence. Besides there is much greater art required in the delivery of even such a song as 'After the Ball' from the platform than is generally supposed. For instance I have noticed more than a hundred times when I have reached and enunciated such commonplace ideas as, 'Have you no babies? Have you no home?' that many in my audiences have been visibly affected."

The *Herald*, in the same interview, stated that, for plugging "After the Ball," Libbey received $500 and a percentage of the sales revenue. He was by no means alone; Jack Allison, Banks Winter, and many others accepted similar gratuities to sing the songs of certain publishers and writers, which often were unsuited to their voice, style, and personality.

This type of plugging persisted throughout the 1900s, until it became a plague and an expense unwarranted in the budgets of many publishers, some of whom contended that, under this questionable procedure, it cost from $25,000 to $75,000 annually to popularize a song. By 1915 it had reached the proportions of an evil that affected everyone in the theatrical and popular-song industry. Each of the publishers was forced to outbid the others to obtain the services of prominent artists to present his songs. That Quartet, the Empire City Quartet, the Avon Comedy Four, Belle Baker, Fanny Brice, Sophie Tucker—all the great and popular artists were besieged by publishers waving checks at them for ridiculous sums. They even paid acrobats to use the melodies of their songs for entrance, exit, and cues.

It was called the "direct payment evil" and it was freely estimated that large firms—Feist and Remick were two—were paying an average of from $15,000 to $25,000 a month to professionals for plugging their songs. It was a nuisance also to the vaudeville managers. For example, one headline quartet sang twelve songs of a certain publisher, who paid the act $100 a song. With this fortification they were heedless of managers and bookers, and of their artistry too, which suffered at the jumbled repertoire.

Thus, the small publisher was threatened with extinction, and *Variety*, the theatrical trade paper, of which John J. O'Connor was business manager, faced the loss of considerable advertising revenue. The publishers could not pay at both ends and eventually would have been forced to drop their advertisements. O'Connor made this clear to Sime Silverman, owner and founder of *Variety*, who told him to go ahead if he had a plan, but to act as an individual and not as a representative of *Variety*.

O'Connor first visited Henry Waterson, of Waterson, Berlin and Snyder. He said he would join in an agreement to stop the practice if the majority of his competitors would similarly bind themselves. Of the thirty-eight publishers O'Connor visited, only three refused—Feist, Remick, and Max Dreyfus, of T. B. Harms. But unfortunately they were among the largest, and O'Connor realized his efforts would be vain without their co-operation.

Vaudeville then being the greatest medium of song exploitation, O'Connor went to John J. Murdock, E. F. Albee's associate and a power in the Keith-Orpheum Circuit. He explained the purpose of the payment system and put it squarely up to Murdock that, if it was not stopped, it would become a malevolent factor in vaudeville because so many singers were unadapted to the songs and because of the audience irritation at their constant repetition. Murdock was interested and agreed to accompany O'Connor that evening to a performance of the bill at the Alhambra Theater. The acrobats opened the show to the tune of the song "I Didn't Raise My Boy to Be a Soldier," published in 1916 by Feist and then, the fall of the year, sweeping the country. In the No. 2 act the man and woman sang it. The dramatic sketch used it for background music. The comedy sketch used it for an entrance cue. The quartet sang its chorus twelve times. In the next to closing act, a boy sang it from a box, and the dog act that closed the show performed tricks to the same number. Murdock was convinced.

The next day, Murdock summoned O'Connor and Maurice Goodman, attorney for Keith and Albee. He instructed Goodman to co-operate with O'Connor in the formation of an organization for the general protection of vaudeville and music publishers and authorized him to announce that the music of any publisher who failed to join such protective association would be barred from the nation's vaudeville circuits.

O'Connor set up a tentative plan for an organization called the Music Publishers Protective Association and called a meeting of representatives of the thirty-five willing publishers at the Columbia Theater, now the site of the Mayfair, at Broadway and Forty-seventh Street. To this meeting O'Connor read a proposed agreement eliminating the payment system, which all of the thirty-five signed. An initiation fee of $1,000 was voted for subsequent applicants.

The following Monday, Sophie Tucker was to open at the Fifth Avenue Theater with a repertoire of Feist songs, and Clarice Vance, the wife of Mose Gumble, professional manager for Remick, opened at another theater with a repertoire of Remick songs. When they arrived for rehearsal in the morning, they were informed that their songs were restricted because the publishers were not members of the Music Publishers Protective Association. At noon, Fred Belcher, of the Remick firm, and Edgar F. Bitner, general manager for Feist, came to the offices of the MPPA in the Columbia Theater building, signed up, and paid their initiation fee in the organization they could have joined previously without cost. Dreyfus, whose music was largely operettas and musical comedies and who had never practiced the "payment evil," also came in. At once the strength of the MPPA was felt when they cracked down on the recording companies, a number of whom were then taking off 10 per cent for what they laughingly called "breakage." The word has since become obsolete in the industry.

For a number of years things moved gently in the industry, until the advent of radio again disrupted normal procedure and the "payment evil" returned with doubled virulence. Throughout the 1930s, an important orchestra leader friendly to the songs of a certain publisher occasionally feigned surprise that a new Buick sedan, parked at his door, was his. Frequent gifts of money were made. And there were instances wherein leaders who plugged a certain song whose sales had scarcely equaled 100 copies were paid royalties on a sales basis of 20,000 copies.

It was common to put the name of an orchestra leader on a song he might agree to plug as co-author and cut him in on the royalties. Or they would just cut him in anyway. The average annual cost to the publishers, during the 1930s, of paying orchestra leaders and prominent singers to plug songs was estimated at $500,000.

The working song pluggers, who are the publishers' contact men, bitterly opposed the practice and set up their own union, The Music Publishers Contact Mens Union, which is an American Federation of Labor affiliate. Still they were helpless to eliminate completely the evil. And in the early part of 1942, O'Connor, who became business manager of Fred Waring's enterprises, was called in. O'Connor reorganized the entire setup, adjusted the errors, flatly stopped all payments over which he had control, and today is the president of the union.

These distinct upheavals—the rationing of profits under ASCAP, the solidarity of publishers in the MPPA—were almost coincidental with a trend in the popular-song expression that was significant and of sociological interest. This was the accent on rhythm at the expense of melody. The great national chorus of song became faint at last, was finally, in our time as a mass expression, stilled. The piano, symbol of middle-class families from the '70s almost precisely to 1914, was now, in the latter half of the new century's second decade, mute in many homes, its "ditties of no tone" a dirge and an epitaph. Briefly it struggled against the phonograph, quickly succumbed to the radio, slain by the knife of science. Mechanical reproduction is an economic spur to artistry, breeding specialists whose excellence is financially rewarded. But it first made us a nation of listeners, and latterly a nation of dancers. In the '90s, a girl's piano lessons were as normal a routine as her needlework. That tradition was no more.

An astonishing confluence of events was responsible for the anemic melodic strain contemporary in our pop tunes. Melody is the bloodstream of song, and for twenty-five years it has grown thinner and thinner. At first imperceptibly, now quite apparent. Where are the composers? The paucity of even a semblance of imaginative talent is proved in today's note-for-note thefts of Tschaikowsky, Grieg, Chopin, Debussy, and Mozart—a current trend inaugurated (with forthrightness; he gave credit to its origin) by André Kostelanetz with his "Isle of May." Who replaced Gershwin? A rather unfair question: Gershwin was not a popular-song writer. The head of a large publishing house told the writer but a few days before these lines were set down that he always regarded Gershwin "a bad proposition commercially." In the industry, Gershwin was known as a "faddist." The definition is found in the characterization of another publisher: "Gershwin was too good to be rated strictly pop tune."

Gershwin did much to improve the standard of American popular music. Yet the zenith of his talent was a death blow at melody, at song. Its sentiment was pseudo, mocking, critical; its essence was mental; its technique, rhythm. It is robot music in relation to the pop-tune genre. It was clad in rayon, not overalls and jumper. It smelled not of sweat and the stale beer of a Sabbath morn. It has the febrile odor of civilization's sickroom. Its pulse was the rivet, not the heart. Its rhythm was geared to the airplane, the microphone, the sound track. In the gamut of his musical span is the notation on the card of a speak-easy, and the causes of war—speed, greed, and the denial of graciousness and freedom.

Yet Gershwin but picked up the torch. Rhythmic influences were apparent long before the world went into its tailspin.

Irving Berlin wrote "Alexander's Ragtime Band" in 1911, unwittingly as a hymn to Gershwin and the feverish beat of jazz,
swing, and boogie-woogie that now contorts the juxtaposed
bodies of Americans everywhere. Here is the top man pop-tune
writer. No one could get near him, this self-inspired little
singing waiter whom they called, rightly in his Bowery days,
Izzy Baline. He is a master of skillful, tricky rhythm, and his
showmanship for a tune is unsurpassed. Unlike Ernest Ball, who
was all but helpless without the aid of a lyricist, Berlin supplied
his own ideas, put his own name on the lyrics of his songs. Recall
some of his songs: "Always," "Call Me Up Some Rainy Afternoon," "Somebody's Coming to My House," "Crinoline Days,"
"A Pretty Girl Is Like a Melody," "Easter Parade," "Isn't This a
Lovely Day?" "God Bless America" . . .

Berlin transcended the "technique" of the pop tune, which
at its average best is a manufactured product. Many regard his
"When I Lost You," with which he commemorated the death
of his first wife, Dorothy, a sister of E. Ray Goetz, as his best
song. Perhaps it is. Of more sociological importance, though,
are his dance songs, "Everybody's Doing It" ("Doing What?
Turkey Trot") and the "International Rag." Here, with the
issuance of these, happened the great confluence—the meeting
of the rhythmic waters of jazz and the feverish tripping beat
of the sensational Castles, Vernon and Irene, who almost overnight in 1914 stopped America's singing and started the sway
that was to end in swing.

Vernon Castle, whose real name was Blythe, was an English
eccentric comedian. Irene, whose real name was Foote, was a
New Rochelle girl who first met Vernon at a swimming party
on Long Island Sound. He was enchanted with her from the
first, and when she asked him to get her a job in his American
musical, *The Hen Pecks*, he seriously entertained her proposal
and succeeded in placing her with the company. She danced
a tarantella in the show and later, in *The Summer Widowers*,
Lew Fields' next musical, she and Vernon became engaged and
were finally married. It all but broke the heart of a little girl

in the show—Helen Hayes—who for all her fourteen years and despite the admonitions of her watchful mother, Mrs. Catherine Brown, who was always with Helen on tour, had fallen in love with Vernon, believing his blandishments, which were meant as a jest.

The following summer, the Castles, who were just another pair of musical-comedy performers in 1912, went to Paris, where, after a poverty-ridden period, they achieved a quick success as a dance team in a French revue and later at the Café de Paris and the Casino de Deauville. Returning to America, they opened as a dance team at Louis Martin's, where they inaugurated a series of tea dansants, which subsequently became the rage of the town. Everyone wished to learn their Castle Walk, a dance they created, and Vernon often taught six hours daily. At odd hours they danced at private parties. Gracious as they were graceful, they soon became society's darlings, and Vernon, a superb showman, proceeded to exploit their acclaim.

He opened, in 1914, a teatime dancing school called Castle House (he appropriated his stage name from the royal residence, Windsor Castle) and accepted a fabulous contract to dance at Sans Souci, a restaurant at Broadway and Forty-second Street, and their opening there in the season of 1914–15 attracted more ermine and mink than a first night of the Metropolitan Opera. Ford Dabney, their Negro music arranger, says that the tables for the Sans Souci opening cost $100.

THE SWAN SINGS ITS THRENODY

PRIOR TO THE INNOVATIONS of the Castles, there were mainly two types of public dancing—the two-step and the waltz. The bunny hug and the turkey trot were only variations of the two-step. The Castles created or developed to perfection and public practice the Castle *valse classique*, the Castle last waltz, the Castle combination, Castle tango, Castle lame duck, the

Castle Maxixe, Castle walk, and a step that never became popular because it was too difficult, the Castle half-and-half. This they danced to an opening measure in 3/4 time, the second bar in 2/4 time, with these rhythms alternately recurring throughout the dance.

There was no music in the industry for the Castles then, and they were forced to create their dances without instrumental accompaniment, until they came upon Ford Dabney and James Europe, both Negroes, skilled musicians, and, still better, aware of that music of three- and four-piece bands moaning in jerky beats along the bayous and the levees of Louisiana, blue in tonal color and startling in arrangement—the musical thing they call jazz.

Thereafter, until Vernon Castle was killed when he crashed his plane at Kelly Field, Texas, in 1917, to save the life of another flier, Dabney wrote all the Castles' music and Europe collaborated. They were representative of a superior group of Negro composers and musicians whose wonderful rhythmic agility was inherent. These included Cecil Mack, who wrote "Teasing" and the score for "Running Wild"; Chris Smith, who wrote one of the most apposite pieces to herald this beginning of the era of dance—"Ballin' the Jack"; William H. Tyers, composer of "Maori" and "Admiration," a tango; Lucky Roberts, composer of "The Junkman Rag" and of the currently popular "Moonlight Cocktail."

In the same group were Noble Sissle and Eubie Blake, who wrote "I'm Just Wild About Harry" and "Love Will Find a Way"; Henry Creamer and J. Turner Layton (now a music-hall star in England), who produced a fine succession of hits—"After You've Gone," "Strut Miss Lizzie," "Dear Old Southland," and " 'Way Down Yonder in New Orleans"; and Shelton Brooks, whose "Some of These Days" has lasted thirty years.

One Negro composer, W. C. Handy, "father of the blues," is internationally known. Handy was of the old school whose work derived from the people. Wandering the St. Louis streets one afternoon, he met a Negress sorrowing for her faithless husband. "My man got a heart like a stone cast into the sea and it's gone so far I can't reach it," she told Handy. And to the theme of her emotional outburst he wrote "The St. Louis Blues."

Most of his blues were similarly inspired by the sayings of his people. But the "Memphis Blues," Handy wrote as a campaign song for Edward H. Crump, Memphis politician. It was originally titled, "Mister Crump," and these lines from it, naturally, were unsung at the rallies:

> Mister Crump doan allow no easy riders here,
> Mister Crump doan allow no easy riders here.
> We doan care what Mister Crump doan allow,
> We gonna barrelhouse anyhow.
> Mister Crump can go and catch himself some air.

(Easy riders: Negro argot for pimps, procurers, and politicians.)

How the Negroes rallied to the rhythmic call! Today they are among the best practitioners of the sting of swing and boogie-woogie. Here is a roster: Thomas (Fats) Waller, superb pianist and composer of "Ain't Misbehavin'" (for which Andy Razaf, also colored, wrote the words) and "Honeysuckle Rose"; Maceo Pinkard, composer of "Mammy o' Mine" and "Sugar"; Clarence Williams, who composed the remarkable "Royal Garden Blues" (it was the pattern for about twenty-five successive numbers); Spencer Williams, who did the lyrics for "Royal Garden Blues," "Tishomingo," and "I Ain't Got Nobody"; and Perry Bradford.

Bradford had one song, "Crazy Blues," and with indefatigable industry he set out to make it a hit. He sold it to fifteen different publishers under fifteen different titles over a period of five years, hoping that one would issue it. They never did. Finally Bradford got Bessie Smith, a colored singer, to record the song for Okeh, and the disk sold well above a million records. Bradford then published the song himself—and the lawsuits started. Because everyone in the industry was amused and astonished at his nerve, they were settled amicably. Later, when Okeh offered him notes (as good as money), for his royalties on the record sales, Bradford declined. "I ain't no goat; I can't eat paper," he said.

Europe, a sound musician, organized the Clef Club in 1916. It comprised a group of colored musicians and composers, among them Will Marion Cook and J. Rosamund Johnson, and he made it an important musical unit in New York. Europe was also a pioneer in promoting jazz. He may well have been the first to bring it north. As early as 1911 he held what today would be called a jam session in a West Fifty-third Street club, and the same year gave a concert of jazz music in Carnegie Hall, which anticipated Paul Whiteman by more than ten years.

A man of considerable personality and wit, Europe, like the Castles, became a society favorite, and it was while he and his band played at a private party that Europe and the Castles first met. Vernon was astonished, first at Europe's rhythms, then at the instrumental color of his band. It included a bandolin, a combination banjo and mandolin and then new. The Castles engaged him immediately as their personal musician and there-after demanded in all of their contracts that Europe's music be used solely. Ford Dabney, the pianist in Europe's orchestra, was hired as the Castles' arranger.

When the Castles signed with Charles B. Dillingham for the musical *Watch Your Step,* they demanded a colored orchestra of forty musicians under Europe and Dabney to play their special dance numbers. It was unusual and expensive, but Dillingham agreed. The show went into rehearsal and was booked to open in Bridgeport, Connecticut. A few nights before the opening, Europe, listening to the siren call of a girl in Chicago, walked out on the show. The Castles accordingly dismissed him, hired Dabney in his place, and eliminated the number from the musical, with the result that forty musicians lost their jobs and $70,000 spent on the sets was needlessly wasted.

But Europe assembled another band, which became even more popular, and at the outbreak of World War I he was commissioned a lieutenant and made the bandmaster of the 369th colored regiment, Colonel William Hayward in command. It was an unusual situation. Up to that time, bandmasters had the rank of sergeant. "And I'm going to turn your band over to one of them and put you in charge of a machine-gun nest," said Colonel Hayward.

"Why that man just wants to get me killed," Jim told his comrades, and at his first opportunity he went to Paris and called on Major Barclay Warburton, attaché at the Paris Embassy. Major Warburton, who married Rodman Wanamaker's daughter and who had often hired Jim to play for private parties, prevailed upon General Pershing to send Jim back to his band to preserve the morale of the troops.

As an overseas bandmaster, Jim's fame became international, and he returned after the war to the nation's acclaim. He held his band together, and on March 17, 1919, at the Manhattan Opera House in New York, he began what was to have been a tour of the country. It ended with his murder during a concert in Boston, on May 9. His assailant, Herbert Wright, the drummer, was irritated at Jim's sarcastic direction, "A little more pep in the sticks," and stabbed him to death backstage during the intermission.

Europe was brought back to New York and buried from St. Mark's Methodist Episcopal Church in West Fifty-third Street after a parade from a Harlem undertaker's parlor. Throngs witnessed it, and among the spectators were his old commander, Colonel William Hayward, and John Wanamaker, Jr. He was buried in Arlington, not in his uniform, but in the fantastic dress clothes that he wore as a jazz-band leader, which included a white, pleated silk shirt and striped vest.

Even the last war with its sentimental songs (Gitz Rice's "Dear Old Pal of Mine" sold more than 3,000,000 copies) failed to restore the melodic line. The nation was not recovered from its jazz jitters; indeed, was beginning to enjoy them. A pronounced success in 1917 was Shelton Brooks' "Darktown Strutters Ball," which was issued by Leo Feist, who also published the Dixieland Jazz Band's "Tiger Rag" the same year.

The following year, "Everybody Ought to Know How to Do the Tickletoe" was a pronounced favorite, and in 1919, Pete Wendling, to the lyric by Bert Kalmar and Edgar Leslie, wrote "All the Quakers Are Shoulder Shakers Down in Quaker Town." "The Jazz Babies Ball," by Maceo Pinkard, was a featured number in the Shubert Gaieties of 1919, and two years later, Richard A. Whiting, with Gus Kahn and Raymond B. Egan, caught the spirit of that era of abandonment with their risqué,

> In the morning, in the evening,
> Ain't we got fun.
> Not much money, oh, but honey,
> Ain't we got fun.

And ending with the eyebrow-lifting,

> The rich get richer, and the poor get children;
> In the meantime . . .
> Ain't we got fun![1]

Whiting also wrote, with W. Franke Harling, "Beyond the Blue Horizon," an excellent melody that captivated everyone in 1930. There were, indeed, a number of good melodies written throughout the depression and even up to the evil of 1939. Hoagy Carmichael, Walter Donaldson, James F. Hanley (especially for his "Indiana" and "Just a Cottage Small by a Waterfall"), Billy Hill, and a few others contributed melodic songs whose strains were of the lyre and the lips. But this was nostalgia; it was not to prevail. Swing and hot-licks bands met the temper of the 1930s, as boogie-woogie is the symbol of today's tragic madness.

Tragic also in a minor key, and proof of melody's swan song, is the statement made to the writer by Jay Witmark, of the firm of his publishers, that Victor Herbert in the last few years of his life could not obtain a commission to compose an operetta. There was no call for his music, and he was forced to write choruses and finales for ballets. Herbert died in 1924.

[1]Copyright, 1921, by Jerome H. Remick & Co. Used by permission.

It's a youth's world, this age we live in; a world of realistic terror, without romance. Nobody writes "I love you" any more, even on fences. We have cashiered the prince and unionized the slavey. Our songs today are written mainly as dance tunes for junior hep-cats and jitterbugs. The ballads of mother and morals in Tin Pan Alley are as passé as the word "demure"; the sweetheart of its songs mature, sophisticated, a crass hussy, rouged and meretricious. Since Pan blew a harmonica, young love and the ministrations of Cupid were as the eternal verities to the ballad mongers. Alas for the influences of realism!

> Accident'ly on purpose you paused while passing by,
> Accident'ly on purpose you tried to catch my eye.
> You made that chance remark . . .[2]

Certainly we knew flirt songs in the '90s; but this little 1940 tramp is strictly two dollars.

In "Keep an Eye on Your Heart" there is a suggestion the girl is promiscuous:

> Keep a look out when you're stepping out,
> You belong to me.
> Keep an eye on your heart, don't upset my apple cart—
> Keep your sweet charms out of other arms . . .[3]

"The Same Old Story" is not only absolute realism; it's defeatist:

> The book reviewers all say it,
> The yarn of love's overdone.
> I guess we'd better O.K. it,
> Nothing's new under the sun.[4]

Trivia? They are only a sample of what the boys and girls danced to last year.

They are an earnest, too, of the social and cultural upheaval in a world of no romance or childhood, an upheaval that has been steady in the terroristic world of Hitler and that has in-

[2]Copyright, 1940, Broadcast Music, Inc. Used by permission.
[3]Copyright, 1940, Broadcast Music, Inc. Used by permission.
[4]Copyright, 1940, Broadcast Music, Inc. Used by permission.

creased with added agony in this Hitler war. Our books today are mainly realistic, factual, informative, historical, speculative, or brutal in style. A year ago the writer asked a Hollywood executive what new trend his studio was expressing in motion pictures. "Well, in the first sequence of our latest film a lady burps," he said. This, he added, was the first belch from the screen by a lady. The picture was *The Lady Eve.*

The hero of Broadway's best musical in 1941—*Pal Joey*— was a heel. Joey was one of a panel of punks spawned by John O'Hara that originally scampered across the pages of the *New Yorker.* O'Hara deloused the magazine of him and leased him to theatrical producer George Abbott. The plot of *The Cream in the Well,* a produced if unsuccessful play of last season, was enlivened by a touch of incest.

A girl's idea of *le dernier cri* today is a tweed coat and a figure like Hepburn's. The number of women who stack themselves up in slacks, tailored suits, plain blouses, and ornamental gadgets that approximate armor plate is daily increasing. The gadgets, of course, went out after December 7. The war, naturally, is a masculine influence. But before Hitler loosed his horror on Poland, girls were having their sports clothes made by men tailors. Fashions—that is, the things women wear underneath and right out loud—derive not from the edicts of Sapphic arbiters but from the economic, sociologic, and cultural trend. Femininity in our times is as rare as a blush.

Most of the college girls today, *and yesterday,* go in for government, current events, business courses, and journalism, and when they graduate, they get themselves up like Greta Garbo off the screen and look for a job. They wouldn't give you a nickel for Tyrone Power, think Errol Flynn is an Irish cop, and are really on the make for Phi Beta Kappa. Home and babies is a course in social service. What they want is a career. Even sex is secondary.

To all of this our popular music, with its swing-arranged murder of such noble melodies as "Jeannie with the Light Brown Hair," "Loch Lomond," and "Sweet and Low," and its boogie-woogie style, is the proper obbligato in tempo and theme to the juvenile beat it is written to stir.

Youth, even prewar, is the conqueror of our society. It is at least arguable that the theater is the one remaining adult expression. But what a social paradox now exists! An adolescent girl today has no childhood. She reads the same comic strips, the same slick magazines, sees the same movies, listens to the same radio programs, dresses in the same style as her mother. And, like Mrs. Pat di Cicco, visits her first night club at fourteen. So, also, is a boy's life the replica of his father's.

Now they are giving their hearts, their hands, their lives in the best of causes—tossed themselves willingly into the world's crucible. We may hope a refining alchemy will result which shall ultimately make precious their steely mettle when the benison of a righteous peace of freedom falls. Youth has taken over our land, our times—a severe victory. It has cost the birthright of innocence, of boyhood's dramatic discoveries, of girlhood's modesty and naïveté. All these once were charming.

However strange it may read, the expression of the American popular song up to as late as the 1920s was adult, or at least intended for adults. It was precisely when youth assumed the songs as a rhythmic media for dancing that the popular song lost its character and became a raucous, incoherent chant, its ditties based on the realism our youth now prefer instead of the romance that marked the boy-and-girlhood of greensick days.

The social conditions, the environmental life of America in the two decades before the treachery of Pearl Harbor, were scarcely conducive to song. The number of distinctive melodies published in that span of twenty years is meager. Mainly they originated in Hollywood or were part of the scores of Broadway musicals—those, say, of Richard Rodgers or Jerome Kern, who had long ceased quaffing at the Alley's Pierian springs. Neither Rodgers nor Kern write in the pop-tune genre. Nor is the brassy sophistication of Cole Porter of that breed.

This interpretation of the popular-song expression in our time is intended as a factual reference. There can be no pessimism in a nation that faces the light more in confidence than hope. Song will never be driven from the hearts of our people. The tragedy of this war must end in a sunny recapitulation of the amenities, the restoration of sentiment, the renaissance of the verities we once considered eternal—and will again. The nostalgic interest in everything American that now kindles our culture—this paradox of a tradition new-found—is an earnest of this promise. Our lyres shall be restrung for new hymns in old thoughts to our land, our homes, our affections.

INDEXES

GENERAL INDEX

359

INDEX OF SONG TITLES

(An asterisk after a title indicates that lyrics of the songs are given.)

371

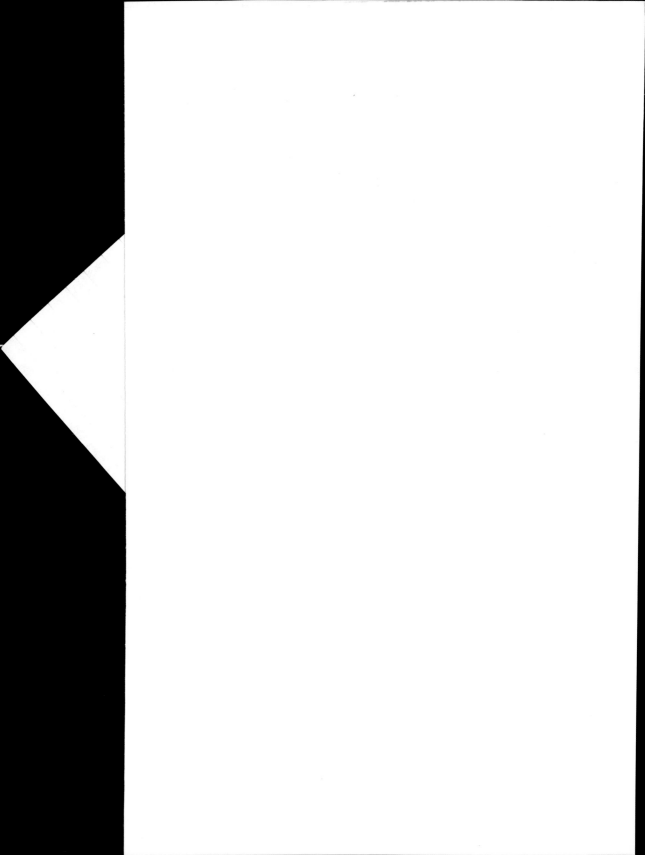

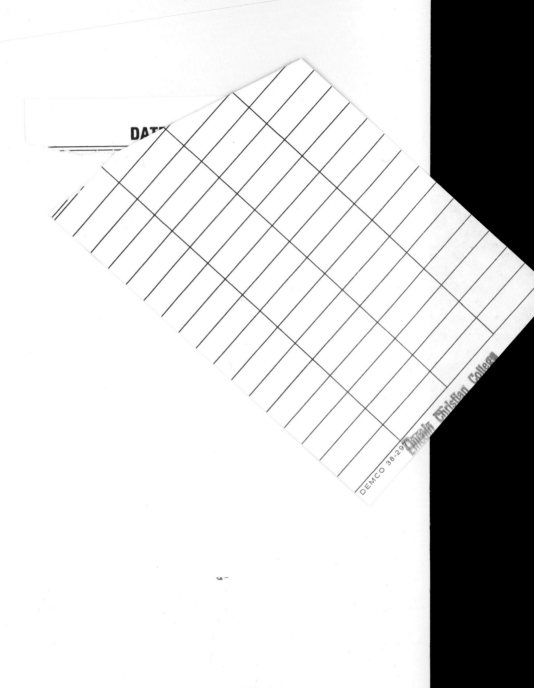

DATE